THE
WIZARD'S
LEGACY

Also by Craig Karges

Ignite Your Intuition

Also by Jon Saint-Germain

Runic Palmistry

THE
WIZARD'S
LEGACY

A Tale of Real Magic

Craig Karges
with **Jon Saint-Germain**

Tell me and I'll forget; show me and I may remember;
involve me and I'll understand.

—CHINESE PROVERB

Leading
Authorities
Press

Washington, D.C.

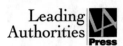

Leading Authorities Press
1220 M Street, N.W.
Washington, D.C. 20012

ISBN 0-9710078-4-5 (alk.paper)

Library of Congress Cataloging-in-Publication Data

Karges, Craig, 1957–
    The Wizard's legacy : a tale of real magic / Craig Karges ;
  with Jon Saint Germain—1st ed.
    p. cm.
  ISBN 0-9710078-4-5 (acid-free paper)
    I. Saint-Germain, Jon, 1960–   II. Title.
  PS3611.A78 W59 2003
  813'.6—dc21   2002069505

Printed in Canada on acid-free paper that meets the American National Standards Institute Z39-48 Standard.

First Edition

10 9 8 7 6 5 4 3 2 1

Dedications

Craig Karges dedicates this book to:
The memory of Mom, Billy, Nan, Willie and, of course, Doc and May.
Each has left a special imprint on my life. And to the one and only
William J. Karges, the best father a boy or man could ever have.

Jon Saint-Germain dedicates this book to:
My wife Elizabeth, the source of all my magic.

Contents

Contents

Preface

I remember reading somewhere that Winston Churchill, when asked for his impressions of Russia, replied that the nation was "a riddle wrapped in a mystery inside an enigma." He could just as easily have been talking about my uncle, Alain (Doc) DeLyle. Clairvoyant, Mystic, Hypnotist, Wizard, Charlatan: he was known by all these titles to his admirers and detractors. No one can deny that he was an extraordinary man.

"Doc" DeLyle was a man ahead of his time in many ways. He espoused herbal medicaments and magnetotherapy back in the 1920s and '30s, long before these alternative treatments became popular during the current New Age. In his heyday, his services were so valued that he earned a thousand dollars a day (this was in 1930; the equivalent today of ten thousand dollars!). He held numerous degrees, among them Master of Herbalism from Dominion Herbal College, Doctor of Psycho-Analysis from American University, and a degree from the Standard Institute of Psychical Training. He also had a Minister's License issued by the State of Ohio. The nickname "Doc" was earned, not honorary.

In the 1930s and '40s he was a theatrical headliner, performing his mind reading and hypnosis show all over the country under various billings, including Zebara, Ramazon, and Alain DeLyle—Supernormalist Supreme. His first large theatrical outing was perhaps his most imaginative: RAMAZON AND HIS TROOP OF HYPNOTIC ZOMBIES. The zombies were stage assistants who walked among the audience in a trance. During the show, my uncle hypnotized members of the audience on stage and performed psychic feats. His show broke theater box office records in small and medium-sized towns up and down the eastern seaboard. After his retirement he concentrated mostly on giving psychic readings and herbal treatments to a devoted body of clients.

But above all that, he was my great-uncle. At the age of thirteen, I spent some time with him and my Aunt May in their home in West Virginia. During that period we played games and had conversations that I realize now were intended to teach me lessons about life and the amazing personal power that lies within each of us. These teachings were valuable, but the best lessons I learned were from his example. I have never in my life known an individual so wise, intelligent, and at ease with himself and with the world around him.

During my period of apprenticeship, I learned that Doc was an extraordinary man (as you'll see for yourself within these pages), but as for the truth—well, at thirteen, I didn't know exactly what the truth was about my uncle, and now, thirty years later, I'm no closer to understanding the real "truth" about him and probably never will. However, I tried not to let this personal failing affect the book. One of the lessons I learned from my uncle was to never, ever let mere truth stand in the way of a ripping good story!

Much of the content of this book is derived from the experiences of a thirteen-year-old boy, as recalled by a forty-two-year-old man. Additional information comes from the confidential client files I inherited from my uncle. Many of these files contain extremely delicate personal information. To protect these individuals, I've made changes to names, dates, and places.

I would like to emphasize that, whereas much of this work is biographical (where my uncle is concerned) and autobiographical (where I am concerned), an equal portion has been condensed and fictionalized, blending fact with imagination, what was with what might have been. I elected to keep the names and relationships of members of my family true to life, but their personalities aren't exactly the same as portrayed in this book. I did this as a tribute to the family I love, and I hope that I caused no embarrassment to anyone. Consequently, this book is labeled fiction, even though the characters and events are grounded in reality.

My uncle always said that his job as a Psychic Consultant was to provide people with information. What they chose to do with this information was their own business. This book is written with that philosophy in mind: think of it as entertainment, amusement, inspiration, or history as it suits you. Believe it or don't believe it, at your discretion. All I can tell you from my own experience is that Alain DeLyle was real, the events surrounding his life actually happened and are well documented, and his teachings helped many, many people at least as much as they did me. While reading this book, it may be helpful to bear in mind Thomas Hardy's injunction, "While many things are too strange to be believed, nothing is too strange to have happened."

I hope you enjoy this book about my great uncle, Doc DeLyle. I also hope you'll benefit from his lessons as much as I have.

—Craig Karges, February 2001

Acknowledgments

This book is the result of much work, creativity, and imagination on the part of many individuals. With this in mind, Craig Karges wishes to acknowledge the following:

All the extraordinary people at Leading Authorities, Inc. for all they do for me both on the platform and in the bookstore.

Northeastern Graphic Services, Inc., for overseeing the design and composition of *The Wizard's Legacy*.

International Publisher's Marketing (IPM) for producing a quality product and for getting that product into your hands.

Christina George and the staff of the Ohio County Public Library for letting me dig in the archives.

Phyllis Sigal and the staff of the *Wheeling News-Register* for supporting my efforts.

Clinton Billups, my personal manager, for opening new doors.

Judith Conkle for taking a look at the original manuscript.

A special thank you to Uri Geller, the world's most celebrated paranormalist, for his inspiration and for giving his blessing to the fictional yet representative account of a 1970s-era Geller television appearance you will find in this book.

Charlotte, my wonderful wife, for 22 years of love, support and shenanigans.

Jon Saint-Germain for sharing my fascination with Doc and his work.

Introduction

Oral tradition, in my opinion, is the most effective learning tool we have. Knowledge—secrets—are passed down from generation to generation, master to student, as Doc DeLyle passed his wisdom to a young Craig Karges. Fashioned from the dream-stuff of ancient folklore, tempered by experience, forged by love and loss, and sculpted into shape by the Word, knowledge is indeed Power. And the most powerful knowledge, the wise ones tell us, is self-awareness. Who are we? What do we want? Why are we here?

The world is a palace of contradictions; a baffling construction that seems hard-wired for confusion and conflict. Finding our soul's path—our one true destiny—is difficult. Torn between the conflicting drives of the need for security and the desire for independence, sometimes we need someone like Alain "Doc" DeLyle to help us make sense of it all.

As the Old Man said, "Mastering others requires strength, but mastering the self requires wisdom."

I was born to a family of psychic readers. My grandmother taught me the basics of palmistry from the age of six. She learned the craft from her mother, who learned it from . . . etc.

Like Craig, as a child I was fascinated by magic and mysticism. I practiced constantly, staying up all night and studying obscure texts with such evocative titles as: *Our Magic, The Amateur Magician's Handbook*, and *Corinda's Thirteen Steps*. I learned that behind the facade of illusion presented by the stage magician there lurked a core of real magic. Real magic, as Doc would say, exists within all of us, lurking in that murky realm between imagination and reality.

Real magic is Life.

I dreamed of being a magician someday, but everyone told me that you couldn't make a living as an entertainer. I listened. I went to school, got a degree in Engineering and worked in the field for nine years. I made fairly good money, but it was killing me. Engineering is a noble profession; building things is a great and fascinating work. It just wasn't for me. As Doc might have told me, I needed something more spiritually satisfying.

Fate took a hand. In the mid-'80s, the country experienced a recession. Layoffs were inevitable. At the urging of close friends (who were honest and insightful enough to tell me I was in the wrong career), I went to my boss and asked if I could reduce my hours to part-time status. He agreed, and I began "developing my market," as we show-business types like to say. I began attending psychic fairs on the weekend as a palmist, sometimes doing as many as thirty ten-minute readings a day. Soon, my after-dinner mind-reading show took off spectacularly and, as the demand for engineers hit rock bottom, I made an easy and painless transition into the field I love.

I never looked back. Today my time is divided between performing, doing readings in my own "Sanctum," investigating ghost hauntings, and writing books on metaphysical subjects. Reading hands and writing books are my two great loves.

Fate performed her own special brand of sleight-of-hand by bringing Craig and me together to give new life to Doc's voice for modern readers. How we two were brought together, the man with a story to tell and the man who ached to tell stories, is a fantastic bit of synchronicity that you'll just have to wait to read about later in the book! As I pored through his notebooks and material, Doc hooked me, just as he hooked Craig in that magical summer of 1971.

To the question of how much of this book is true and how much is might-have been, I can only respond with a saying that is attributed to the Buddha: "Believe nothing, no matter where you read it, or who said it . . . unless it agrees with your own reason and your own common sense."

So listen, O King, as we tell you of marvels and wonders, and of a Wizard the people called Doc, for he was exceedingly strong and wise . . .

—Jon Saint-Germain, March 2001

THE
WIZARD'S
LEGACY

PART I
A Summer
of Magic

The Passing of a Wizard

NOVEMBER 8, 1971. I AM THIRTEEN YEARS OLD. As I stand by my great-uncle's grave, I can't help but think how much he would have loved this day: the cloud-filled, faded-denim sky reaching toward the mountains, broken with sporadic thunder, flashes of lightning, the threat of a winter storm. Against the grumbly, unshaven heavens fly a flock of geese, honking loudly. It was as though Nature herself conspired with us to give my uncle a dramatic send-off. I look around at the other mourners. Our breaths form ghostly plumes in the frigid air.

Brother Carl, one of the few spiritualists that my uncle respected in the area, raises his arms toward the turbulent sky. "Let us pray," he says:

> *"The LIGHT of God surrounds us;*
> *The LOVE of God enfolds us;*
> *The POWER of God protects us;*
> *The PRESENCE of God watches over us;*
> *Wherever we are, God is, and all is well. Amen."*

"Amen," we say. I look at my uncle lying in the coffin. An expression of peace is on his face. For the last time my eyes take in familiar details: white hair combed neatly back behind his ears, prominent nose and well-groomed mustache, eyes that in life were usually curled into crescents of amusement or compassion. Eyes that missed nothing. He's smiling slightly, as though enjoying a private joke.

Maybe he was. With my uncle, you never knew.

There are many mourners, especially impressive for the small town of Wheeling, West Virginia. Here are men and women from the coal mines and steel factories, many of who had been his clients, come to pay their respects. Scattered among them are reporters and magicians (the stage kind, you know, who pull rabbits from empty hats and coins from youngsters' ears) gypsies, carnies, hypnotists. And us, of course. The friends and family of a Wizard.

Brother Carl closes the coffin. My father nods to me. It is time. I follow my father to the coffin and grasp the brass rails. The other pallbearers move into position. At a prearranged signal, we all lift together. Shared among us, the burden is surprisingly light. Together, we convey Alain "Doc" DeLyle to his final resting-place. The coffin is lowered into the ground; my father and I pick up a couple of shovels and throw in the first few spadefuls of dirt.

Just as the clods of earth thud against the coffin, the sky breaks open and an icy rain begins to fall.

■ ■ ■

Aunt May said, "Byrel, would you and William like something to eat? Some coffee?"

"Nothing for me, May, thanks," my father said. He was thumbing indifferently through a magazine. My little brother Brian rolled on the floor with the two resident Persians, Chester and Angelica. Both felines looked at Brian like he was an idiot, in that barely tolerant way of cats to remind us who's really boss.

"Some coffee would be great," Mom called. "Need any help?"

But Aunt May had already glided into the kitchen. I heard the sounds of china clinking and cabinets opening and closing. Aunt May was one of those people who couldn't sit still for a minute. Though recently widowed, the rules of hospitality required that she make her guests comfortable.

I was soaking wet; the storm had moved in so suddenly that none of us was prepared for it. I took off my drenched raincoat, stepped onto

2

the front porch, and shook it out. A dog was sniffing around the lawn jockey that guarded the driveway. The lawn jockey always made me laugh. Doc had painted the ebony face and hands an ethnically ambiguous tan color, as a humorous reminder not to read a person based on external appearances.

I came back into the living room and hung my overcoat near the hearth to dry. Aunt May reappeared, carrying a tray laden with coffee and small pieces of cake. "Here you go, dear," she said. Dad took the tray and sat it on the coffee table while she went over and fussed with my dripping overcoat. "Craig, you'd better get those wet clothes off or you'll catch pneumonia."

"Yes, Aunt May." I wrestled my way out of my suit jacket and hung it over the back of a chair near the crackling fireplace. The constricting tie followed the jacket and soon I was reasonably comfortable again. She handed me a cup of hot chocolate and a handful of ginger cookies—my favorite. I grinned at her. "Thanks." I sipped the rich chocolate, letting the cup warm my hands.

"It was a beautiful service, wasn't it?" my mother said.

Aunt May bustled about the living room, straightening up. Boxes of Uncle Alain's effects were stacked in every corner. He had been a collector of many things throughout his life. She nodded. "Yes, he would have been pleased at seeing all his friends there." She dabbed at the corners of her eyes with her apron. "I know he wouldn't want us to be sad, but I miss him."

Mom said, "I guess a lot of people are going to miss him. So many depended on him." Dad leafed through the magazine, saying nothing; I knew he didn't quite approve of my uncle's "fortune-telling."

"They'll have to find someone else to take care of them," Aunt May replied. "Alain's gone to his rest. After all he did for other people, he deserves it."

"I'll miss his tricks," my brother interjected from the floor.

"He didn't do tricks," I said. "He did magic."

"Whatever," Brian muttered.

I began emptying the pockets of my dress suit, cluttered with the usual assortment of junk thirteen-year-olds collect and carry as personal talismans. A battered harmonica I was trying to learn to play. A garnet I had found by the river. A pocketknife. The service sheet from my uncle's funeral.

My mother continued. "How are you going to get the word to his clients? Not everybody will have seen the obituary in the paper."

"I don't know," Aunt May said. "I suppose I'll just have to tell them when they call for an appointment. Or drop by, as they usually do."

I found something else in my pocket. I was puzzled, because I usually knew the exact contents of my personal inventory. I pulled the foreign object out and looked at it.

Suddenly, icewater ran through my veins. What I saw was impossible.

Mom said, "Maybe we could go through his appointment book and send cards—Craig!" she cried.

"Son?" I heard the anxious voice of my father as though it were coming down a long tunnel. "Are you all right?" I felt Mom's cool hand on my forehead. The cause for their alarm was the shattered cocoa mug lying in pieces on the floor, hot chocolate running in rivulets across the tiles. The mug had slipped from my hand. Later, they told me my face had been as white as a sheet.

"Son, are you all right?" he repeated. The wind howled outside; sleet hammered against the windows like buckshot. I could not answer. All I could do was stare, shocked, at the square of paper I had just found in the pocket of my jacket. A small square of my uncle's magenta notepaper, slightly damp from the storm, with five words scrawled on it in his distinctive handwriting. Five words that meant something to me and only me:

Craig—Believe in real MAGIC.

It hadn't been in my pocket when we left for the funeral. I swear it hadn't.

"You made a mess, you dope," my little brother said.

■ ■ ■

That was thirty years ago. Today, I can look back on this incident and theorize a dozen ways that square of paper had ended up in my pocket. Doc had passed away on November 5th and on the next three

The Wheeling Suspension Bridge, gateway to Wheeling Island
and the "Wizard's Den"—the home of Alain "Doc" DeLyle.
—"River and Mist" photo by Benjamin J. Schneider, Schneider Studio,
Wheeling, West Virginia.

days I had been helping Aunt May pack Doc's belongings. Perhaps I
absent-mindedly slipped it into my pocket without noticing it. Maybe
on the day of the funeral I picked it up on the way out the door, along
with my wallet. Possibly it was my older brother Bill's idea of a joke;
Bill shared Uncle Alain's odd sense of humor.

Yes, I can think of a dozen logical reasons how that paper could
have wound up in my pocket—but in my heart of hearts, I don't really
believe any of them. You see, I had spent the summer with my uncle
and had learned that sometimes, whether you want it to or not, magic
happens. I believed then (as I sometimes do now) that Uncle Alain was
reminding me of the time we shared before his death, when he taught
me there was more to the world than what could be seen with the eyes,
heard with the ears, or grasped by the hands.

He taught me that the world was full of Magic, if you only gave
yourself permission to believe in it.

CHAPTER ONE

I Discover Magic

AT THE AGE OF THIRTEEN, THE DIRECTION OF MY LIFE CHANGED FOREVER.

On a beautiful summer evening in early June, it was warm and clear with a million fireflies flickering around the honeysuckle bushes in the back yard. I had just finished the last homework of the school year, and all of summer stretched out ahead of me like a new and unexplored territory. Three long months were filled with endless possibilities of adventure and new experiences. Dinner that night had been meat loaf and chocolate cake (my favorite), and I was feeling quite happy and satisfied. It was a great day to be a kid.

I sprawled across the couch watching television. The country was still buzzing about the successful Russian launching of Salyut, which, along with Skylab, was one of the first spacecraft designed as a space station. My dad had retreated to his den to spend some quiet time alone. My older brother Bill (home from college for a few days) was out with friends, Brian was conked out on the floor, and Mom was on the phone. I had the television to myself for a change.

The movie on that night was *The Great Houdini* starring Tony Curtis and Janet Leigh. It was a curious coincidence. Just a couple of weeks ago my seventh-grade class had gone on a field trip to Niagara Falls. While there, we had toured the Houdini Magical Hall of Fame. At first only mildly curious, by the end of the tour I was intrigued by the flamboyant, death-defying magician. I bought a poster and a couple of pocket tricks from the souvenir shop.

Magic had cast its lure, and I nibbled at the bait. But it was about halfway through the movie, when Houdini is trapped under the ice of the Detroit River, that I became fatally hooked.

It was definitely a turning point in my life. Up to that moment, if anyone had asked me what I wanted to do when I grew up, I wouldn't have had the slightest clue how to answer them. But by the time the final credits of the movie rolled I knew what I wanted to be: a man of mystery, a wizard. I imagined what it would be like to become one of the selected few who had mastered the secrets of magic, how great it would feel to look out from the stage and see a theater full of people with mouths hanging open in wide "O's" of astonishment, knowing that I—the Amazing Craig!—had inspired that sense of wonder.

Fame. Riches. Admiration. It all sounded pretty good to me. I mounted the poster of Houdini on the wall just over my desk, next to the one of Raquel Welch in a bikini. Like I said, I had it bad.

I haunted the library looking for books on magic and illusion. I found a few and devoured them hungrily. I was fascinated by the intricacies of the art of legerdemain, by how much practice even simple tricks, like making a quarter vanish at your fingertips, required. Most of that stuff you see magicians do so effortlessly is hard! Ease of execution comes only with year after year of devoted rehearsal.

I stayed up late into the night practicing esoteric sleights like the classic pass, the top change, and the second deal—essential components, I read, of a magician's toolkit. I learned about the Si Stebbins system, the Downs Eureka Pass, and how to make a little red ball jump from one inverted cup to another. Man, it was fun!

After several weeks of practice, I learned to do a few tricks moderately well and immediately looked for "guinea pigs." In the timeworn tradition of all young magicians, I tormented my entire family with constant demands of "pick a card!" To this day, the sight of a deck of playing cards can cause my younger brother to run screaming from the room.

I had found my true love. Wheeling, West Virginia in the '70s was a curious mixture of industrialization and natural woodland beauty. Although we had the Ohio River winding through the green, rolling hills and valleys, and woods of almost supernatural peacefulness (not to mention several great parks), I spent most of my time in my room. I had my magic. I practiced and practiced. I was happy.

■ ■ ■

One day, after I had asked my mother to "pick a card" for the thousandth time that week, she said, "If you want to know about magic, you should go talk to your great-uncle Alain. He used to be a mentalist and magician, a long time ago."

Of course, my interest was immediately piqued. I knew from my books that a mentalist was a magician who specialized in illusions of mind reading and psychic powers. I later learned just how limited and misleading this definition was.

Alain "Doc" DeLyle was my grandmother's brother-in-law, who had been born in California in the late 1800s. Apparently, he'd moved away because the family disapproved of his psychic activities. Mom told me that Doc DeLyle worked as a fortune-teller or psychic reader. I knew who he was, of course. He was married to Aunt May, who always helped with the larger family functions, birthday parties, anniversaries, and funerals. Alain rarely attended any of these. I found out later this was because my grandmother didn't approve of him and called him a bad influence.

My mother told me that Alain was pretty much retired these days, doing the occasional "reading" for people now and again. I could tell from the tone of her voice she didn't take these "readings" seriously. Apparently, he had made a great deal of money back in his days as a performer and had retired quite comfortably.

To this day I don't know if it was my obsession with magic or a desire to get me out of her hair that prompted my mother to make the introduction. Probably the latter. The charm of selecting cards from the dog-eared family deck had long since worn off. Sensing that an adventure was afoot, my little brother Brian insisted on going too.

After making a phone call, she drove us over to his house, located on Wheeling Island. The island was on the West Virginia side of the Ohio River, accessible by the Wheeling Suspension Bridge. I loved the old, picturesque bridge. It had been built about the time of the Civil War, and the original stone masonry and anchorages still stood intact. With its huge towers and fairy-tale-like structure of wire and steel, it seemed like the entrance to a magic kingdom.

We pulled off the highway into a driveway that wrapped around a restored Victorian mansion. It had a nice back porch, a circular veranda, and even a cylindrical tower! At the turn of the twentieth century Wheeling Island had been a very elite place to live. Several wealthy families built their homes there, until they found out the Ohio River tended to flood now and again, including a great 'Big One' every decade or so. When the wealthy abandoned their castles and island paradise for dryer land, most of the edifices became apartments and offices. Mom told us that Alain and May had gotten a great deal on a house that sat on high ground and completely restored it.

There was a chopping block with a stack of cordwood along the side of the driveway. (Even at his advanced age, Uncle Alain still chopped his own wood. He also grew his own vegetables.) I noticed an expansive herbal garden and a field of sunflowers near the river. Apparently, my uncle liked to keep his hands busy. We parked next to the most impressive car I'd ever seen and got out. Mom rang the bell.

A stocky man with a thick mustache and an amazing head of white hair answered the door. He wore a red smoking jacket, just like an English lord in an old movie. Uncle Alain seemed glad to see us. His eyes glittered as he smiled. "Byrel, come in," he said, in a deep, well-cultivated voice. He pecked her on the cheek. "You're looking lovely today. This must be Craig and Brian. How do you do?" He shook our hands.

"Fine," Brian said. "I'm hungry."

"Glad to meet you, sir," I said, elbowing my brother.

Alain looked me over, a long speculative look. "Call me 'Doc,' boys. So you're the magician?"

"Yessir."

He nodded. "Bravo. Come on in."

Aunt May appeared from the kitchen. "Oh good, you're just in time for lunch."

Over lunch, the grown-ups talked about various things while Brian and I ate in silence. At least I did; Brian interrupted every few minutes to ask questions. The two resident felines, Chester and Angelica, rubbed across our ankles as we ate. My uncle seemed a little shy, preferring to watch the conversation rather than dominate it. However, in some way I didn't quite understand, he participated without talking. Mom and Aunt May included him in the conversation, unconsciously looking at him as though seeking corroboration or approval. Most of his conversation consisted of nods and smiles. When he did speak, it was to interject a bit of humorous insight.

Mom and Aunt May went into the kitchen to clean up. Uncle Alain —Doc, I reminded myself—turned to me. "Show me something, son."

"What do you mean?"

He smiled. "Show me a trick."

"Oh. Okay." I reached into my pocket and removed a silver half-dollar, placing it in my left hand in position to do a move known as the French Drop. I took the coin in my right hand, blew on my fist, and opened my hand. It was gone.

"Ah, it's in your other hand," Brian said.

"Shut up, dope," I told him. "You've seen the trick already." I looked at Uncle Alain for his reaction.

He nodded. "That was good, Craig—really good. Your body language was a bit inconsistent, though, and I don't think you really believed the coin was gone. That's why Brian here was on to you. He sensed your lack of conviction. Let me tell you the real secret of good magic: If you really believe in your own magic, others will too. Let me see that coin."

Doc took the coin and held it at his fingertips for a moment, letting the light twinkle from it. Then he began his moves. For the next two minutes we saw that coin do impossible things. It vanished from his fingertips, only to reappear at his elbow. He handed it to me, and as my fingers closed around it the coin melted into thin air. He found it behind Brian's ear. My brother giggled and rolled on the floor in delight. "He's better than you, Craigy."

Indeed he was. The coin seemed to have a mind of its own, dancing mischievously around without the aid of my uncle. In fact, the coin's antics seemed to surprise him as much as us. Suddenly, the coin vanished.

"Now where could it be?" he mused, looking around the dinner table. "Aha!" Doc picked up a roll and cracked it open. The coin was nestled inside!

"There you are, you scurrilous rascal," he said. "Better take it back, son." When he handed the coin to me, I looked at it closely, almost expecting it to disappear before I could return it to my pocket. I was entranced. "Teach me to do that."

Doc patted me on the shoulder. "You already know how to do it, Craig. You just don't know that you know . . . not yet, anyway." While I tried to figure out what he meant by that, he walked over to his desk and came back with a stubby pencil and a square of his magenta notepaper. "Here's a little experiment in telepathy," he said. "Just write a single word or name, something that means something to you and you only." He turned his back to us. "When you finish writing, fold the paper in half, and in half again. Make sure no part of the writing is visible." I did as I was told. I folded the paper and held it up to the light. Nope, no way to see through it.

He turned back around and extended his hand out for the paper. He held it at his fingertips for a moment. "Concentrate." With a quick gesture, he tore the slip of paper into fragments. "Here, quickly, hold out your hands." He dropped the pieces into my cupped palms, like confetti. "Hold them tight."

Holding my hands between his, he looked at me intently. His dark eyes bored into mine, as though looking through them into my mind. It was an unsettling feeling.

"Ah," he muttered. "You're thinking of a man, someone whom you admire . . . a role model. I see handcuffs, chains . . . spirits. A man buried alive, trapped under ice and struggling for air." A smile spread across his face. "I see the initials HH. Harry Houdini. Is that correct?"

I nodded, stunned. It was the best trick I'd ever seen. I had no idea how he had accomplished it.

"Ha, ha!" Brian yelled. "How'd he do that, Craigy?"

"Shut up, dope," I said. I thought about how deeply the trick had moved me. This was something more than just making a coin appear inside a lemon, or finding a chosen card in your pocket. This was more intimate, going inside a person's mind and revealing their secret thoughts.

"I understand your fascination with the late great Houdini," Doc said mildly. "But I'm afraid there's a huge difference between the man and the legend. Houdini was always a bit of a bore; he had to be the center of attention every minute of the day. A frightened, insecure man. When the public began to lose interest in his tricks, he tried to garner headlines by exposing psychics and mediums. Most of his "exposures" were pure bullcrap of course—pardon my language, boys," he said, as Brian collapsed into giggles. "He didn't have the slightest idea what was going on."

I was amazed at Doc's dismissal of Houdini, who I thought was the greatest magician who ever lived. He seemed to sense my discomfort and smiled again.

"But no matter," he said. "Magicians have always looked at the paranormal with a skeptical eye." He winked at me. "And now I'm going to tell you the biggest secret of all, Craig. You may not believe it now, but someday you will. Here it is." He leaned closer and I smelled the mingled aromas of cigars and whiskey; a fragrance that would become very familiar to me over the summer. "Not everything in this business is fake, son. Oh no, not by a long shot."

"Are you going to show me how to do that?"

"Perhaps. Maybe it's another trick you already know but don't know that you know. Let's go into my office and I'll show you another one."

We followed him through the den into his office. My eyes wandered around the room. Crystal balls, ancient books, and old vaudeville posters were everywhere. A leering gargoyle served as a bookend over the mantle. In a glass case (like you would see in a doctor's office) were jars upon jars of various herbs, with names I had never heard of before: John the Conqueror Root, Ginseng (quite popular now, but in the '70s practically unheard of), Echinacea, Hellebore.

It was an amazing room. A matched pair of Romanesque statues, man and woman, held large crystal orbs over their heads. There were gold Buddhas, incense burners, and a large Chinese gong. On a table near one wall was a crystal ball, several decks of tarot cards, and about two-dozen small stones with symbols carved on them. A vague smell of incense and cigar smoke permeated the room. There was no doubt in my mind: this was the den of a real wizard.

He pointed to a tall bookcase, one of several. "Now, Brian, here's one for you. Go over there and take out a book, any one you like. Open it to any page and pick out a word in your mind. I won't peek." He turned around and covered his eyes with his hands. My brother ran to the bookcase and selected a volume of Edgar Allen Poe's short stories. He opened the book and glanced at one of the pages. "Okay. Got it."

Doc nodded. "Put it back on the shelf—no, not there. Poe lives next to Hawthorne. Kindred spirits, you know." I wondered how he had known which book Brian had selected while his back was turned, but I knew better than to ask. It was probably another trick I already knew without knowing I knew. Whatever that meant.

"Now look at my eyes and think of your word." Brian looked at him seriously, blinking like an owl. "My, what an impressive word for someone your age, Brian. You're thinking of the word *invisible.*"

"That's right!" Brian yelled. "Like the Invisible Man! Do another one."

Alain patted us on the shoulders. "Showtime's over, boys. I'd love to continue, but there's work to do. I'm glad you came today. Let's go outside. You can help me in the garden."

Uncle Alain's back yard slanted down through a patch of woods all the way to the river. As we followed him to the garden I thought about the book trick. I corrected myself. It wasn't a trick; tricks were what magicians did. People who read minds were psychics. Such people possessed gifts that other people didn't have—gifts that were sometimes scary, linked to the occult and black magic. I thought I could never perform such miracles.

Doc was just as amazing in the garden as he had been in the den. Although from my thirteen-year-old perspective he was as old as the hills, he easily worked circles around the two of us. We pulled weeds and dug potholes for a couple of hours. By the time Mom called for us to leave, Brian and I were both exhausted.

Doc DeLyle walked with me over to the car. "Magic is a two-way street, Craig," he told me. "It's a collaborative art. It's not you against them. You and the audience have to work together to accomplish miracles. It's a lot like gardening: sometimes the thing to do is just relax, enjoy the experience, and let the work take care of itself."

I was too tired to ask for clarification. I simply nodded my head. My hands ached from pulling weeds. Brian fell asleep as soon as his head hit the car seat.

Mom and Aunt May exchanged farewells. As we pulled out of the driveway, Doc nodded to me. "Come back sometime and I'll show you that coin trick."

"What about the mind-reading trick?" I asked.

"Ah, that's another story," he replied, eyes twinkling. "Let's start with the simple stuff and see where it leads us."

We pulled onto the highway, and I looked at my uncle's silhouette against the fading skyline until we drove out of sight.

C H A P T E R   T W O

The First Rule of Magic

TWO DAYS LATER I RODE THE BUS INTO TOWN and walked across the bridge to Wheeling Island. It was fortunate that we lived just a few miles away, but I would have traveled a lot farther to learn the secret of the coin trick.

I had given up on the book trick. All weekend long I had Brian look up words in books while I attempted to read his mind. "*Briefcase!*" I'd guess.

"No, *chocolate!*" Brian would reply, collapsing into a fit of giggles. By the twentieth attempt, I was ready to kill him. I concluded that such miracles were beyond my skills. *Maybe some day*, I consoled myself.

Doc was out in his garden, waiting for me.

"I knew you'd be back. Was it the coin trick or the book trick?"

"The coin trick." Doc's parting remark a couple of days ago about "starting with the simple stuff" confirmed my belief that his mind-reading abilities were beyond me. For now, anyway.

His eyebrows rose like two bushy caterpillars. "That I *didn't* know. I would have guessed the book trick." He stood up and stretched, clapping his hands together to shake loose the garden soil. "Let's go inside, I need a drink."

"The coin trick, eh?" He lit a cigar and rocked back in his chair. Aunt May was in the next room, dressed in a leotard and exercising to classical music. I could see her quite well from where I sat, and considering her age, her flexibility (not to mention her figure) was nothing short of remarkable.

Doc puffed at his cigar. "I learned the coin trick from a fellow named Tommy Downs, back in the twenties. Great coin man. Funny as hell, too. Let me see that half-dollar."

I fished it out of my pocket and handed it over. He looked it over critically and rubbed it on his pants, grimacing. "What's that on it—bubble gum?" he asked, flipping it toward me.

I reached for it. It twinkled away in mid air. I looked at Doc, puzzled. His eyes glittered back at me. He raised his hand from where it rested on his knee. Under his hand was my half-dollar.

He picked the coin up and waggled it at me. "You see, it all depends on belief. You believed the coin was in my hand, but it was really somewhere else."

I thought about it. I had actually seen the coin flashing through the air. Or had I?

"Where is it now?" he asked.

"There," I pointed at his hand.

"Nope." He opened his hand and it was empty.

"—but I saw it!"

"No, you *believed* you saw it." He pointed, and I realized the coin was still resting on his knee. He had only pretended to pick it up. "You see, Craig? It all happened in your mind. I didn't do anything. You did all the work. Real magic begins in the mind."

That was the first lesson. But I still didn't understand what *belief* had to do with making a coin disappear. He coached me for about an hour on the use of body language to control the audience's attention. How a seemingly innocent gesture can make a coin appear to be someplace where it wasn't. Suddenly, it all made sense. He had been right when he said it was a trick I already knew how to do. My body seemed to carry out the correct movements instinctively once I had them clearly in my mind. It even surprised *me* when I made the coin jump from hand to hand!

"You got it?" he asked, grinning.

I returned his grin. "I'm getting it."

"Bravo! Practice it for a bit. I'll be right back."

Doc retired to the bedroom and returned in a few minutes dressed in a jaunty blue-and-gold workout suit. I gave him a quizzical look. "May and I are going to do some Tai Chi," he said. Care to join us?"

I didn't know what he was talking about. He said, "Tai Chi is an ancient form of exercise from China, designed to energize the body, relax the mind, and bring harmony to the spirit."

I'll admit I was a bit intrigued. "Okay, I'll give it a try. What do I have to do?"

"It isn't hard. Just do as we do."

May put on a record of Oriental music and we began. Tai Chi was more like dance movements than calisthenics. I tried to imitate the smooth, flowing movements, but had difficulty at first. It was a lot harder than it looked. Doc told me to concentrate on my breathing and coordinate my movements with my breath. "In . . . out," he said softly, "back . . . and forth." After a while, I got the hang of it, but I felt a little foolish. I didn't quite see the appeal it held for my aunt and uncle.

Old folks are weird, I decided. This wasn't exercise; it was ballet. But at the end of an hour, I was surprised to find I'd broken quite a sweat. And I did feel more relaxed. Doc told me he and May practiced Yoga, Tai Chi and other esoteric disciplines on a daily basis. The exercises were not only excellent for the body, he said, but expanded the mind as well. I didn't see how wrapping your foot around your neck and trying to sit on the back of your own head improved one's mind, but I kept my skepticism to myself. And I will admit my sleep that night was deep and refreshing. Today, when sleep eludes me, I run through a couple of Tai Chi routines and sleep like a baby.

■ ■ ■

A few days later, a major turning point in our relationship occurred. After the regular exercise session, Doc pulled out his old-fashioned pocket watch and checked the time. "Craig, I have a client coming in a few minutes. Why don't you wait in the den and read for a while? There are some interesting books on the bookcase next to the fireplace." Just then the doorbell rang. "That'll be her," he said. "I'll be finished in about thirty minutes, son. Have fun. Try to learn something."

I went into the den and sat in the big chair near the window. From the chair I had a clear view of the front porch. Standing at the door was a worried, fretful-looking woman, about my mother's age, wringing a tissue into pieces. I saw Doc answer the door with a comforting smile. He took her by the arm and gently led her inside.

I know what I did next was wrong, but the drama of the situation piqued my curiosity. I had to see what would happen next. Doc's office adjoined the den, separated by a thin panel door. I hurried over to the door, carefully opened it a crack and watched as Alain led the crying woman to his table and urged her into a chair.

Taking her hands in his, he looked into her eyes. "My dear, you've been through a difficult time. You've experienced great loss. I'm here to help you." The woman could only nod. "How did you hear about me, Miriam?"

The lady—Miriam—sniffed. "Some friends of mine a-at work said you c-could help me . . . I've never done anything like this before, Doctor DeLyle. I'm not sure what to do."

Doc nodded. "I understand." Although his back was to me, I could hear the gentle smile in his voice. "I can't promise you anything except that I'll do my very best." He released her hands and rubbed his palms together. "Do you have anything belonging to the boy?"

Miriam opened her purse and brought out a beaded chain with a tag of metal hanging from it: a set of dog tags. Doc looked at the tag.

"Robert," he read. "Did you call him Robby or Rob?"

Miriam nodded. "Most people called him Robby, but we always called him—"

"—Butch," Doc interrupted. "You called him Butch, and he called you his pretty Mommy."

Miriam's face went through many expressions. Amazement turned to fear, then grief. Her face crumpled and my uncle pulled her to him, holding her until her sobs abated. I looked away, embarrassed to be an uninvited witness to this private sorrow.

Miriam said, "When I got the news, I couldn't believe it at first. I thought, this must be some kind of mistake. It's somebody else, not my boy. Then they sent the body home and I knew." She clutched my uncle's arm. "I just need to know that he didn't suffer! Please tell me that the Lord took him quickly."

"I'll do my very best," Doc said, so softly I could barely hear him. He took the dog tags and held them between his hands. For the space of at least five minutes he was totally silent. I barely breathed.

Alain lifted his head. "I see a man, but it isn't Robert. This seems to be an older male, perhaps an uncle, who is wearing a uniform. He's showing me his chest," Doc gestured toward the center of his body, "and seems to be telling me this had something to do with his death. He died in the war. Not Vietnam, though, one before."

Miriam nodded. "Yes! That's my husband's brother. He was killed by machine gun fire in Korea."

"His name is something like Nathan or Nate . . ."

"Neddie."

"Yes . . . Miriam, I can't get through to your son, but Neddie's telling me that he helped the boy cross over. He was with Robert at the moment of his death, and he wants me to tell you that the boy died peacefully. Your son is being comforted right now. He's with friends and family, who are taking care of him and seeing that he has everything he needs. The shock of his death was severe; he apparently lost both legs and an arm. However, there was no pain. Neddie wants me to emphasize that point, Miriam—no pain at all." He was silent for several moments.

I watched, fascinated, wondering how my uncle could have known so many personal details about the woman's family. The light in the room shifted as the sun moved behind some clouds. I peered through the crack intently and had to muffle a small gasp. Was it my imagination, *or was there a shadowy figure standing behind the woman, its hands on her shoulders?* I blinked, and the apparition was gone. I decided it was just my imagination, fueled by the power of my uncle's voice.

"Neddie says that in a couple of weeks, Robert will show you a sign. He doesn't want you to be sad, he says. You'll be together soon enough. Heaven is so much better than you can even imagine. Look for the sign."

"A sign," she repeated.

Doc raised his head. "I'm sorry, that's the best I can do right now. Does it help at all?"

Miriam told him that it did. She was still crying, but the fretfulness and tension seemed to have disappeared. She seemed . . . I don't know—*changed* somehow. Relieved. Like a burden had been removed.

"I can't tell you how thankful I am," she said. "How much do I owe you?

Alain waved it away. "No charge."

Her eyes widened. "But . . ."

"No charge," my uncle said firmly. "I'm glad I could help. Your son died bravely, doing what he felt was right. It's the least I could do." He stood up, and reverently handed back the dog tags. "Miriam, I want you to believe what you've heard today. You'll get a sign from him. The love you'll feel will be so pure and strong you'll hardly be able to stand it. I'll give you some medicine to help you sleep tonight."

He showed her to the door, talking in a confidential tone of voice. I hurried back into the big chair and pretended to read a book I grabbed from the table.

Doc came into the den and chuckled. "Learn anything?" he asked, pointing to the book sardonically. I looked at the title: *Sexual Dysfunctions in Pathological Medicine.* I put the book down hastily, blushing. I could tell from the tone of his voice that he knew I'd been listening.

"I, uh . . ."

"I asked you a question, son."

I looked at the floor. "I'm sorry, Uncle Alain. I didn't mean to eavesdrop . . ."

He was silent. I looked at him, expecting him to banish me from his house forever. But he was smiling gently. The expression on his face told me he wasn't angry. I realized then that he had wanted me to witness the reading. He had set me up! The chair by the window, the slightly open connecting door—not to mention the natural curiosity of a thirteen-year-old.

"Call me Doc," he reminded. "You're still avoiding the question. Did you learn anything?"

I thought about it for several long moments. Doc waited patiently, an amused expression on his face. "I guess I did," I finally answered. "I learned that there's more to magic than making coins disappear."

He laughed. "Ah yes, there is indeed. Come with me."

■ ■ ■

During the next few weeks, my training began in earnest. I learned a lot about my uncle, probably more than anyone else in the family—with the exception of Aunt May, of course—had even suspected. I began to understand why some members of my family, devout Catholics every one, looked askance at his activities. Some of his work almost bordered on witchcraft.

During this time, he saw clients two or three times a week. Sometimes they wanted readings, other times my uncle would give them herbs, crystals, or small magnets to help with their aches and pains. He would read crystal balls, tarot cards, or palms, depending on the client's preferences. Many of his clients were poor, and very rarely did he charge for these services.

One day a woman came by who insisted that someone had cast an evil spell on her. Doc listened very seriously as she described an endless succession of bizarre accidents, bad luck, and health problems that had plagued her during the past two years. It all stemmed, she said, from the time she angered a gypsy woman at a county fair. "That gypsy put a hex on me, I know she did," the woman insisted. "She looked at me funny and made a sign with her hand. Ever since then, nothing's gone right for me or my family."

Doc frowned. "Yes, this is quite serious. I can definitely see a dark, evil cloud surrounding you, full of hostile energy. Have you been feeling tired and run down? Hard to get out of bed in the morning; joints aching, pounding headaches just behind the eyes?"

She nodded vigorously.

"Gypsy magic is very powerful. No wonder you've had such a bad patch of luck. However, your luck's about to change. It so happens that I studied with a band of gypsies while traveling in Cornwall several years ago. It won't be easy, and you'll have to be brave, but I think we can lick this."

He made the woman lie down on a table and spent several minutes carefully adjusting the position of her arms and legs. Then he placed crystals, magnets, and colored stones on her forehead, chest, and shoulders. While he made these preparations, I was busy lighting several candles, as he had instructed me to do. He took a raw egg and placed it in her left hand, admonishing her to hold onto it no matter what happened. "And for God's sake, don't break it." The woman looked suitably impressed, and more than a little scared.

He had me shake a rattle made from a tortoise shell over her while he chanted a long prayer. Occasionally, he'd toss herbs and powders at the reclining woman. I watched in fascination as she writhed, groaned, and perspired during the ritual. I had no clue what was happening.

Finally, at the end of an hour, Doc collapsed into a chair, the picture of total exhaustion. His neat hair was askew, and even his mustache looked rumpled. "That should do it," he gasped. "It was a tough battle, but we beat it. How do you feel?"

The woman rolled her eyes as she took a mental inventory of her body parts. "I feel a bit better, I think. Yes, I believe I do."

Doc nodded, holding her hand. "A curse is very similar to having an infection. It will take a few days for your body to expel the toxins it's built up. There's only one thing left to do, and the curse will be completely lifted." He sent me into the kitchen to fetch a saucer. I brought it back and he handed it to the woman. "Crack the egg open, and let's see if we've been successful in capturing the evil energy that's been causing all your troubles."

The woman cracked the egg and poured the contents into the saucer. Alain gasped in horror. The woman screamed. I must admit I almost did, too. Lying amid the goo was a small, malformed figure, like an embryonic demon. The creature had small horns, and its tiny eyes seemed to glitter malevolently in the candlelight.

"Quickly!" Doc touched a candle to the small figure. It immediately burst into flames and was soon incinerated. Only a wisp of greasy, foul-smelling smoke remained. He breathed a sigh of relief. "That was close. Too damned close. It was a lot worse than I thought. That gypsy must have been an amazing sorceress. But you're free now, and I'm sure you'll find your luck has changed for the better." He gave her a package of herbs to put in her bathwater to complete the cleansing, and once again, when the woman tried to pay him, he wouldn't accept it.

After she left, he confided to me that he really didn't believe in curses and spells. "She cured herself through the power of suggestion."

"Why didn't you just explain to her that curses don't exist?" I asked him.

He raised an eyebrow. "I didn't say they didn't exist, Craig. I said I don't believe in them. However, that lady *does*, so for her the curse was real and extremely powerful. It was a dark cloud that overshadowed her natural happiness." He handed me an ice-cold cola and poured himself a glass of whiskey. "If I had tried to tell her it was all in her head, she would've gone away and paid six hundred dollars to some fake." He sipped the whiskey and sighed. "I can't emphasize this enough. If you believe in something strongly, it is real—at least it is for you. Her belief in the curse made it real, not only for her but for her entire family. Belief is contagious, son. It's the most powerful thing in the world. Don't kid yourself for a minute. We lifted a terrible curse from that poor woman."

I asked him about the demon in the egg.

He waved it away. "It's an old gypsy trick. She believed the curse was created by gypsy magic, so we used gypsy magic to dispel it. Cause and effect; the power of belief. The first rule of magic. Got it?"

I nodded. "I think I'm getting it." Then I asked him something that had been on my mind for a long time. "Can you really talk to the dead?"

He gave me one of his enigmatic smiles. "Anyone can talk to the dead, Craig. People do it all the time. The trick is getting them to answer back." He stood up and yawned, and I heard his joints crack. "I'm hungry. What do you say we go get a pizza?

CHAPTER THREE

The Power of Intuition

IT SEEMED AS THOUGH DOC'S PATTERN OF INSTRUCTION was to blow my mind with miracles, and then bring me back down to reality by explaining the phenomena in everyday, down-to-earth terms. I had been a bit disillusioned with him after he admitted that the "cleansing" that ended with the devil in the egg had been a trick. But after thinking about the results of the deception, how the woman believed she had been released from a dark curse, I saw that perhaps the most effective way to get a point across was to provide visible evidence that magic had occurred. The existence of the trick didn't mean that real magic hadn't happened.

The idea excited me. Perhaps visible confirmation increased the power of suggestion, sort of like when a doctor gives a patient a sugar-pill placebo. And there was no denying that Doc had *something*—call it intuition, psychic powers, or whatever—that connected him to a source of information I didn't understand. Gypsy tricks aside, I'd seen him tell people things about themselves and their departed loved ones that he had no way of knowing.

Helping Uncle Alain lift spells wasn't the only thing I did that summer. In between visits from his clients, we played odd little games that were designed to enhance my powers of intuition. One of these exercises involved trying to guess which one of four objects my uncle was thinking of. Jotting a quick note on a piece of his magenta paper, he placed four coins—a penny, nickel, dime and quarter—in a row on the table and had me touch one. I thought about it carefully. The dime was the smallest coin, the quarter the largest. But the penny was the only copper coin. The nickel seemed innocent enough. I touched it.

Doc smiled. "Read my prediction."

I unfolded the square of paper. *"You will reject the dime and the quarter as too obvious. The penny will attract your attention for a moment, but I really think you'll settle on the nickel."*

"Do that again," I challenged.

This time I vacillated between the quarter and the penny. I finally chose the penny.

He had predicted that too. I was completely baffled.

"Craig, it's fairly easy to determine which coin someone will choose if you just try to get inside their mind and think as they think. You try it."

I took the pencil and wrote, *"You will pick the dime."*

Doc picked the quarter.

"I just don't get it," I said.

My uncle patted my shoulder. "You will. You just have to quit thinking about it so much. Use your instincts. Try to sense what my actions will be *before* you make the prediction. Try it again."

I wrote the prediction and set it aside. "Now," he said, "look at me and use your will power to reinforce your initial impression. Try to *make* me pick the coin you want."

I looked at him and concentrated. He reached over and touched the penny.

Amazed, I turned the prediction over. *"You will pick the penny,"* I had written in block letters. It was an incredible feeling, esoteric and magical.

He touched the back of my hand. "Good! Now do it again!"

We performed the experiment at least two dozen times that day, and my accuracy rate climbed impressively. By mid-afternoon, I was getting it right four out of five times!

"Now you got it," Doc said.

Another game we played utilized his antique pocket watch. It was one of those old ones with the hinged metal case that you had to pop open to see the face. Doc had me set a random time on the watch and he'd guess it, usually to within a minute or so of accuracy. Sometimes he had me close the case and spin the hands, so that neither one of us knew where they stopped. Yet he could still guess the hour and minute with amazing precision.

Then it was my turn. He set the watch to a random time and challenged me to guess it. I tried several times but I was always way off. I just couldn't see how it was done. This wasn't like making a coin disappear or finding a chosen card. Those tricks had certain mechanics that made them work. As far as I could tell, there were no rules to Uncle Alain's magic. He just seemed to expect me to do it. I gave up in frustration.

"You're trying too hard, Craig," he said gently. "Just relax. Look at me."

His eyes caught mine and wouldn't let go. "Relax . . . relax," he urged me. "Now, close your eyes and imagine the face of a clock in your mind. Really see it. Imagine the hands are spinning, spinning. Let them come to a stop by themselves; do not try to anticipate or influence them." He snapped his fingers, and I jumped. "Now. Tell me what time it is."

"Three forty-six," I replied, without thinking.

He popped open the case and showed me. The hands were set at 3:49. "Not bad. You'll get better."

While we took a break he introduced me to my first real magic word—and it wasn't *Abracadabra* or *Hocus Pocus!*

"*Intuition*," Doc said, portentously. "The most magical word of all. The source of all real magic."

"But what is it?" I asked.

He scratched his chin, thinking. "It's a small voice inside you that tells you the correct answer. A sense of rightness that goes beyond logical thought. You see, underneath the surface of your mind there's a machine that ticks away, observing, analyzing, constantly weighing information. Most of the time, we're unaware of this machinery, but sometimes—usually when we least expect it—we get a flash of insight.

Like when you get the punchline of a joke. Your head lights up and everything makes sense."

"Like when I knew you'd pick the penny. It just popped into my head."

He nodded. "Yes. A very crude application of this wondrous sense, but it's a beginning."

Like any skill, intuition can be refined and trained, my uncle said. Most of us simply ignore that inner, nagging voice. We concentrate on rational thought and the "real" world so intently that we exclude this magical sense. "We just don't use it any more." He puffed at his cigar and chuckled. "Back in the Stone Age, when man was just another food source for predators, it was extremely useful to have a sixth sense that shouted '*Run!*' when something big and hungry was about to pounce on him. Intuition often speaks to us in dreams, when the conscious mind is asleep. We'll go to sleep with an insurmountable problem, and in the morning—*voila!*—like magic, we have an answer."

He told me that Aunt May was the most naturally intuitive person he'd ever known. "That's what first attracted me to her. She always knows what people are *feeling*; what they need to make them feel better about themselves. She's a natural healer, a genius in her own way. She does effortlessly what took me decades of practice—and does it better! Some people are geniuses with their minds, like Leonardo da Vinci and Einstein, and some are geniuses with their feelings, like your Aunt May. I'd trust her feelings over a barrelful of logical arguments any day."

He shrugged. "I guess the bottom line is that nobody really knows what intuition is. Perhaps it's our link with the Divine. Maybe it's just the ability to make good guesses and listening to feelings rather than thoughts. There's nothing supernatural about it, though. I suspect that a psychic is just a person who's trained his intuition to make good guesses based on limited data." He jumped to his feet. "Let me show you a tool that taps directly into the intuitive machinery."

He led me to his table and picked up a long, black leather case. He opened it and removed a nine-inch length of chain with a bead at one end and a small brass plumb-bob at the other.

"This is a pendulum," he told me. "I use it quite often to help my clients tap into their subconscious minds and ferret out the answers to their own questions. You hold the bead and let the pendulum dangle, like so." I took the pendulum between thumb and forefinger, as he showed me. The tip of the bob was so sensitive it trembled and twitched from my slightest movement. "Now," he said, "concentrate your thoughts on making it swing back and forth. Don't move it consciously, try to keep your hand as still as possible. Do it only with your mind."

After a couple of minutes, the pendulum slowly began to swing. I watched it in amazement. I could have sworn I wasn't doing it.

Doc nodded. "Good. Now, I'm going to suggest to you that the pendulum will stop swinging back and forth, and will start swinging in a small circle. Again, do not do this physically. Let your thoughts push it."

Again, seemingly with a mind of its own, the pendulum swung in a tight circle.

"Excellent. Now let's try a little experiment. Think of a question that can be answered either *yes* or *no*. Hold the pendulum at arm's length and concentrate on your question. If the pendulum swings back and forth, the answer is *yes*. If it makes a circle, it's like the 'O' in *no*. Give it a try."

I held out the pendulum, wondering if he was pulling my leg. I jumped. Almost immediately, the pendulum described a large circle.

"Whatever you just thought, the answer is a strong *no*," he commented. "Try it again."

Again I held the pendulum at arm's length and asked, "*Is this what I want to do when I grow up?*"

A strong *Yes!*

I felt Doc's eyes on me and I looked over at him. He had an intense expression on his face that startled me. "What is it?" I asked. "What are you looking at?"

Doc shook his head. "Whatever you were just thinking ignited a light in your eyes that I haven't seen in a long time . . . Craig, make me a promise?"

"I don't know. It depends on what it is."

Doc laughed. "Suspicious, eh? All I ask is that you never let that light go out."

31

I admitted I didn't understand what he meant. Doc rubbed his chin. "All children have a light burning within them, a wonderful power that represents their talents and limitless potential. Have you ever noticed that all parents think their children are beautiful and talented little geniuses? Well, they are! All children are special, small beacons of illumination. The problem is that, as they grow up, often that light begins to dim. It becomes overshadowed by the pursuit of wealth and prestige or simply by the mundane tasks of day-to-day living. We're trained to use our brains more and listen to our hearts less. That inner, playful being withers and disappears. The sense of wonder dries up, the harsh realities of life snuff out our imagination. And when the fire dies it is incredibly difficult to rekindle. While you were operating the pendulum I saw a wonderful gleam in your eyes. What I want you to promise me is that you will never, ever let that light die out. Always keep that inner child alive. Will you do this for me? It's the only price I ask for the lessons I will give you."

I stared at Doc's eyes, trying to comprehend what it was he wanted from me. And then for a moment—just a moment—I understood. I saw Doc, not as an old man but as a young boy, eyes filled with wonder and amazement, eager to embrace any adventure the day might offer. The little boy still lived inside the old man!

"I promise I'll try, Doc."

He gripped my arm affectionately. "That's all I ask."

The lessons continued, but we still hadn't attempted the word-from-the-book test. After playing with the pendulum for a while, I asked him about it. "Are the mind-reading tricks done with intuition?"

He looked delighted at my curiosity. "No. To read a person's thoughts, you have to go beyond intuition into *visualization*." He rubbed his chin, looking at me speculatively. "I think you're ready."

Uncle Alain made me spend the rest of the afternoon blindfolded. And I don't mean with a handkerchief tied around my eyes, like pin-the-tail-on-the-donkey. Oh no. He taped my eyelids shut ("to prevent peeking," he said with an evil chuckle) and covered my face with a thick wool cloth that practically smothered me. "Visualize your surroundings!" he called to me, as I bumped and thumped across the cluttered office. "You've been here enough times to know where everything is!"

"It's impossible," I told him. "Nobody could do this."

He proved me wrong. Doc allowed me to blindfold him with the tape (I deliberately stuck some in his mustache) and wrap his eyes with the cloth. He proceeded to navigate the room effortlessly. I wasn't too impressed; after all, he'd lived here for years and had plenty of time to perfect this routine. I think he must have read my mind, because he stood in front of me and asked me to remove a dollar bill from my wallet.

"What for?"

"You'll see."

He instructed me to fold the bill in half and stare at the serial number, to let my eyes track the digits without any conscious effort. He reached out, touched the bill briefly with his index finger, and began calling out a string of numbers and letters. "H86, 024 . . . 3 —No, wait a minute, that's an 8 . . ." My jaw dropped. He was telling me the serial number of the bill I was holding! I looked closely to see if he was peeking somehow. It was impossible. I knew the tape held his eyelids shut. He couldn't open his eyes if he wanted to.

He correctly named every one of the digits. I was floored. "How do you do that?"

"I told you: *visualization*." He painfully stripped the tape from his eyes, grimacing as it tugged at his eyebrows and mustache. "I knew a blind newspaper vendor in Times Square who could tell the denomination of any bill as soon as it was handed to him—and give you correct change. Want to try it again?" he asked, with a twisted smile.

I found I could construct a mental map of the house and, eventually, the yard. Chester and Angelica made the test more challenging by staying under my feet most of the time. Then, while still blindfolded, Doc made me go into the kitchen and make a cup of tea for him, complete with honey and lemon. Aunt May worried and fretted around me as I fumbled through the cupboards, but I managed to complete the task with only minor burns.

"Bravo," Doc commented, as he sipped his tea. "Just right. You're beginning to get it."

I felt a great sense of accomplishment, but there was no way I could duplicate the dollar trick. I knew better than to even attempt it.

Of all the lessons, I think he enjoyed the blindfold exercises the most. At least he seemed to, judging from his laughter as I stumbled around the house. I was afraid he'd give himself a heart attack.

Over dinner, he explained the pendulum to me. "It's not witchcraft or magic that makes it swing," he said. "But your own unconscious signals. It's a valuable tool because your subconscious mind cannot lie to you. It always gives you the right answer. In other words, the pendulum amplifies your own intuition."

I was a bit disappointed. "You mean it was me doing it all along?"

"Well, yes—of course. Who else?" He must have sensed my disillusionment, because he added, "Craig, there are two ways to look at the world: either nothing is magical or everything is magical. I leave it as an exercise for the student to figure out how I choose to see the world."

Aunt May added, "Shoo, that's an easy one. Craig, your uncle is amazed every morning when the sun comes up."

"You bet," Doc said, reaching for a biscuit. "One of these days it might not. There are no guarantees in this life." I didn't know if he was serious or not. As I've said before, with my uncle, you never knew.

CHAPTER FOUR

Dark Car, Dark Clouds

UNCLE ALAIN DROVE ONE OF THE MOST BEAUTIFUL CARS I'd ever seen, a jet-black 1961 Jaguar Mark 10 Sedan, just a step behind a Rolls Royce in luxury but a step ahead in performance. The car had been a present from a grateful client. When I discovered the price of the car, I concluded it must have been a *very* grateful client! I asked Doc about it, and he told me the following story:

"By 1962, I'd pretty much retired from the road, and your aunt and I had just bought this place. It needed a lot of repair, so I was doing as many readings as I could. One day a man came to me for a reading. He pulled into my driveway at the wheel of this car,"—he patted the hood—"and I thought it was the most magnificent vehicle I'd ever seen. But I was driving a rusty '49 Buick at the time, so of course anything would look pretty good to me. This fellow was well groomed, successful, and obviously wealthy. He carried himself with the air of a self-made man, but he had the saddest eyes I'd seen in a long time. I'd seen that look before. He'd lost something a long time ago, and was at the point where he'd do anything to get it back.

"'How can I help you?' I asked him.

"He looked at me and sighed. 'I'm tired,' he said. 'I've worked hard all my life. I'm at the top of my field, and have all the money I need. But . . .'

"'Ah,' I said. 'There's always a "but," isn't there?' The man with the nice car went on to tell me that he had grown up under incredible poverty. As children, he and his sisters never had enough to eat or clean clothes to wear. He swore his children would never do without, as he and his family had done. To this end, he devoted his life to work. He got a job in sales with a major corporation, and saved his money and invested wisely. He scrimped and saved. You know, he followed the American Dream. Eventually he had enough money to start his own company, which took off like a rocket. He was wealthy and successful. 'But,' he said, 'I seem to have never gotten around to having a family of my own. You see, a long time ago, there had been this girl . . .'

"It was an old story, Craig. As a young man, the businessman had been engaged to a young woman whom he felt was his one true love, but the job offer in Saint Louis was too good to refuse. She wanted him to stay; he couldn't bring himself to turn the job down. She told him they didn't need the money; he told her she was being selfish and unrealistic. The two argued. In anger he called off the engagement and went to Saint Louis to follow his dream.

"However, he learned that money and success are not necessarily equivalent to happiness. Always, in the back of his mind and during the lonely times, he thought of the girl he'd left behind. When he came to me, all he wanted was a chance to explain to the girl how he felt. 'The family moved away, and nobody knows where they went,' he said. 'I suppose she's married, with a family of her own, but I just want to see her again, and make a clean slate of it. It's been tormenting me. Can you help me find her?' I told him I'd try.

"I asked if he had anything that belonged to his lost love, a picture or a piece of jewelry. He handed me the girl's engagement ring, which he'd had with him for years. 'Perfect!' I told him. I remembered a trick I'd learned in Scotland, when I was traveling there years ago. The locals used it to track down missing persons and livestock. I got out a map of the United States and spread it on a table. Then, I tied the ring to a length of string and asked the man to hold it over the map, thinking about the girl as he last saw her, holding her face in his mind. If there was any connection between them at all, I reasoned, this very special pendulum would help bring it out.

"Eventually, the pendulum swung back and forth—you've seen how it works. He was amazed, and almost dropped it. 'Careful,' I cautioned him. 'Concentrate!' The pendulum zeroed in on Florida. We were quite certain; I had him repeat the procedure several times, from several different directions. We even managed to narrow the location down to Fort Lauderdale."

Doc puffed his cigar. "It was all I could do for him. It was a long shot, but he traveled to Florida and made inquiries. Money was no object to him, of course, and he had plenty. He was willing to spend it all to find her. *Did* he find her, you ask? Seven months later, I got a letter from him saying he caught up with her just outside of Fort Lauderdale. She'd been recently widowed and was living with her children. Did I mention that the letter ended, 'I saw the way you admired my car. Please accept it as a token of my—OUR—appreciation.' The car was delivered to my driveway. And that's how I got it, cross my heart and hope to die."

I looked at Doc skeptically. "Is that the truth?"

He stubbed out his cigar. "What is truth? Craig, I firmly believe that one shouldn't let truth interfere with a good story. Believe it or not as you choose; I also believe in free will."

And that was all I ever got for an answer.

■ ■ ■

That jet-black Jaguar was a sweet car nevertheless, low and crouching like a Bombay panther. As you can imagine, this car was well known in Wheeling. Everyone recognized it as belonging to "that psychic guy who lived on the island." This notoriety often led to some very interesting encounters. Some people would go out of their way to talk to Doc and try to get free advice—which he willingly gave—while others made a point of crossing the street and walking on the other side of the road to avoid him.

One day we roared across the bridge into town to run a few errands. Mom had invited Doc to dinner that night (I think Dad just wanted to know a little bit more about the old guy his son was spending so much time with). That was the day I learned that not everyone admired my uncle's abilities. That some people, in fact, feared them.

We had just emerged from the liquor store with a bottle of wine. I noticed a piece of notebook paper flapping under the Jaguar's windshield wiper. I thought it was probably an advertisement of some kind, but when I pulled it off and read it, I was shocked. BURN IN HELL! it read, in large, sprawling letters. Then I noticed the long, jagged scratches in the car's paint. I looked at my uncle. His lips were pressed together. "Who did this?" I asked.

"An admirer," he responded curtly. He pointed to the radio antenna, which someone had broken off. "One of my more zealous fans. Get in the car—I'll try to explain."

As we drove across the bridge, Alain explained to me that a number of people believed his abilities were nothing more than Black Magic. "Some of the more conservative religious groups shy away from anything dealing with psychic abilities or the paranormal. They occasionally feel that they must make their sentiments known to me. This isn't the first time this has happened."

I had a flash of realization: an *intuitive* flash, you could say. "You know who did it, don't you?"

He nodded. "Yes, we go way back. He has a bit of a local following."

I remembered the violence implied in the hateful note, scratches and the broken antenna, and thought that Alain was understating the case. "Are you going to tell the police?" I asked.

He shook his head. "No, the person who did this truly believes he's serving God . . . at least his interpretation of God. At my age I'm reluctant to engage in a Holy War with the local Fundamentalist congregation. Besides," he continued. "One thing I've learned in my lifetime is to be tolerant of other's beliefs."

"But he broke your antenna!"

His voice remained mild. "No big deal. I can get a new one. I've had to address this issue all my life. I left California because my family was embarrassed to have a psychic in the family. The more famous I became, the worse it was for them. When I married your Aunt May, I thought her family would run me out of town on a rail. You may have noticed the clan acts a little standoffish towards me."

I had noticed. It was the reason it took me thirteen years to meet him. But I was confused. I had learned in church that God was tolerant and forgiving, not violent and spiteful. However, there seemed to be an endless series of rules, some of which didn't make much sense to me. I mentioned this to Doc.

He laughed. "I don't blame you for being confused. People make it a lot more complicated than it is. God is basically Love. His prophets taught compassion and forgiveness. 'Do unto others as you would have them do unto you,' is another way of saying 'try to see the other fella's side of the story.' Unfortunately, many people project their own fears and attitudes into their beliefs. It's easy to make yourself feel better by pointing fingers at other people. The Bible clearly says in several places that the devil cannot bestow paranormal powers upon a person. Oh, he can promise them, but he never delivers."

"I never thought of that."

"God created the mind, and everything in the mind, for a purpose: God wants us to be happy and free. He wants us to love one another and use our talents to make the world a better place for everybody. If your talent happens to lie in the arena some people call 'paranormal,' and you can use this talent to help others, what are you supposed to do—ignore it? To me, that would be a great sin. Craig, I've made a lot of money with my own peculiar talent, and some would say that in itself is a sin. But I've helped more people with my readings than I can count, and made thousands of others laugh and have a good time with my show. I've never made anyone pay who couldn't afford it. I give away more readings than I get paid for, and I've never harmed anyone. So where's the problem?"

We rolled across the suspension bridge. Down below, several families played along the bank of the Ohio River. "Why are people afraid of what you do?" I asked.

"We fear what we don't understand. Most people get their ideas about the paranormal from bad novels, and even worse movies. Understanding ourselves is vital to living an intelligent life, but it's also scary. God gave us a mind as well as a spirit. Unfortunately, it's a lot easier to get by on faith alone without even trying to understand reality. You're beginning to understand that what I do isn't a power, but a developed skill that anyone willing to apply themselves can learn." An unreadable expression appeared on his face. It might have been nostalgia, or it could have been regret for opportunities lost. "There's a big difference between faith and fantasy. The secret is to not get lost in your own dream world and try to project your own human failings onto God. Wishful thinking, fantasies, might-have-beens. No one is immune to these. We all do it, I do it, and so do you. But no matter how much we may want to, we can't go back and rewrite history. Far better to look ahead."

"It just all seems so complicated," I sighed.

He then told me that the highest law was compassion. "Compassion is beyond law and ethics. Compassion is beyond debate or intellectualization. Any action that rises from compassion is a moral act, regardless of what the law and the rules say. When in doubt, always ask yourself: 'What is the most compassionate path?' You'll never go wrong if you do that."

I told him I didn't think the person who broke his antenna was very compassionate.

"Depends on how you look at it." We pulled into his driveway and he opened the door. "Remember what I said about the power of belief? Well, today someone broke my antenna." He turned and looked at me, eyes somber. "Three hundred years ago they would have burned me at the stake—and you too, as my apprentice. Personally, I think we've come a long way."

Doc changed into a tank-top shirt and old jeans, and I helped him buff the scratches from his car. I was amazed at the large slabs of muscles on his chest and arms. He was old enough to be my grandfather, and yet he looked like he could wrestle a grizzly bear into submission if he wanted. We installed a new antenna and the job was done. Doc had a few extras in his garage. Apparently this wasn't the first time this had happened.

After we removed all evidence of the vandalism, we went to the back garden and collected a basket of vegetables to take to my mother. Doc seemed to put the whole incident behind him.

Aunt May saw us off. "You two have fun. And Alain—behave," she said.

Doc chuckled. "May, I'm going into the lion's den. It's your family. Won't you reconsider, come along and protect me?"

"You're on your own, dear. I'm chairing the Garden Club tonight." I thought it was interesting that Aunt May wouldn't be joining us. I suspect she may have hung back so my family could scrutinize Doc by himself. Maybe she had one of her "feelings," as Doc called them.

That night, Doc was his usual quietly charming self. He and my dad discussed politics (I noticed Doc veered toward the conservative point of view in order to agree with my dad), and I was glad to see my dad become more relaxed around him. Doc cracked him up with the quote: "Those who enjoy politics and sausage shouldn't look too closely at what goes into either."

After dinner he amused Brian with some magic tricks—"paying for his dinner," he told me with a wink. He concluded his performance by folding a paper napkin into a beautiful facsimile of a rose, which he presented to my mother. "It was a lovely meal, Byrel," he said, bowing and kissing her hand. "Thank you for inviting me." My mom got all flustered. Dad snorted and rolled his eyes.

As most families did in the '70s, we retired to the living room after dinner to watch television. After a typical debate over what to watch, we settled on a variety show. The host, a red-haired country singer, did his turn and introduced the guests. Wayne Newton came out and sang; George Carlin told some jokes ("I don't get it," my Dad muttered throughout); a juggler did his bit. Then the host introduced his next guest, a young Israeli whose name was not familiar to us. However, the guest was introduced as a "psychic," which caused Doc and me to sit up and pay attention.

"Laydeez and Gennlemun," the host drawled, "please welcome Uri Geller!"

A young man with black hair and dark eyes came out and immediately dominated the stage with his infectious enthusiasm. He asked audience members to bring him keys, rings, knives—anything metal. He stroked keys and they bent into odd angles. Rings sagged into ovals, knife blades drooped like taffy. It was simply the most incredible thing I'd ever seen.

"Nice trick," my dad observed. "Can you do that one, Craig?"

I just looked at him and he laughed.

Geller had come to the United States after blowing minds throughout Israel and Europe with his displays of *telekinesis* (the ability to affect solid matter with the mind) and took the country by storm. I suppose it was a sign of the times that a charming guy who could bend spoons just by stroking them could set the entire world on its collective ear.

Doc was impressed with the young performer. "Incredible. To think that one of us would make it on television . . ."

Geller pointed into the camera and spoke directly to us, the home viewers. "I want every one of you to get a spoon, fork or broken wristwatch. Go—go now, and hurry back. I'll wait." He crossed his arms, and the studio audience laughed. Brian ran into the kitchen and returned with a handful of cutlery, doling them out to us like a blackjack dealer.

On the television, the host supplied a handful of silverware. Geller's eyes reached out from the screen and grabbed us. "Now, do just like I do. The power is within you. *You* can do this; just believe it can happen." The spoons and forks melted like putty as soon as Geller touched them. I was astounded. "Now, *you* do it," Geller urged, "picture the metal softening . . . becoming liquid . . ."

I rubbed and stroked the spoon I was holding, but nothing happened.

"Look, I did it!" Brian held up a spoon, twisted into a weird angle. I laughed to myself, thinking he had cheated, then I looked down at my own spoon. The bowl had bent to about a forty-degree angle. I was speechless.

"My silverware!" Mom cried out.

"You boys quit messing around," Dad said.

I would have sworn I hadn't bent the spoon manually, it just seemed to go limp by itself. I made a mental note to investigate this phenomenon further. Mom took the silverware away and we turned our attention back to Geller.

His repertoire seemed endless. He rotated the hands of a wristwatch and deflected a compass needle, all the while encouraging the audience to believe in their own incredible powers. I went over to Doc, who seemed entranced. "How is he doing that?"

During the late 1800s and early 1900s Wheeling Island
was in its heyday—it had lost some of its sparkle but none of its
character by the time Alain "Doc" DeLyle took up residence in
the mid 1900s. —*Island Homes–From the Bridge*. From Art Work of
Wheeling, West Virginia. Chicago: The Gravure
Illustration Company, 1904

"He has an intuitive understanding of the fundamental nature of
matter and energy. He can manipulate objects with his thoughts."

"But how did he bend *my* spoon?"

Doc looked at me mischievously. "Weren't you listening? He didn't
do it. YOU did. Geller is a catalyst. He can trigger the psychic power
in others."

"It's a good trick," my father repeated. "He must have a laser con-
cealed in his belt or something.'

Doc winked at me as though saying, "Ah, skeptics."

Geller concluded his performance by psychically duplicating a
drawing the host had made and sealed into an envelope before the
show. He seemed as excited as the audience did when his feats worked.
"The power is in YOU,' he told the audience. "I'm not doing this;
YOU are!" He strode from the stage, leaving the host and his guests
goggle-eyed.

When the banjo player came out, Doc and I retired to the back porch to watch fireflies and discuss what we had just witnessed. I thought that Geller was the most incredible performer I'd ever seen. I couldn't imagine anyone doubting the authenticity of his powers— no props, no boxes or assistants, just a handful of everyday objects. "Now everyone will know that these abilities are real," I said.

Doc shook his head. "Not everybody. That boy is really going to catch hell from skeptics. They'll be on him like locusts on a wheat field."

I looked at him, puzzled. "Why?"

He rubbed his chin. "Well, some people believe it's their duty to protect the gullible public from scoundrels like Geller. And me, for that matter. And you, should you decide to follow in my disreputable footsteps."

I thought about Uri Geller, the young, enthusiastic performer whose extraordinary feats of mental abilities had amazed me. He was so likable. So believable. "What do you think will happen to him?"

Doc shrugged. "Who can say? Probably, a few jealous magicians will crawl from the woodwork and 'duplicate' his feats, riding his coat-tails all the way to the bank—like Houdini did with the spirit mediums of his time. If Geller's smart, he'll turn this to his advantage. Use their own tactics against them."

Doc went home and I retired to my room. I really didn't know what to think about my uncle. My head spun with new and sometimes con-flicting concepts. I thought about Doc's clients, who came to him for reassurance and peace of mind; the faceless vandal who had damaged Doc's car over a difference in beliefs; a young Israeli who had mastered the power of mind-over-matter; and skeptics, who categorically denied the existence of paranormal phenomena of any kind. Who was right? Who knew the truth? What was the truth? I heard Doc's voice in my head:

Perhaps truth is whatever you want it to be.

That last was too much for my exhausted brain. I went to bed.

CHAPTER FIVE

Spirits and Other Matters

THE NEXT FRIDAY DOC CALLED and said he had a surprise for me.

"What is it?"

He chuckled. "We're going to a séance."

A séance! I could hardly wait. I fidgeted around the house, killing time. My mom, irritated by my restlessness, finally put me to work in the kitchen helping her paste trading stamps in books. It helped pass time, but I'll never forget the taste of those stamps, like alum-coated bananas.

Doc drove by just after dinner and picked me up. He was wearing a spiffy charcoal grey suit and a matching fedora.

"Where are we going?"

"To Madame Adele's Friday night spook show," he answered.

He told me there was an elderly woman (whom we will call Madame Adele) who gave public séances in her home near Wheeling. These séances were usually by invitation only, and free of charge—except it was strongly hinted that attendees could leave a "love offering" in the basket near the door. Often these love offerings amounted to several hundred dollars a night. Tax free! Madame Adele, according to Doc, was a good example of how low some people will stoop to deceive the innocent.

"Her real name is Mildred Statz and she used to work for a collection agency. Check out her advertisement." He handed over a flier and I laughed. It read: MADIM ADELE, PHYSIC EXTRORDINAIRRE.

"She can't spell," I observed. "Is she any good as a psychic?"

Doc grinned. "You'll see for yourself. I got us in for the eight o'clock show."

We pulled up into the driveway of Madam Adele's studio. Judging from some of the expensive cars in her driveway, her clients were pretty well-to-do. We parked and walked over to the main entrance. Two of the largest men I had ever seen in my life stood near the door, checking invitations and instructing people where to go. Their sloping foreheads and large jaws made them look like gorillas dressed up in expensive suits.

Doc nudged me. "Her sons," he whispered. "Living proof that Darwin was right." I bit the inside of my cheek to keep from laughing aloud. Neither one of the two goons looked like he had much of a sense of humor. Doc handed over our invitation and, grunting, they motioned us in.

We were directed through a hallway that smelled of roses and incense into a drawing room set up as a small theater. About fifty wooden chairs (the kind they used to have in old churches) were in rows in front of a small elevated platform. A single antique chair sat on the platform, next to a small table with a pitcher of water. Every seat was occupied, and the rest of the room was packed with standing guests. We took a spot along the wall where we had a clear view of the stage. Gospel music played from hidden speakers.

I saw the famous collection basket near the door, guarded by another one of Adele's apelike sons. I nudged Doc and pointed. It was already brimming with bills, and nothing less pious than tens and twenties were allowed to profane the sacred pot. He nodded.

"After the show, there'll be ten times that much. Ah, here comes the esteemed Madam herself."

The audience broke into applause as a door opened and Madame Adele (PHYSIC EXTRORDINAIRRE) swept into the room blowing kisses to her fans and admirers. She was a large woman, with a great love for red-and-gold silk kimonos. Her round face was surmounted by the biggest blonde beehive hairdo I've ever seen. She held up her hands and the applause subsided.

"Thank you for coming, my dear children." She smiled, showing a mouthful of large white teeth. It was scary, like the grin of a predatory animal. "Tonight in this circle of love, we will be reunited with our dear departed. Death isn't the end, my beloveds; oh no—it's only the beginning! Our Father's house has many mansions, and there is one waiting for each of us, where our loved ones wait to greet us with open arms!" After delivering this corny pabulum, she sat down in the chair and began massaging her temples. "I must have silence, now, as I communicate with my Spirit Guide, Lotus Blossom . . ."

According to the flier, Lotus Blossom was a Chinese slave girl who lived and died around 1000 B.C. I watched, intrigued, while Madame Adele writhed and moaned in her chair, struggling to make contact with the other side.

Suddenly, she opened her eyes, blinked rapidly and smiled at us. "Herro, my fliends," she said, in a high pitched, sing-song voice. "Me Rotus Brossom. I bling gleetings flom the other side!"

"Is she serious?" I whispered to Doc.

"Keep watching. It gets better."

She continued into a long, incomprehensible sermon urging us all to love one another and pursue our own unique spiritual path. Doc told me later that most of her discourse came from newsstand astrology books and fortune cookies. The audience ate it up, though, staring at the stage with rapt adoration. Several faces were streaked with tears.

Lotus Blossom answered a few questions from the audience and delivered words of good cheer from departed relatives. With a shuddering gasp, Madame Adele woke up. One of her sons brought her a glass of water, which she sipped daintily. She smiled at the audience. "Now we will hear from my Indian Guide, Chief Raincloud."

Again Madame Adele went into a trance. She was an Academy Award waiting to happen. When she opened her eyes this time, her face was woodenly stolid. She raised a hand in greeting. "Ugh. How, Pilgrims," she intoned in a deep voice. "Many moons have I dwelled in Happy Hunting Grounds. I bring greetings from Great Spirit . . ."

Doc looked delighted. "This is new," he whispered. "I haven't seen her do this routine before."

Even for the '70s, it was undoubtedly the worst impersonation of an Indian I ever heard, as racially offensive as the old burlesque minstrel shows. I felt Doc trembling next to me and, alarmed, I looked at him to make sure he was okay. To my amazement he was trying his best not to laugh out loud! He gestured with his head toward the stage, telling me to keep watching.

Madame Adele was oblivious, deep in her trance. "Ugh. Great Spirit say Happy Hunting Ground is for all peoples. I prepare a teepee for my white children as well as red . . . much wampum for all kemosabes—"

I think it was the word "kemosabe" that did it! Doc couldn't take it anymore. He began giggling loudly. Shocked faces turned in our direction, wondering who would dare disturb such a sacred moment. After all, this was Chief Raincloud! I heard outraged exclamations; one woman began crying.

I can't tell you firsthand what other pearls of wisdom the Chief might have had for us, for at that moment a large hand descended on the back of my neck and lifted me from the floor. I was pinned in the steely grip of one of Adele's sons, like a fox in a spring trap; he hurried me through the hallway and flung me out the front door like a Frisbee. I flew through the air and landed painfully in the driveway, rolling over several times before the momentum of my flight expended itself. The gravel tore at my knees. I got up on my elbows in time to see Doc land nearby with a loud thud, still choking with laughter. He had a black eye.

"What's so damned funny?" I asked him, wondering how I was going to explain to my parents exactly why I came home with bleeding elbows and torn pants.

"Ha haaa!" he howled, slapping his knee. "Oh my. Hee heee! Son of a bitch!"

"What?"

"Oh my God, that was beautiful! That was *choice!*"

"What?"

He threw his arm around my shoulder and stuck his face so close to mine we were nose-to-nose. "Didn't you hear, *kemosabe?*" he gasped,

"Lotus Blossom was bad enough, but there at the end she outdid herself. She summoned *Tonto!*"

I looked at him in shocked amazement, and then it hit me. I started to laugh, and that got him going again. I never laughed so hard in my life. Anyone seeing us would have thought we were crazy, clinging to each other as we rolled in the dirt.

It was a lovely moment.

■ ■ ■

"Do you believe in spirits?" I asked him the next day. I'd been comparing the shoddy performance of "Madim Adele" with the incredible readings Doc performed for his clients. Miriam had been back several times to seek information about her son. It seemed to me that Doc's abilities were as real as Adele's were bogus.

"What do you mean?"

"Do spirits really talk to you?"

He chewed his moustache for a moment, thinking. "I don't know," he finally answered.

"You don't know?" My face must have reflected my puzzlement, because he laughed.

"That's right—I don't know. All I can tell you is that I usually know exactly what my client is supposed to hear. My intuition tells me to say certain things. I don't know if I believe the information actually comes from spirits, but on the other hand, I don't completely dismiss the idea either. The simple truth is, I don't know. Just because I haven't experienced something directly doesn't mean it isn't possible." He scratched his chin, searching his memory. "A good friend of mine in New York, who works under the name Brother Shadow, says that spirit mediums who convey messages from the dead do not have direct contact with souls of the departed. He believes that the departed are with us, not floating around somewhere in space, but alive and well within the subconscious of everyone they ever came in contact with when alive. Those we know leave an imprint on our minds that continues after their death. He says his job is to help the client bring these memories back and relive them."

He went on to explain that some psychologists speak of a cosmic consciousness that exists on another dimensional plane, which occasionally breaks through into normal awareness. "I believe the mind has access to all information, past, present, and future—kind of like a huge, universal library containing all the information that ever was and that ever will be. Carl Jung explored this possibility quite a bit. Why do two people often open their mouths at the same time and start to say the same thing? Sometimes the phone will ring and you just know who it is? Or you hear a song playing in your head, turn on the radio and the same song is playing? Jung called this phenomenon 'synchronicity.' Perhaps a psychic event is what occurs when two or more people tune into this huge, cosmic pool of knowledge at the same time."

He paused. "The bottom line? Craig, I wish I knew. Intuition appears to be the key that unlocks this vast body of information. But as to the why and how—it's anybody's guess. I think this is why science has such a hard time investigating psychic abilities. The cause or source of the power seems endlessly elusive."

"But it *could* be spirits? Is that what you're saying?"

He looked at me. "Come with me, I'll show you something."

We retired to his den. He poured a glass of whiskey and told me to help myself to a soda. "Back in the early '40s, when I was making a bit of a reputation for myself, a representative for the American Psychical Society contacted me. The Society was a group of scientists who investigated the paranormal to determine if there was anything to it or not. I was naïve. I agreed, thinking that I'd simply show my skills and participate in a scientific discussion."

He laughed. "I was mistaken. Out of the group of ten investigators, maybe two of them were open-minded to the possibility of ESP. The others were hardcore skeptics, determined to debunk everything I did. They simply refused to believe what they were seeing was real. My scores were so high they were convinced I was cheating, so they brought in a magician to 'debunk' me." Alain smiled. "This guy strode in like he owned the place, and with his bald head, white beard and burning eyes, he looked like an Old Testament prophet. He watched me for several days and told the scientists he had it all figured out."

"What happened?"

"Well, he showed the scientists a few card tricks, said my readings were vague generalities that applied to everybody . . . completely ignoring the very specific details I gave, mind you . . . collected his check and left. The investigators divided into two factions; those who believed I was real and those who didn't. I was tired of being a lab rat anyway, so I quit. The last I heard, the results of the tests were listed as 'inconclusive.' So ended my attempts to scientifically investigate the existence of spooks." He took a sip from his glass. "I remember hearing a story once about a skeptic who said, 'God, if you really exist, make a rainbow appear in the sky right now.' Suddenly, a beautiful rainbow appeared, arching across the sky in magnificent splendor. The skeptic remarked, 'What a coincidence! A rainbow!'"

I laughed; it reminded me of my father.

"You see Craig; it's a matter of belief again. Or, more specifically, disbelief. Skeptics believe only in science and rationality, and anything that doesn't fit in the parameters of the scientific method simply doesn't exist. Psychic phenomena have no clear place in a structured cause-and-effect worldview, so they chuck it out. They believe nothing. In this sense, they're really not much different from Madame Adele's clients. Those people you saw last night represent the other end of the spectrum—they're willing to believe *anything*, no matter how ridiculous it seems to you and me, as long as it supports their view of the world. The best thing, in my not-so-humble opinion, is to keep an open mind to all possibilities."

I didn't ask him if the demonstrations he performed for the scientists had been tricks or the real stuff—or a mixture of both. I knew that he did tricks sometimes, but I also knew he could do things that were definitely not tricks. I also learned from experience that he had a wicked sense of humor, and it may have amused him to lead the skeptics down the garden path with a little sleight-of-hand. "What were you going to show me?" I asked.

He looked at me. "Oh yes, I went off on a tangent, didn't I?" He got up and rummaged through a closet, bringing out a dusty glass box. "By any chance have you ever heard of the Dunninger challenge box?"

I told him I had. Dunninger was the preeminent mentalist of his time, a headliner back in the vaudeville days. When my class toured the Houdini Magical Hall of Fame, I saw Dunninger's challenge box on display, an odd little contraption designed to test spirit mediums. It was a simple device but very clever. A pencil was suspended in the middle of a glass box, point down, its tip barely touching the surface of a piece of paper. It was impossible to manipulate the pencil in any way.

Doc wiped the dust off the box. "This is a replica that an acquaintance of Joe Dunninger's gave me years and years ago. Joe was a die-hard skeptic when it came to matters of the spirit world. He was against the whole idea. He went after mediums every bit as ferociously as Houdini did. He designed the box and offered ten thousand dollars to any medium who could cause the pencil to write something—anything—on the paper."

"Did anyone take him up on the challenge?" I asked

"Some did. None succeeded."

"Can you make it write?"

"Nope. Couldn't dot an 'i' or cross a 't' if my life depended on it." He handed the box over to me. "This is for you. It needs a little work, but I think you can fix it." He grinned. "Conduct your own investigation. See for yourself. If you get any messages from the spirits, be sure to let me know!"

I still didn't know whether or not Doc believed in spirits. And although I concentrated on the box for hours, I couldn't so much as make the tip of the pencil tremble. I guess I had to be content with a definite 'maybe' for my answer.

■ ■ ■

Two days later I experienced one of the most frightening events of my life. In fact, it was so terrifying and otherworldly that I decided I'd had enough of Doc and his magic.

It began innocently enough, with a morning spent working in the garden behind Doc's house. He asked my help clearing away a dense undergrowth of brush around his boat dock. His back yard slanted down to the river and was a jungle of trees, bushes, and vines. We attacked the brush with razor-sharp machetes and a savage conviction to finish the job by late afternoon. I've already mentioned that my uncle was incredibly agile and alert for a man of his age. I should add at this point that nobody knew exactly what his age was. Doc seemed ancient to me at that time, but at the age of thirteen my fifty-year-old father was "old." Doc seemed to enjoy keeping his age as much a mystery as his past. He liked to keep people guessing.

He usually worked several hours each day and took long walks in the evenings. I don't remember him ever being sick or under the weather during the entire time I knew him. His health and energy seemed inexhaustible. I've always been active; I love the water and swimming, but Doc could work circles around me.

By eleven o'clock I was becoming tired, although Doc seemed as energetic as ever. I wondered if the secret to his vitality lay in the strange herbs and potions he kept in his cabinet. Perhaps he'd discovered the Fountain of Youth?

Between my exhaustion and daydreaming, I was an accident waiting to happen. Doc was chopping away at a tangle of honeysuckle, lecturing me on how to make the maximum use of my energy. "Quit fighting the weeds," he called out. "Work with them. Follow the path of least resistance." I was ready to finish the job and get something to eat, so I raised the machete and chopped at the base of a thick sapling, intending to sever it with one blow. However, my grip was weak from fatigue, and the repetitive drudgery of the work had lulled me into a state of carelessness. Instead of cutting the sapling, the machete deflected from the tree and hit me in the leg.

At first I didn't realize I was injured. I lifted the blade to eye level and noticed the edge looked different. It was flecked with not only green tree sap, but a bright red, sticky liquid as well.

Blood! My brain screamed.

Then I looked down at my leg and saw the deep gash along the side of my shin, just above the ankle. I still couldn't comprehend that it was *my* leg, *my* blood I was seeing, pumping out of the jagged wound.

Then the pain hit me!

I felt the world spin around and around and I sat down heavily. I guess I almost fainted. Blood spurted from my leg onto the grass.

The whole thing couldn't have taken more than a couple of seconds. Doc ran over and held my head up as I swooned backward. "Ah shit," he said. "May!" he yelled toward the house. "Bring bandages! Craig's hurt!"

I felt weak and dizzy; my hands and feet were numb. Doc held my head between his hands and caught my eyes with his. "Look at me, Craig. Don't give in. Stay awake now. We're going to try something, and if you'll just trust me, everything will be okay."

"It hurts," I said. I was trying very hard to keep from throwing up.

"I know it does. We'll take care of that, too. Just listen to me. Take a deep breath and relax . . . in, out." I took a shuddering breath and let it out. "Again." He made me breathe deeply until my respiration was smooth and even. All the while he applied firm pressure to my leg to staunch the bleeding.

"Concentrate on your leg, the source of the pain. Examine the pain—don't shy away from it. Feel it, sense it, be aware of it . . ." He urged me to focus only on the throbbing pain that radiated from my leg up into the rest of my body. "Relax . . . let it go, just clouds fading on the horizon. No pain. No pain at all. Imagine a cooling hand stroking your leg, erasing all the pain. Like ripples in a pond, and the ripples fade away into nothing . . ."

May ran out with a first aid kit and quickly examined the cut. "He needs stitches," she said. "He's cut pretty deep. What happened?"

"Craig cut himself with the machete. It was my fault, I should have kept my eye on him . . ." I heard their voices abstractly, like they were in another room discussing a subject in which I had no interest. "Right now we have to slow the bleeding. Craig, listen to me. Does it still hurt?"

To my surprise, the pain had subsided to a barely noticeable dull throb. "No, it's better now."

"All right then. Imagine your blood as it flows from your heart, picture each beat. Blood flowing through your body to your limbs. Your arms and legs . . . now, slow the beat of your heart, just tell it to slow down. Slower . . . slower . . ."

I don't remember exactly what he said as his voice carried me away, but I began to actually feel the blood circulating through my body—a strange, hot/cold sensation as though my blood was alive and communicating to me. It was a peaceful, sleepy feeling, as though time stood still. I willed my heart to slow down, and I think it did.

Portrait of a Wizard, artist's interpretation of Alain "Doc"
DeLyle during the mystical summer of 1971.
—Artwork by Jon Saint-Germain

"Good," Doc said. "Now I want you to focus your attention to where I'm touching you. Open your eyes and look at your leg."

I did as he asked and felt a shock of horror. Blood everywhere; the leg of my pants was drenched in it. Again I felt that sensation of floating away as the world spun around me.

"No!" Doc's voice was sharp. "Don't pass out. Look at it. Be aware of it. I want you to concentrate on stopping the blood flow to your leg. Just imagine the veins and capillaries closing up, clenching like a fist. Stop the bleeding, Craig, I know you can do it."

He ran his finger along the edges of the gash and urged me to stop the bleeding. Perhaps it was the state of shock I was in that allowed me to summon abilities I didn't know I had. Maybe it was belief in Doc's magic. I don't know . . . but I saw the flow of blood slow to a trickle, and then stop completely.

Doc sighed in relief. "Good boy. I knew you could do it." May stepped in and bandaged my leg, turning the gauze expertly. Doc ran to the house, returning with one of his herbal concoctions, which he urged me to drink. I grimaced at the bittersweet taste, but it did seem to calm me down.

Even though the bleeding had stopped, I was seriously scared. Not so much from the cut, but from what I had just seen my uncle do, an impossible, unheard of thing: he only touched me and healed my injury, an injury so serious that only a couple of minutes ago I was worried I might bleed to death.

No, no, my mind insisted, *he can't do that. That would be . . .*

Let's face it. That would be a *miracle.*

May called my mother to meet us at the hospital. As we drove into town, I lay down in the back seat and pretended to sleep. But my mind was whirling with questions.

A few stitches and I was as good as new. I've already said this was the most frightening thing I'd ever experienced. Not the bleeding (I'd been cut before), but Doc's uncanny healing abilities. In short, I was sure that my uncle was either a witch or a saint. And from what I learned in church, saints didn't drink whiskey or smoke cigars!

It was too much for me. I decided my apprenticeship had come to an end.

CHAPTER SIX

The River Shaman

MY PARENTS NEVER KNEW the full extent of my injury. Mom worried and fussed, of course, but Dad knew that teenage boys were likely to get scraped around a bit. "It's not like he almost bled to death, Byrel," he said. I saw no reason to correct him. If it hadn't been for Doc's intervention—his *magical* intervention—I probably would have bled to death.

Neither one of them blamed Doc for the accident, which is what I feared. However, this left me without a good excuse to avoid him. I'd been holding out a vague hope they would forbid me to see him anymore.

I was scared of Doc—and a little bit angry with him, I had to admit. I felt like he'd been holding back, just showing me the tip of the iceberg—minor party tricks—while all the time he possessed magical powers like a wizard from a fairy tale. I decided that the psychic stuff wasn't for me. I didn't want to do real magic. From now on I'd stick to simple tricks, where at least I knew what was going on and where I was in control of the how and why.

That night I was up late watching Tom Snyder, who was interviewing magicians Mark Wilson, Doug Henning, and Walter Gibson (creator of The Shadow). I had a piece of rope in my hands, trying to imitate a trick Mark Wilson was doing. I heard the front door open and my older brother Bill came in, returning from a night out with his friends. Bill was home from college for a couple of weeks, but spent most of his time away on business of his own.

Bill seemed surprised to see me. "Up late, Bear," he said. ("Bear" was his nickname for me—to this day I have no idea why.) He went into the kitchen and I heard him making coffee. "Want some?" he called out.

"Sure," I said. Actually, I'd never had coffee in my life, but I didn't want to appear immature in front of my older brother. Soon he returned with two steaming cups.

"Here you go," Bill said. "How do you take it?"

I sipped it and tried not to grimace at the taste. "I like a little cream and sugar," I said, and went into the kitchen and practically filled the cup with the two items. I noticed a bottle of Jack Daniels on the counter and grinned. Apparently Bill liked to dilute his coffee, too.

When I returned to the living room, I found that Bill had pre-empted my seat in the comfortable chair. "Finders keepers," he said, lighting his pipe and peering at me through the smoke. I admitted he won the chair fair and square and sat down on the small sofa.

"So what have you been doing with yourself all summer?" Bill asked.

I shrugged, sipping my coffee. "Nothing much. Practicing magic mostly."

He nodded. "Mom says you've been spending a lot of time with Doc, the family outcast. That should be fairly interesting."

I was surprised that he knew about my visits to the island. "How so?" I asked him.

"It's not everyone who gets a chance to learn at the feet of a shaman." He puffed at his pipe. "I'd pay attention if I were you. You'll learn more from Doc than you will from any class you'll ever take. What has he shown you so far?"

"He's shown me a few things," I said evasively. "What's a shaman?"

Bill laughed. "A shaman is a wise man, a teacher, one who communicates with the spirits. A practitioner of healing magic. Keeper of knowledge. Medicine man." Bill looked toward the darkness outside the window and for a moment he was somewhere else. Bill was always the smartest of us, a genuine scholar, and he kept to himself a lot. He was twenty at the time, seven years older then me. I hadn't seen much of him since he'd left home three years ago to go to college and join the Marist Brothers, a religious order of the Catholic Church. The Brothers teach, do missionary work, and the like, and Bill was gone most of the time.

"I really should go out to the island and visit Doc," he said. "He helped me get my head together a couple of years ago when I didn't know what to do with myself." He drained his cup and looked at me. "Ready for a refill?"

"Okay." I was enjoying the time with my older brother and wanted to prolong it as much as possible. I handed him my cup. Bill retreated into the kitchen, whistling.

This time I drank the coffee black, and I noticed that whether through intent or absent-mindedness Bill had added a little bit of the Jack Daniels to the brew. The combination tasted awful, but I drank it nonchalantly. At least I hoped I did. Other than my sessions with Doc, this was the closest to being treated like an adult I'd ever experienced.

"Shamans have always been an integral part of any human tribe," Bill said, plopping down into the overstuffed chair. "Keepers of the tribe's legends, folklore, and history. Physician, teacher, wizard, and psychologist all rolled into one. Since Freud, though, we've exchanged the shaman's rattles and incantations for the analyst's couch and the mysteries of the Oedipus complex." He jabbed his pipe at me to emphasize his point. "I don't necessarily think this is an improvement. One of my professors taught me that when a society loses its folklore and its dreams, it begins to decay. History proves this over and over again. Any civilization that becomes too cerebral loses its heart and begins to die."

I listened to him, my head pleasantly buzzing from the alcohol. If Bill was talking about this stuff in college, maybe there was something to it after all.

Bill leaned back and put his feet on the ottoman. "Which brings us to our dear great-uncle, Alain the suburban shaman. People bring problems to him that they can't discuss with a modern psychotherapist. When someone tells Doc they see spirits and hear voices, he considers the possibility that maybe they really do. If the same person went through our enlightened mental health system, they're likely to wind up lobotomized or locked away in a nice white room somewhere far away. After all, sane people don't see things that aren't there, do they? Doc provides alternatives that modern science has yet to recognize."

I considered it. "That makes sense," I said, "but . . . Doc's scary sometimes. He knows things that he shouldn't. You never know what he's going to say or do." I took a deep breath. "He scares me. I don't plan on going to see him again."

Bill frowned in surprise. "Why? I would think this is a golden opportunity for a budding magician to learn the craft from a master . . ."

So I told Bill about how Doc had healed the cut on my leg. I was a little high from the liquor, or I probably wouldn't have said anything about it. Bill followed me intently, asking questions occasionally.

"And the bleeding stopped?" He took a big sip of his drink. "Incredible."

I nodded. "It was witchcraft," I concluded.

Bill laughed. "Bear, it wasn't sorcery or necromancy. Doc helped you call upon your autonomous nervous system. The body has a hell of a lot of ways to fix itself. We just forgot about them while we were busy building better indoor plumbing. It's not unheard of—scientists say we have a lot more control over our autonomous nervous system than we realize. You know how Indian fakirs can slow down their bodily functions and go without air for hours or days?"

"Yeah . . ."

"It's the same thing: control through concentration. Even the archskeptic Houdini discovered he could stay in an underwater coffin over an hour, if he consciously slowed his heartbeat and breathing." He paused to relight his pipe. "Let me give you an example. Remember last fall when you dreamed about Brian falling from the oak tree in the back yard, and the next day it happened? What did I tell you?"

"You said it was a precognitive dream. Dad said it was a coincidence."

He looked delighted. "You remembered; there's hope for you yet. You're right, Dad doesn't have much use for the paranormal. But think about it: you predicted the future. Are you some kind of witch or warlock?"

"No."

"Okay then. Neither is Doc. A lot of people think psychic ability is a lot of crap or dangerous superstition, but believe me the Russians take it very seriously. As does our own government. ESP is either a very old or a very new ability in the human race. It will be interesting to see where it leads us."

We spoke long into the night about parapsychology, life in general, and girls. About 3:00 A.M. I couldn't hold my eyes open any longer. My head was spinning with new ideas and alcohol. Bill clapped me on the shoulder. "Go to bed, Bear. Sleep well. And give Doc another chance. No matter what, the show must go on, right?"

"Maybe," I said, but in my mind I added, "Nope. No way." I staggered into my room and fell asleep immediately, determined to have nothing further to do with Doc, whether he was a shaman, magician, or whatever.

But Doc had other ideas.

■ ■ ■

About a week later (I remember because it was the first day of August) I was playing ball in the park with some of the neighborhood kids. I was beginning to notice girls then, and looked for any excuse to show off a little for them. After the game, some of my friends wanted to see a few tricks. By a fortunate coincidence (?) I happened to have a deck of cards with me. And my lucky silver half-dollar, of course.

I ran through my limited repertoire of card tricks, concluding with the coin routine I'd learned from Doc. The coin appeared, disappeared, penetrated my hand, and re-appeared behind the pretty ear of my down-the-street neighbor Rebecca Simmons. Teenage boys tend to be a bit skeptical toward conjuring. I remembered how my classmates had heckled the magician at the Houdini Magical Hall of Fame (and to tell the truth, the guy hadn't been all that good), so I expected my friends to tease me a little. They didn't disappoint me. The girls, however, seemed impressed by my performance. Their admiration irritated my friends, who proceeded to give me a hard time. Robert Davis—no tactician—said the whole thing was a bunch of crap. "If you really want to impress me, let me take the deck into my own hands and pick a card."

Without thinking I replied, "I'll go one better. How about you just think of a card and I'll try to find it."

"Bullcrap. Who do you think you are, Nostradamus?"

I looked at him, trying to appear mysterious. "Go ahead—think of one." I fanned the deck in front of his face, giving him a choice of any card in the deck. He looked them over for a few seconds. "Got one."

"All right. Whisper it to Rebecca."

"Why?"

"Because when I blow your mind I don't want you lying to me about it."

This provoked lots of laughter and good-natured punches to Robert's arm. He grinned and whispered the card to Rebecca, hiding his mouth with his hand so I couldn't read his lips.

I went through the deck as Doc taught me, trying not to think, listening for the whisper of intuition. Everyone fell silent; I could hear children playing in the park, the funky rhythms of the theme from *Shaft* floating over from someone's transistor radio, tuned to the local AM station WKWK.

One card seemed to stand out from the rest: the Seven of Spades. I removed it from the deck and held it, face down, in my left hand. "I think this is it . . . the Five of Diamonds." I deliberately miscalled the card to make Robert think I failed. I handed the card to Rebecca, still face down. "What card are you thinking of?"

He smirked. "Seven of Spades, you goof. I told you you couldn't do it."

I made a magic gesture toward the card in Rebecca's hand. "Turn it over."

She did. Robert's jaw dropped when he saw the Seven of Spades. My friends applauded, but the look on his face was better than any applause. The look Rebecca gave me was even better.

Robert admitted that he was impressed. He wasn't a bad guy at all, just one of those people who let his mouth run away with him at times (well, in Robert's case it was most of the time). He slapped me on the back. "Pretty good, Karges. You're not as big a dork as I thought." It was suppertime, so my friends trickled away, leaving me alone with a warm feeling in my belly. Karges the Great, magician supreme.

"Bravo!" I heard a familiar voice behind me. Doc had been standing near the swings, watching the whole time. He walked over to me, clapping his hands. "You did that very well."

I took a deep breath. "Uh . . . hi, Uncle Alain. What are you doing here?"

He looked around the park. "Just enjoying this beautiful day. I haven't seen you in a while. How have you been?"

I didn't know what to say. "I'm doing all right. I've been pretty busy." It was a lie; I hadn't been busy at all. In fact, I'd spent the last week bored out of my mind. Nothing seemed to hold my interest very long.

Doc chuckled. "I'll bet you have. So little time before school starts, and so many things to do before summer ends." He smiled. "Which reminds me: I'm glad we ran into each other. I wanted to invite you on a boat ride. I'm going out to see some of the islands while the weather is good. Care to come along?"

What was I supposed to do? Say to him, *No, Doc, you scary old warlock, I think I'll pass.* Before I could formulate a polite refusal, I heard myself saying, "Sure, that would be great."

His smile widened. "Excellent. Why don't you come out Friday and help me get the old boat ready? You can spend the night and we'll get up early Saturday and go out to the islands." He pulled out his watch and glanced at the time. "I have to run, Craig, I've a few errands to see to. It was good seeing you perform. Good job!"

Doc turned and hurried off.

Now I was in a real predicament. I'd pretty much made up my mind to cool off the relationship between us, and now I'd agreed to spend a couple of days with him. But after all, I consoled myself, it was only a boat ride, and I was curious about seeing some of the other islands on the Ohio River.

It could be an adventure, I thought glumly.

■ ■ ■

"So what do you two talk about out there?" my Dad asked me as he drove me to Doc's place on his way to work Friday morning. Summer was giving way to autumn, and the early morning sky was foggy and timeless. As we drove through Wheeling's downtown area, I recalled the time Doc's car was vandalized by someone who feared him and his powers. A wave of shame swept through me when I realized that I was guilty of the same type of superstitious dread.

"Nothing special," I answered. "Magic and tricks and stuff. Show business."

Dad nodded. "Just don't take it too seriously, son. It's time you started thinking about what you want to do when you grow up. Your uncle is retired. He can afford to spend his time playing around. He likes being the Mysterious One. That's okay, but just remember that you're going to have to make a living someday."

"Why can't I make my living as a magician?"

"Because it's not a 'Real Job'." The way he said it, I could hear the capital letters. "No security. Craig, when I was your age I wanted to fly airplanes. At night I dreamed about being a fighter pilot, going on secret missions, air-to-air combat, you know, be a hero. But as I got older I learned to tell the difference between dreams and reality."

I thought that Doc would have argued that dreaming is just a step away from reality, but I didn't say anything.

"I'm just saying you need to be practical, son." Dad reached over and ruffled my hair, a gesture he'd done ever since I was a little kid. I rolled my eyes to show him I wasn't a little kid anymore, but I didn't really mind. Dad was pretty neat, as Dads go.

Doc met us at the end of the driveway, near the back yard. He held a large bucket full of cleaning supplies. Standing there in bib overalls and a straw hat, Doc didn't look scary. In fact he looked like a kindly old maintenance man, the farthest thing from a Wizard I could imagine. But I couldn't forget how he touched my leg with one finger and stopped the flow of blood from the cut.

Why don't you just ask him about it? a voice in my head nagged.

Because I'm afraid of what he might tell me. Maybe I don't want to know.

Doc and my Dad exchanged greetings. "I hear you and Craig are going on a boat ride," Dad said. "Sounds like fun. Are you going to do any fishing?"

Doc smiled. "No fishing, Bill. Just a little archaeology, perhaps." He straightened his straw hat. "Fishing in the past. I thought we might go out to some of the islands and poke around a bit."

Dad looked interested. "We used to do that as kids. The islands are a long way down the river, though. What kind of boat do you have?"

"Come down to the dock."

We walked down the path through the back yard to the boathouse. I noticed Doc had finished the weeding job we'd begun. I almost shuddered at the memory of blood spouting from my leg, and the stitches above my ankle throbbed and itched in sympathy.

My uncle's boat usually stayed under a canvas tarp in the boathouse at the end of the dock. He'd removed the tarp and brought the boat onto land, resting it on a tube-metal cradle. My dad whistled when he saw it.

"She's a beaut," Dad said. "What is that, a Chris-Craft?"

It was a pretty thing, two-tone natural wood finish, brass fixtures, and smooth curves that were more appropriate to a piece of sculpture than a boat. Its name glittered in gold letters on the hull: *River Shaman*. My mouth dropped open in surprise at encountering the unfamiliar word again. Doc nodded. "Yep, a 1948 Custom Runabout, double-planked mahogany hull, white oak and spruce inlays." He ran his hand lovingly across the bow. "I haven't had it out in a while, but with a little elbow grease it'll be ship-shape in no time."

Dad was amazed by the elegant craft. "Where'd you get one of these, Alain? They cost a fortune."

Doc laughed. "One of the indulgences of my youth. When May and I bought the house and I saw it had a boat dock, I convinced her it would be a shame to waste it. I bought the *Shaman* from one of my clients. His business was doing poorly and he needed the money." Doc shrugged. "I paid him more than it was really worth. It was in bad shape, took me months to restore."

Dad was impressed. I wondered if he'd changed his mind about the practicality of making one's living as a performer. "She's a beaut," he repeated. "Wish I could go with you." He looked at his watch. "I have to get to work. You guys have fun. Bye, Craig."

Doc turned to me. "Grab a rag."

We didn't talk much as we polished the brass and chrome fixtures and cleaned the boat's cockpit. Sometime around noon we took a break. May brought us a pitcher of iced tea and sandwiches. We ate in silence.

"Are you a shaman?" I finally asked.

"Eh?"

"My brother Bill says you're a shaman."

"Ah." He wiped his hands on a napkin. "Perhaps I am."

"Is that where your boat got its name? Is it magical, too?"

He laughed at the nervousness in my voice. "Craig, don't be scared of what happened the other day. I don't have any magic powers. I'm not a witch or a sorcerer. All I did was catalyze your body's ability to heal itself. I didn't stop the bleeding. You did. I helped you, but you did it yourself. All a shaman does is help you summon abilities that you already have, though you may not realize you have them. The mind has an incredible influence on the body and spirit. 'Right thinking,' as the Buddhists call it, leads to good health. Fear, arrogance, negativity, despair: these are worms in the apple of the soul, gnawing away the core. A shaman nourishes the spirit, helps a person focus his or her mind to remove these negative energies, so the body can heal itself. You understand?"

"I think so."

He looked at me for a moment, and I got that feeling again that he was reading my mind. "You stayed away because you were scared of me, is that it?"

I never felt so ashamed in my life. I dropped my eyes to my hands, green-stained from the brass I'd been cleaning. "I'm sorry, Uncle Alain."

He laughed. "You only call me 'Uncle Alain' when you think you're in trouble. You're not in trouble, son, so go ahead and call me 'Doc.' I don't blame you for being afraid. You're beginning to learn that most of the things people believe are out of their control are *not*. Glimpsing the full potential of the mind is a scary thing. And the realization that you, and you alone, are the master of your Fate is enough to frighten anyone. I'll let you in on another secret. All the people who come to me for advice, even those who want reassurance from the spirit world, could do it for themselves if they only learned to listen to their intuition. And their dreams. Dreams are one way the subconscious mind sends us messages." He shrugged. "Perhaps most people just need a second opinion. Maybe it's impossible to be totally objective about your own life. Perhaps this is why we need shamans to help us understand ourselves. Some people seek advice from a minister or psychologist, others from a psychic. All want the same thing: answers to the riddle of their existence. Who am I? What am I here for? Is there more to life than this?" He got to his feet. "Ready to get back to the boat? A couple of coats of wax and she'll be as good as new."

We returned to our task. I felt much better, my good spirits renewed—the worms removed from my apple. I grinned. Doc had healed me again. We talked as we worked, with the ease and comfort of old friends. I realized I'd missed Doc and resolved to spend as much time as possible with him until school started. Our suburban shaman, Bill had called Doc.

By six o'clock, the *River Shaman* gleamed in the fading sunlight like a jewel. Doc stood back, nodding, and admired our work. "I think the old girl's ready."

May prepared a huge dinner, after which we listened to the radio in the den for a little while. "You'd better get to bed," May told us. "Dawn comes early."

I yawned. I was ready. May led me from the den toward the guest room.

"Interesting dreams," Doc wished me as I shuffled off to bed. I thought it was a funny thing to say. Not 'sweet dreams' but '*interesting dreams.*' I was too tired to wonder about it, though. Exhausted from trying to keep up with him all day, I fell asleep almost immediately.

People shouting, screaming; horses galloping and snorting. Guns firing. Flames from the burning house dimly illuminate the night.

The burning house.

"Fire!" a woman's voice screams. "Won't somebody do something about the fire?"

I am an observer, coolly watching the pandemonium. Soldiers, dressed in long coats with dozens of brass buttons, are running everywhere.

"Where is he?" a general on horseback demands.

"He's not here, Sir," a young soldier replies.

"Damn him, he's escaped downriver! Find him!"

I look back at the house. It's a beautiful plantation-style mansion. But not for long. The flames rise up to lick away the roof. Servants and groundskeepers scatter in all directions, soldiers waving sabers and pistols in close pursuit. Smoke billows through the hot air, suffocating and harsh; the roof collapses— screams of despair pierce the night!

The air tastes like smoky terror.

A word floats through my mind, borne aloft by wisps of smoke: Blennerhassett.

I don't know what the word means, but a chill of fear shivers up my spine. The word tears into tatters, scattering to the four winds like embers.

One of the mounted soldiers gallops straight toward me! I step back into the sheltering woods, terrified . . .

I jump at the touch on my arm. "Don't be afraid, Craig," a soothing, familiar voice whispers. "They can't see you."

"Aunt May?" She stood there, shimmering, wearing the clothes of an eighteenth-century housemaid.

She smiles. "It's just a dream. It can't hurt you."

The burning house and sounds fade as the image of a map superimposes itself across my vision. A parchment map of a rectangular island. I see a large 'X' near one end. The 'X' catches fire, and the flames spread until they consume the map. A hot blast strikes me in the face; the world is on fire. I raise my hands to protect my eyes—

I sprang awake and looked around the room in confusion. A cool breeze blew from the window, drying the sweat that had broken out on my forehead. The dream was so vivid I thought I still smelled smoke. 'Interesting dreams' indeed. Doc had planted one of his suggestions, and I fell for it hook, line, and sinker.

Thanks, Doc.

I shook my head and went back to sleep, determined to have no more dreams that night.

CHAPTER SEVEN

The Alchemist's Island

AFTER AN INCREDIBLE BREAKFAST (at Doc and May's house you had your choice of two kind of meals: large and huge), we walked to the boathouse. Doc wore a tan fisherman's vest with dozens of pockets and his straw hat, and he carried a heavy canvas bag. I brought along our provisions. We lowered the *River Shaman* into the water and jumped into the cockpit. Doc fired up the engine and we were off to explore the islands. He didn't ask me if I had experienced any "interesting" dreams, nor did I volunteer any information.

The river was covered with a dense fog, made rosy by the dim light of the rising sun. Within a few minutes we'd lost sight of shore, suspended in the blankness of the mist. It was eerie and timeless, like being in another dimension. A lone car horn hooted from the mainland like a lost owl. After about an hour I was eaten alive by curiosity about our destination. "Where are we going?" I asked.

"Hmm . . . you'll see." Doc consulted a map. "We'd better take it slow until the sun burns off the fog."

I pointed to the large canvas bag. "What'cha got there?"

He patted the bag. "I want to collect some plants and herbs while we're out." He peered into the fog. "And maybe some other things if we're lucky." He reached into the bag and removed a shovel, giving me a sly look. "Buried treasures."

I groaned. More digging!

It took most of the morning to get to our destination. By the time we saw the dim outline on the horizon, most of the fog had lifted. Just enough rolled along the ground to create an eerie effect, like the moors in a Vincent Price movie. I halfway expected to hear wolves howling in the distance. Doc jumped nimbly to the bank and gave me a hand up. I scrambled to the rocky shore and looked around. I'm not sure what I had expected to see on our "island adventure," but I was a bit disappointed. Though beautifully wooded and tranquil, the island seemed no different from any other that I'd seen—including Wheeling Island, where Doc and May lived. In fact, the landscape seemed indistinguishable from their back yard. Doc, however, seemed excited. "Let's take a look around." He pointed toward an overgrown path that led through the trees. "That way."

We walked through the woods for a while, Doc stopping now and then to collect a bit of fungus, wild herb, or mushroom, which he transferred to small bags and tucked away in his vest pockets. The air was bright and lovely, the fog completely gone and the sky a clear, blue-crystal goblet. Birds sang, woodchucks chirruped, and squirrels chattered around us.

"Beautiful," Doc commented. "Like Lord Byron, I'm most religious on a sunshiny day."

Suddenly Doc exclaimed in excitement. Completely disregarding the wet ground, he dropped to his knees and scraped away earth and leaves from around a small plant. "Great! This is phenomenal good fortune!"

It looked like any other small flowering plant to me. "What is it?"

Doc carefully removed the plant from the ground with a small scoop, taking care not to damage the roots. "This is a rare orchid called *Saloop* or *Lucky Hand*. See the shape of the root?" He held it up. The roots grew in the shape of small human hands! "One of my clients has been bugging me to make him a good luck charm to help his business bring in more money."

70

"What do you do with it?"

Doc transferred the plant to a small jar and tucked it away in his bag. "You dry the root and place it in a small green flannel bag, along with a silver Mercury-head dime, two nails from a horseshoe, some chamomile and nutmeg, and a chip of lodestone. Then you carry the bag on you, being careful not to let anyone else see it or touch it. It's called a Mojo. Supposed to bring the wearer prosperity and luck."

"Does it?"

Doc smiled at me. "It does if you believe it does."

I made a noncommittal grunt, and he laughed. "I found some wild catnip and goldenseal, too. Good for the development of psychic powers. Want some?"

"No thanks. What about those mushrooms you picked, do they do anything?" I had heard about hallucinogenic mushrooms, and I wondered if Doc occasionally experimented with something a little stronger than whiskey.

He leaned closer, conspiratorially, rolling one of the odd-looking mushrooms between finger and thumb. "Ah, *morchella semilibera*. Quite hard to find. These are the greatest treasures of all."

My curiosity was aroused. "What are they?"

He winked. "Morels. Sautéed in port wine and butter, they are exceptionally delicious."

I was still laughing at Doc's mischievousness when we came out of the woods into a broad clearing. The grin vanished from my face. There was something ominously familiar about the shape of the ground, something that triggered latent memories of fear and pursuit.

"This is the main reason we came," Doc said. "There's something I always wanted to look for here. The remains of an old house. The only problem is, nobody knows exactly where it stood."

Tattered remnants of mist clung to the ground like smoke.

(*"Fire!" a woman's voice screams. "Won't somebody do something about the fire?"*)

(*"Damn him, he's escaped downriver! Find him!"*)

My voice was barely a whisper. "There was a fire here . . ."

Doc turned around and looked at me. His eyebrows knitted into a quizzical expression. "What's the matter? Are you all right?"

I nodded, although my throat was dry and my heart was a wounded bird fluttering in my chest. I walked around the clearing, sure I'd been here before. It was the first time in my life I'd experienced the phenomenon known as *déjà vu,* and the experience was unsettling. I pointed in the direction of the rising sun. "I dreamed about this place. Over there, where all the brush is. There used to be a big house there. Blenner-something."

"The Blennerhassett mansion," he muttered.

"The what?"

His expression was thoughtful. "In the late 1700s a wealthy Irish aristocrat named Harman Blennerhassett settled here. He was routed a few years later when it was rumored that he and Aaron Burr were planning to establish a kingdom in the American Southwest and secede from the United States. He was arrested for treason. He was released, but his house had burned to the ground and he was ruined. I've been interested in his story for years. Where did you hear of him?"

I shook my head. "I dreamed about the fire last night. I thought it was just a nightmare."

Doc looked at me and nodded thoughtfully. "May had one of her dreams last night too. She said she dreamed you were scared and she comforted you. She also dreamed that we would find what I've been looking for."

"What are you looking for?" I asked.

He rubbed his chin. "I'm not sure. We'll know when we find it."

■ ■ ■

"The problem is, the house was huge, with many outbuildings. We could dig for weeks and never turn up anything but rusty nails." Doc walked around the flattened area where the house lay in my dream. "We have to narrow down the search a bit. Ever use a divining rod?"

I told him I'd never even heard of a divining rod.

"Ha!" he laughed. "Let me show you how to make one, then."

Doc searched the surrounding woods until he found a tree he liked. He removed his pocketknife and cut a fresh branch, removing all the twigs and leaves until he had a Y-shaped forked twig about a foot long. "The secret is to relax your mind and let it happen on its own. Try not

72

to get too caught up trying to figure out how it works. If you start analyzing it, you'll never get any results. Just hold one end of the 'Y' in each hand, and walk back and forth until you feel something tugging at the end of the stick . . ."

I took the stick from him and held it awkwardly. "I've never done this before. Why do I have to do it?"

Doc shrugged. "Hey, it was your dream."

So it was. I took the stick firmly as Doc showed me and walked around the area for a while, feeling foolish. At least there was no danger of anyone else seeing me march around waving a forked stick around like an idiot. I kept glancing at Doc to see if he was laughing at me. However, he squatted on his calves and watched with solemn, glittering eyes, apparently very interested in the results of our experiment. The rough ends of the stick chafed the palms of my hands. My hands were beginning to sweat, and I held on to the stick with difficulty. It seemed to vibrate and twitch.

After fifteen minutes I was discouraged. I looked at Doc, hoping he'd say to forget the whole thing. However, he gave me an encouraging nod to continue. I gave an exasperated sigh and trudged on.

Ten more minutes passed, then fifteen. Sweat ran down my face, burning my eyes. I fell into a sort of waking doze, not really aware of anything except marching back and forth, back and forth . . .

Damn! The stick jumped in my hand, pointing downward. I almost tripped over my own feet in amazement. Doc jumped to his feet. "Do it again," he called out. "Try it from a different direction!"

I stepped back about twenty feet, regripped the stick and approached the spot where it had twitched. Once again it pivoted in my hand and pointed downward. The stick felt heavy, like it had a weight tied to its end. At that moment, I was exhilarated and amazed. I looked at the stick in awe. It seemed to have a mind of its own.

Doc ran over and marked the spot with a rock. "Try it again, from over there."

We did it three more times (once, while I was blindfolded with a bandana) before he was satisfied. He encircled my shoulders with his arm and gave me a hug. "Go sit on that log and rest, Craig. Have a bite to eat. You've earned it." He unrolled his bag, removed a short-handled spade and commenced to dig. After I gobbled down a peanut butter sandwich and some lukewarm lemonade, I joined him.

"Dreams are the doorway to the unconscious," he said, as we sifted through the hard-packed soil. "It was great good fortune that your nocturnal vision narrowed down our search."

I told Doc how I had once dreamed about my little brother Brian falling out of our tree. But I couldn't understand how it was possible to dream of a place you've never been.

Doc leaned on his shovel and wiped the back of his neck with a bandana. "Dreams can provide you with incredible insights, if you let them. Clairvoyant dreams are one of the more common psychic phenomena, you know. Even people who don't believe in ESP have them sometimes, though they usually explain them away as coincidence. I suspect that what happened last night occurred with a little help from your Aunt May. May often walks about in her dreams, and last night her activities probably triggered your own dreamtime awareness." He grabbed his shovel. "Good thing, too, or we'd be digging all day! Craig, it's important to pay attention to your dreams. Not only your nighttime visions, but the hopes and dreams you hold dear in your heart. Too many people place their dreams aside to follow a 'practical' or 'sensible' path, looking for that elusive brass ring called security. But what good is security if you're not happy?"

"My dad says that security is important."

"He's right. But so is happiness. Why settle for one, when you can easily have both?"

I was listening to him, digging in the soil with a garden trowel, when the blade scraped against something harder than the dirt. "I found something!" Dropping the trowel, I scooped at the earth with my hands.

Something shiny glittered from the dark earth: a chain of some kind.

"Careful . . ." Doc cautioned.

Gently I removed the object from the ground and wiped it off with a bandana. It was a small silver locket, hanging from a gold chain. The locket was in surprisingly good condition. I handed it to Doc, whose eyes danced in delight. "It's definitely late seventeenth or early eighteenth century. First blood goes to you, Craig. See if you can open it!"

I carefully pried at the latch with a grimy thumbnail and the locket popped open. Inside was a faded lock of auburn hair. "Look!" I handed the locket to Doc. There was a watercolor portrait of a young woman with clear green eyes and red hair.

Doc looked at the portrait and nodded. "Blennerhassett was chased out of Ireland for marrying his underage niece. It caused quite a scandal, according to the books. He said she was his one true love. I'll wager even money that this is a picture of her."

"What do we do with it?"

Doc handed it to me, folding my fingers over it. "You keep it. A souvenir. A reminder that true love is a precious treasure."

"Don't you want to give it to Aunt May?"

He smiled. "She already knows." He gripped his shovel. "Let's keep digging!"

We dug around the area for about an hour, then Doc tossed his shovel aside. "Aha!" he crowed. He dropped to his knees and burrowed in the ground. "Look at this!" Doc produced a massive, dirt-clotted gold ring. He wiped the dirt from it and I saw that the ring was fashioned in the shape of a cobra, with a diamond on its head, and dark rubies for eyes. It was kind of creepy looking, and I said so.

Doc nodded. "The snake is a very old symbol of spiritual protection, believed to frighten away negative influences—evil spirits, if you will. To the alchemist, the serpent represented Eternity. Judging from the magical symbolism, I suspect this item belonged to Harman Blennerhassett himself."

Aha! That's why Doc was so interested in coming to this particular island! As Doc would say, I 'got it.' "Was he into magic?" I asked.

Doc shrugged. "Blennerhassett was known to conduct secret experiments in physics on this island. I suspect some of these experiments involved the magical science of alchemy. Do you know what alchemy is?"

I nodded. "Alchemists were people who tried to turn lead into gold, a long time ago."

Doc smiled. "So they did. Alchemists paved the way for the modern science of chemistry. But the quest was more than just a search for instant wealth. Alchemists saw the transformation of base metals into precious elements as a metaphor for the soul's search for perfection. Just as a lump of lead can be turned into gold, so can the human being overcome the baseness of the flesh and become something pure and precious." He closed his hand around the ring and wiggled his thumb. "I'll keep this as a souvenir of our trip today—and a reminder that all things are possible." When he opened his hand, the ring had vanished.

He walked toward our equipment. "Let's go, May will be waiting for us."

I was dumfounded. "We're leaving?"

Doc looked at me in gentle surprise. "Yes. We got what we came here for."

"But why are we quitting now? There's got to be more stuff buried here."

Doc smiled. "Undoubtedly. We'll leave it to future treasure hunters. No need to take more than our share."

I followed Doc to the boat, sure that I would never understand him and his strange ways.

■ ■ ■

Doc opened up the engine on the way back to the mainland. I grinned into the cool spray. It was exhilarating, and the cold mist felt good after a day of hiking and digging.

To my surprise, Doc wasn't traveling in the direction of his home on Wheeling Island, so I asked him where we were going. My stomach ached with hunger, and I was looking forward to one of May's exquisite meals. I didn't know if I was up to any more adventures this day.

Doc laughed. "Don't worry—we're going to eat at the restaurant at the old hotel in Marietta. A special treat to celebrate the return of two brave treasure hunters."

Doc idled into one of the docks at the marina and secured the *River Shaman*. I noticed the other boaters casting envious glances at the elegant craft. I already knew it was a lovely boat, but judging by the way people looked at it, the *Shaman* must be something special indeed. We were walking to the clubhouse when a large, middle-aged man ran over to us. "Hey, hold up," he called out.

Doc turned around. "Yes?"

The man came up and introduced himself. His eyes sized up Doc and dismissed him as an easy touch. "I couldn't help but notice your boat." His voice was arrogant and commanding, a man used to getting his own way. "1949 Custom Runabout, isn't it?"

"1948," Doc corrected him.

The man's eyes narrowed. "I've been looking for one of those for years. You wouldn't be interested in selling it, would you?"

Doc shook his head. "I'm afraid not. Sorry to disappoint you."

The man's face clouded in arrogant anger. "Do you know who I am?"

"Yes. I've seen your name around. I must admit I voted for your opponent. My answer is still *no*." Doc took my arm and we walked off.

The man hurried to catch up with us. His arrogant manner had left him. "I'll pay you whatever you want." He named a large sum of money that made me breathe hard.

"Sorry, not interested," Doc kept walking.

The man followed us, insisting that he *must* have the boat. A pleading tone entered his voice. He doubled his offer. Tripled it. It was more than my dad made in a year!

Doc turned around. The tables had turned; Doc was in total control of the situation. Now it was his eyes that appraised the man.

"Cash?"

"Cash, check, whatever you want," the man said. His eyes burned with lust for Doc's boat.

"Okay. A check will be fine. After all, I *know who you are*." The man either ignored or didn't catch Doc's sarcastic emphasis. Doc handed over the keys to the *River Shaman* while I watched in total shock. The man gripped the keys like they were to the Gates of Heaven and wrote Doc a check for a staggering sum of money. Doc scratched out a receipt for the man and signed it. "I'll send you the papers early next week. I hope you enjoy the *Shaman* as much as I have."

"I will, I will," the man said. "Thank you so much. You don't know how much this means to me."

Doc looked at him in amusement. "Perhaps I do," he said, waving the check.

We walked away. As soon as we were out of earshot I said, "I can't believe you sold your boat. And I really can't believe how much he paid you for it!"

Doc laughed, pocketing the check.

"A thing is worth whatever you're willing to pay. Today, that man got his heart's desire. And paid well for it, I might add."

"But you loved that boat."

His voice softened; I thought he sounded a little sad. "There comes a time to let things go. May never really liked boating, and she'll have more use for the money than for a boat she'll never use. That man will love the *Shaman* every bit as much as I did. Besides, he got the boat, while you and I have the memories of our trip. No amount of money can buy such a day. Let's go, Craig—dinner's on me."

It occurred to me that we were stranded many miles from home with no way back. I asked Doc about it and he told me not to worry. We went into the old hotel. I was hungry enough to eat a horse.

As my eyes adjusted to the dim light of the lobby, I heard a voice say, "You boys are right on time."

"Aunt May?"

Doc winked at me. "She had another one of her dreams, Craig. She suspected we'd need a ride home. I've wanted to sell the *Shaman* for a while, but I was concerned I wouldn't find the right buyer. May dreamed that this would be the best time and place to do it."

I decided she was right. After all, Doc got three times what his boat was worth.

"May is one of the most intuitive people I know," he reminded me. "Want my advice?"

"What?"

He bent over to whisper loudly, "Let her order for you." They both laughed at the expression on my face, and we went inside the restaurant.

CHAPTER EIGHT

Reality Reasserted

AFTER OUR TRIP TO BLENNERHASSETT ISLAND, my belief in real magic was complete and unquestioned. Doc had finally gotten the message through my thick skull that you didn't have to be gifted to call upon the magic of the universe, just open-minded enough to let it happen. I was so exhilarated by the adventure that I fell into a lapse of judgment.

I told my Dad.

Halfway through the story (when I saw the expression of his face) I knew I'd made a mistake. I told him about my precognitive dream and, although he didn't say anything, his lips curved into a skeptical half-smile. I knew he was thinking about the time I claimed to have dreamed about Brian falling out of our oak tree the night before it happened. He didn't comment about my story of the dream (though the look on his face spoke volumes!) but when I got to the part about how we found the locket and the ring with a forked stick, his self-control reached its limit. He laughed, not unkindly. "Come on, son. Don't pull my leg too hard—it'll come off in your hand."

"But I saw it. Doc was there, ask him."

He waved it away. "Think about it, son: nobody can find buried treasure with a piece of applewood. If it were that easy, we'd all be millionaires. He was just fooling with you. He probably planted that junk out there so you'd stumble across it."

Mom was sitting at the dining room table, reading a book with the somewhat odd title *Watership Down* and staying out of the discussion. Her policy was to stay out of discussions between my father and me. I wasn't surprised by Dad's skepticism, but I felt compelled to at least try to convince him. "It wasn't a trick; I found it myself. He didn't show me where to look."

Dad rustled his newspaper. "Look, Craig, I don't mean to rain on your parade. Alain is a slick magician, I'll give him that, but there's no such thing as real magic. You're old enough to know better. He probably led you along and palmed that stuff into the hole you dug."

I was stubborn. "But what about my dream? How did I know about the fire, and Blennerhasset's name?"

Dad looked at me patiently. "There's no real mystery about that. Didn't you learn about it in West Virginia history class? I'm pretty sure you must have." He looked at my stubborn expression and said kindly, "Maybe it's something you forgot you knew. While you were asleep it came up in a dream. People do that all the time, especially when they get older. The other day I almost drove myself crazy trying to remember where I left a book I was reading. I went to bed worrying about it. The next morning I woke up and remembered I'd left it under the couch. It's not magic, Craig, it's just the way people's brains work."

"But—" I shut up. I knew Dad was skeptical about such matters and I decided to withdraw from the battlefield. "I guess you're right," I said.

He returned to his paper. "Alain was just having fun with you, like when you were little and we used to put cookies out for Santa Claus. Now you know it was just make-believe. You'll understand when you get a little older. All I'm saying is don't take it too seriously, son. I'm glad you had a good time, though."

I wasn't too upset by my father's refusal to believe my story. As Doc often reminded me, most people don't recognize real magic until it hits them between the eyes. And even then, they're just as likely to dismiss it or explain it away. After all, I was there. Dad wasn't. I couldn't blame him for finding the whole thing hard to swallow.

When I told Doc about my father's reactions, he nodded. "Your father's a practical man. He grew up during a very difficult time, a time when the future of this country was uncertain. Times were tough and people had to be tough to survive. He decided the 'real' world was enough for him—and that's perfectly natural. He has no use for magic, and you're probably not going to be able to change that. Even the people who come to me for readings have real-world problems and want real-world answers. They could work the magic themselves, if they'd surrender their self-control enough to let the magic happen on its own."

The idea that my Dad had deliberately denied himself the richness of the magical experience made me feel vaguely distressed. I asked Doc if there was any way to help people experience magic on their own.

He lit a cigar while he gathered his thoughts. "It's difficult," he said, "because people who don't believe in magic will probably never experience it. It's impossible for our brains to process everything it experiences, so the mind filters out whatever it doesn't want to deal with. Life's more comfortable that way." He waved his cigar at me. "Do me a favor and pour your old uncle a glass of Scotch, would you? BS-ing is thirsty work. And grab yourself a root beer."

I complied, handing him the glass of amber liquid. Knowing Doc as I did, and not wanting to interrupt his train of thought, I placed the bottle within easy reach. He raised his glass. "To magic!" I seconded the toast. He took a sip and sighed contentedly. "Have you ever wondered why people like to watch magic shows?"

I shook my head. "I never really thought about it."

"A magic show is a safe way to experience miracles. It reminds us of what it was like when we were kids. To the very young, the world is an extremely enchanted place, full of wonders and mysteries and magical beings."

"Like Santa Claus," I said, grinning.

Doc grinned back. "Why not? In a world of infinite possibilities, who's to say there's no such thing as an obese and benevolent old elf who likes to reward kids for being good? However, on the other end of the spectrum we have the Bogeyman, who lives in your closet at night, waiting for you to fall asleep so he can come out and dine on your toes. After all, the existence of good magic implies the existence of bad magic, doesn't it? So all you have to do to get rid of the Bogeyman is to quit believing in Santa Claus as well. It's a tradeoff. For some, skepticism has its own rewards," he added dryly. "Those who firmly deny the existence of ghosts are rarely troubled by them."

"So what about magic shows?" I reminded him.

"Ah yes. As we grow older, we tend to limit our possibilities to what we think of as real and obtainable. In other words, we 'grow up.'" He paused, puffing his cigar. "A good magician can make us experience that childlike sense of wonder again—if for only a short while—and remind us of a time when we truly believed we could be anything we wanted to be. The magician takes us back to when we believed we could fly if we filled our heads with happy thoughts, and when we believed we would live forever, or fix broken toys—and broken hearts, perhaps?—with a sincerely spoken magical spell. In other words, it's a fantasy of having real power over the sometimes frightening universe. That's the best part of being a magical performer, Craig: when you look out into the audience and you see that gleam in their eyes; when you know you've cracked through the walls of rational thought and rekindled that inner light, you know you've done your job."

Although it was a little too deep for me at the time, still I enjoyed listening to the sound of his voice. I knew that what I didn't understand at the moment would become clearer to me as I got older. In the meantime, I had my memories and the locket we found on Blennerhassett Island. That night, I went to my room and retrieved the locket from my dresser drawer. I opened it and looked at the picture again, admiring the skill of the artist who'd captured the girl's fair skin, green eyes, and auburn hair, Harman Blennerhassett's true love. She looked like she was about my age, young and pretty. What was it like, I wondered, to find someone with whom you were destined to spend the rest of your life?

Probably pretty nice, I decided.

■ ■ ■

Doc's comment about ghosts brought back a memory I hadn't thought about in years. When I was six years old, I woke up one night with the conviction that someone was standing beside my bed looking at me. I rubbed my eyes, trying to peer into the darkness. "Mom? Dad?" I mumbled. But it wasn't either of my parents. In the dark silence, I could hear my father's snores from the bedroom across the hall. Mom muttered something in her sleep.

Something rustled near the foot of my bed.

Terror so strong I could actually taste it (for me, fear tastes like a mouthful of pennies) coursed through my body. A white figure stood near the window, gazing at me with large dark eyes. I opened my mouth to yell for my parents. Nothing emerged but a weak, breathy noise. The white figure—I could tell now that it was a woman wearing a long, flowing gown—shook her head almost sadly and lifted one pale hand to point out of the window, toward the woods in the back yard. Then, while I watched her, she faded away. One moment she was there and the next, gone! It was almost sunrise before I got back to sleep. I never saw the apparition again, and I never told anyone about it. Over time I came to the conclusion it was just a bad dream. After all, kids are always imagining things. Some nights Brian would wake up yelling that there were porpoises under his bed.

Now, I wasn't so sure. Later I heard that the previous owners of the house had suffered an extremely tragic and horrendous event. Their four-year-old daughter had vanished into those woods, never to be seen again. The girl's mother grieved to death in her bedroom. The question was, did I hear this story *before* I saw the ghost (perhaps I'd overheard the grownups talking about it) or sometime after? I couldn't remember. Maybe my conviction that the spirit of the sad woman wasn't real prevented me from seeing it again.

I thought about Doc saying, "*Those who firmly deny the existence of ghosts are rarely troubled by them.*" I pictured a little child, lying awake at night, chanting over and over, like the Cowardly Lion from the *Wizard of Oz*—"I don't believe in spooks—*I don't believe in spooks*," programming his or her young and impressionable mind to *not see* anything that causes fear or discomfort, to not see spooks and bogeymen and goblins (and to banish kindly old Santa Claus, the Tooth Fairy, and other guardian spirits—but hey, that's the price you pay for peace of mind), learning the parents' skeptical attitudes, building a wall of rationality against the uncertainty of the Unknown.

For some, skepticism has its own rewards, Doc had said.

But so does belief, perhaps infinite rewards. Dreams could come true. A person could transform him- or herself into anything he or she wanted to be. Every fairy tale I'd ever read as a child taught that Good Magic—real magic—always overcame Bad Magic. The power of imagination. The power of dreams. The power to *become*. For a moment— just a moment—I understood the viewpoint of the alchemists and the whole universe opened before me. I saw the true extent of its limitless potential: an infinite dance of life, death, change, transformation.

My head hurt from thinking so much, so I went downstairs to watch television. And as though to reinforce the idea that real magic not only existed, but was perfectly natural, there was a program on PBS exploring the powers of the mind and body. A surgeon narrated a segment about a young girl in China whose leg had been seriously lacerated in an explosion. She somehow stopped the flow of blood to the injured limb until medics could get to her. According to rescuers, this action undoubtedly saved her life. The doctor commenting on the incident remarked, "There's a lot about the mind and body we haven't learned yet."

I thought that Doc would agree.

CHAPTER NINE

Doc Knocks 'em Dead

THE CLOCK WAS RUNNING OUT on summer vacation. I had just a few weeks re-maining before it was back to the books and classes. Furthermore, it was going to be my last year of grade school at St. Vincent de Paul. I looked forward to this because in parochial school eighth-graders got to enjoy one year of being the "anointed ones," the kings and queens of the school, before moving on to freshman status at Wheeling Cen-tral Catholic High School. Childhood is measured in summers and holidays, and the older I became the shorter the intervals seemed be-tween these signposts. My summer vacation sped by like a movie on fast-forward.

Most of my time was spent with Doc, honing my intuitive skills. Even though I'd made remarkable progress during the summer, there were two feats of perception that still eluded me: the book trick and the ability to sense objects while blindfolded.

"Don't worry," Doc assured me. "It'll come. Just relax, keep prac-ticing, and let it happen in its own time. One day you'll look up and say, 'I've got it!' and you'll just do it, almost by accident, and wonder why it took so long to get the hang of it."

Doc scurried around his study, removing various items from his shelves and closets and packing them in a small bag. Occasionally he checked the items against a list. I asked him what he was doing, and he announced that he was coming out of retirement, "for one show only." May had agreed to host a benefit for her Garden Club, and she persuaded Doc to be the featured entertainer. He asked me if I wanted to go along and help out. Eager for the chance to see Doc at work on a stage, I readily agreed.

■ ■ ■

On the day of Doc's show I encountered a snag. I intended to bring along the locket we'd found, but I couldn't find it. After two solid hours of searching, I was frantic. I collared my little brother Brian, who was sprawled on the floor, eating a dripping jelly sandwich and watching *Scooby Doo*. "Were you messing around with my locket?" I demanded.

"I haven't seen your stupid lockup," he said. "What's a lockup, anyway?"

I didn't have any more time to look for the missing locket. Doc's car horn blared from the driveway.

I grabbed my jacket on the way out, dismissing the locket from my mind for the time being. *It'll probably turn up*, I thought. But I was still anxious.

■ ■ ■

Doc said, "I'm actually a bit excited about this show. After all, I haven't performed it in oh . . . twenty-five years or so. But I figure it's like swimming or riding a bicycle: you never really forget how to do it."

I looked at Doc's bag, resting on the back seat. "Have you rehearsed?" I asked.

He tapped his forehead. "In here. I've gone over the show at least ten times."

The venue was the Country Club in nearby Weirton, West Virginia, adjacent to the golf course and protected from prying eyes by tall hedges and thick boxwoods. The people who lived in the bluffs were from "old money" and had built on high land, providing a great view of the river. We pulled into the parking area near the rear entrance (the employee's lot) and got out. The thick perfume of hydrangeas and lilacs seized me by the throat and made my eyes water. We walked through the kitchen, past the food prep area ("the glamorous world of show-biz-ness, kid," Doc drawled) and into the room where the fundraiser was to take place.

The setting was a typical Country Club layout. If you've ever been to a wedding reception, you get the idea. Twenty round tables, each designed to seat ten people, were arranged in staggered rows. If everyone showed up, Doc would have a great audience for his coming-out-of-retirement performance.

Doc carried his entire act in a small case that reminded me of a doctor's bag. Mentalists work with simple things—a few slips of paper, a couple of paperback books, a small chalkboard—which is one advantage over being a magician: not a whole lot of props to carry around. But the burden of showmanship is far greater for the mentalist. He or she must make up for the paucity of stage dressing through charisma, humor, and personality. But Doc didn't seem worried about his long hiatus from the stage. He spent all of ten minutes arranging his act and then took me by the arm.

"Now it's time for a piece of pie. What d'you say?" He didn't seem to be nervous at all. Doc actually had two pieces of pie with his coffee; he seemed in exceptionally good spirits.

■ ■ ■

From the moment of his introduction, Doc owned the stage. He looked magnificent, black pants pressed with a razor pleat, red velvet dinner jacket, white silk shirt, and a cravat. He immediately had the roomful of people in the palm of his hand. I sat near the back of the room, where I could observe audience reactions.

He opened by asking everyone to concentrate on a single playing card. "Just picture it in your mind. Don't say anything aloud. How many of you are thinking of the Queen of Hearts? Raise your hands." Gasps filled the room when almost every hand shot into the air. Doc followed this miracle by predicting three numbers the audience selected at random.

No one in the room had ever before seen anything comparable. His performance was very well received. Doc was charming and urbane in an old-fashioned way. I think part of his appeal was that he reminded everyone of their favorite uncle. The rest came from his genuine pleasure at performing for the group.

Halfway through the show he encountered a glitch. Doc asked for a volunteer. "Me!" a loud voice called out from the back of the room. "Read MY mind!" A large, middle-aged woman pushed her way through the room to the stage. I saw eyes roll when the other members realized who it was. *Uh-oh, trouble,* I could almost hear them think.

But Doc was unperturbed. "What's your name, my dear?" he asked. She smirked. "You tell me—you're supposed to be the psychic."

From the audience someone called out, "That's Beatrice, and she thinks she knows everything!" The audience laughed at this summation of Beatrice's personality.

I was worried, but Doc proceeded as usual. He handed the woman a paperback book and asked her to turn to a page and think of a word. I knew she was going to be trouble by the amount of time she spent making her decision. She took the thick paperback with a skeptical look, then carefully went through the entire volume. It appeared she was trying to read it!

"Sometime tonight, if at all convenient," Doc urged her. The audience laughed.

But the stubborn Beatrice would not be rushed. She leafed through the book, finally made her decision. "Got it."

Doc smiled at the audience and gave Beatrice his full attention. "Now, concentrate on your word, seeing it form in your mind in bold, clear letters. One letter at a time . . . the first letter, the second . . . keep going . . ."

The woman looked at Doc with a crooked smile that said: "I'm not buying this act for a minute!" The audience laughed again; they were obviously enjoying the little drama.

Doc suddenly looked at her. "Beatrice, the word you're thinking of is 'trapping.'"

Beatrice jumped, and then gave a large smile. "No."

Not a single sound from the audience. I sat up in my seat, suddenly alert. She was lying! Even I could see she was deliberately trying to mess Doc up. But how could he prove it? Doc took it in stride. "Ah, I see. Do you mind telling me what word you *are* thinking of?"

The woman looked amazed. "You want me to just tell you?"

"Yes, please—or mail it to me." Again the audience laughed.

"I thought you were supposed to read my mind."

"Everyone's entitled to one mistake. Please tell the audience the word you're thinking of."

She looked around the room, quickly. "*Pocketbook.* I knew you couldn't do it."

The audience had been following this exchange like spectators at a tennis match. Now they gave a collective "*Ah-h-h-h-h.*"

Doc turned to the audience. "Ladies and Gentlemen, as you have seen, what I do is not an exact science. The human mind is a complex thing, and there's a certain amount of error which must be allowed for." He paused. "The key phrase here is 'allowed for.' For you see, I suspected something like this might happen—and I allowed for it." He turned to Beatrice. "Beatrice, would you please look on the inside back cover of the book you're holding. Earlier today, I wrote a simple note—a prognostication, if you will, a premonition of something that might happen. Would you please read the note out loud?"

She did as Doc asked, turning to the inside back cover. Her jaw dropped. She looked back at Doc, scowling. "It's a trick of some kind. You set me up!"

Doc answered calmly, "My dear, you acted freely, of your own volition. The choices you made were yours and yours entirely. Please read the note out loud."

"Read it, Beatrice," someone called out. The audience gave a nervous laugh.

Beatrice must have realized that if she didn't comply, she'd look like a bad sport in front of her friends. Looking like she had just bit into a parsnip, she read: "'This is Dr. Alain DeLyle. I have a feeling that tonight, during the show I will perform for the Wheeling Garden Club, an audience member will volunteer to help me. She'll first think of the word 'trapping,' but change her mind and select the word 'pocketbook.' I hope my impressions are correct. I also hope everyone is enjoying the show.'"

The crowd ate it up. All rose to their feet, applauding wildly. I had a feeling of my own, an impression that Beatrice wasn't exactly the most popular member of the Garden Club. However, Doc was gracious, offering to help the woman back to her seat. Beatrice made her way to the back of the room, muttering, "It's a trick."

Doc now had his audience warmed up for the last half of his act. He invited two women to the stage and provided tape, coins, and a thick scarf to seal his eyes. With vision rendered completely impossible, Doc described various items held up by the audience, concluding his demonstration by successfully reading the serial number from a borrowed bill with his fingertips. Applause followed as Doc moved into his finale, which began with his borrowing personal objects from five audience members. Three women and two men volunteered. He passed around a black velvet bag, asking the five volunteers to drop their items in while his back was turned away. The objects were mixed, and the bag handed to Doc. The five volunteers stood in a row behind him, like a police lineup. Doc turned to address the audience.

"The name of this game is *Psychometry*. It's based on the theory that when an object comes in contact with a person, it retains a trace of energy from their aura—just as a needle rubbed across a magnet will absorb some of the charge. As I touch these borrowed objects, they will whisper stories to me, little facts and quirks about you—their owners. Armed with this information I should be able to zero in on the person fairly quickly." He smiled. "And if I sense anything particularly tasty, we'll discuss regular monthly payments to keep me quiet."

He picked up a small diamond ring and closed his eyes. Seconds passed, and the audience dutifully became quiet.

Doc opened his eyes. "I will tell you a few things about the owner of this ring. She's an old-fashioned romantic, someone who enjoys music and art. She understands people's problems and can sympathize with them, but she becomes impatient when confronted with obstinacy or stupidity. She has a deep affection for small animals, and I see her surrounded by pets of all kinds." He stepped in front of a small blonde woman. "Does the name 'Oliver' mean anything to you?"

She answered, "He's my cat!"

"Your vibrations are strong." He took a deep breath and cleared his throat. "Ah, I see it now. The clouds are lifting, the veil is cast aside, and it's all good news. I see a long life ahead of you, Angie. Your days will be filled with love and happiness."

"How'd you know my name?" The audience laughed at the amazement in her voice.

"I know all and I see all, but I tell a hell of a lot less." Laughter. "By the way, is this your ring?"

"Yes, it is."

The audience gasped. Doc beamed at them, nodding his appreciation. He took Angie's hand and laid the tiny ring in her palm. "You've been a terrific sport, and as a token of my gratitude I'd like to give you this ring as a souvenir."

"Thanks." She laughed at the joke as she returned it to her finger. "How amazing! It's just my size."

"Uncanny isn't it? Thank you, Angie. Let's all give her a big hand."

■ ■ ■

That was Doc's style—easy, conversational, intended to put his audience at ease without overwhelming them with his almost supernatural prowess. He moved about the stage with an erect military authority that belied his age. I won't go into detail about all the readings, but each one revealed personal (but never embarrassing) facts about the person. Two in particular stand out in my mind. Doc turned to a reading of one of the gentlemen on stage. "Are you planning on going fishing this weekend?"

The man was startled. "Yes. Will I catch anything?"

Doc considered it. "I think you'll catch two, maybe three speckled trout—and a magnificent case of poison ivy on your backside." The man laughed so hard he turned red.

The second reading that stands out in my recollection wasn't delivered by Doc, but by me!

It was the third item, as I recall. Doc touched the objects for a moment, smiling. Then he looked straight at me. "Ladies and Gentlemen, if I may digress a moment, I'd like to take this opportunity to introduce my protégé—my nephew, who's been studying with me all summer. Come on up, Craig!"

Everyone applauded. I got to my feet and approached the stage. If looks could kill, the one I gave Doc would have blasted him on the spot. I was absolutely terrified. Every eye in the room bored into my back. Doc rested his arm around my shoulder and whispered, "Smile, Craig." I grimaced at the audience. He continued. "It's long been my contention that anyone, given the proper amount of practice, can do anything that I do. My nephew will prove this." Doc gestured at the three remaining items on the table: a ring, a pocket watch, and an emerald earring. "Go ahead, Craig."

I looked over the three items and decided the pocket watch would be the easiest. After all, there were two women and one man left standing on stage. I figured it was a fifty-fifty shot if I went for the ring or the earring; the pocket watch seemed a no-brainer.

As I reached for it, Doc interrupted me. "You're trying to figure this problem out logically, son. Don't do it with your head. Use your heart. The obvious answer isn't necessarily the correct one."

Shrugging, I picked up the pocket watch. All I wanted to do was complete the task and return to my seat. I wasn't ready to try my skills out in front of a live audience. But as soon as I touched the watch, an eerie feeling came over me. I felt a warmth in my hand; a sensation of pulsating energy. It felt good, comforting.

I looked at Doc. He nodded. "Go ahead, Craig. You got it."

I examined the three remaining volunteers: a teenage girl, a thirtyish man, a middle-aged woman. I walked over to the older woman and held out the watch. "This watch belonged to your father. He loved to travel, and I think he picked this up when he went to Europe."

"Is that correct?" Doc asked the woman. She nodded. "Continue . . . ," Doc said.

I closed my eyes. "I hear the sounds of a crowd, laughing and having a good time. The sun is warm . . . I smell popcorn. There's a feeling of great fun in the air, like a party. I can't quite tell . . . oh wait! I just heard the crack of a bat! It's a ball game. A baseball game!"

I opened my eyes to see if the nice woman was laughing at my overactive imagination. I was so frightened at being in the spotlight that I'd spoken off the top of my head with no real thought about what I was saying, just babbling away. But to my surprise she was smiling, and her eyes glistened with tears. I looked at her, puzzled, and she took me by the hand.

"You have a wonderful talent," she said. "My father took me to a baseball game right before he got sick. It was the best time I ever had in my life." She leaned down and kissed me on the cheek. I felt my face turn bright red. She whispered in my ear, "Thank you for bringing my father back to life for me."

Well, I was stunned. My face burned like I'd contracted a fever. I could feel the woman's kiss on my cheek like it was branded there. Doc led the applause.

He gestured toward the other items, nodding slightly. "Want to finish up?"

I shook my head. "No, once is enough for me." I went back to my seat as the crowd applauded and laughed.

Doc picked up the last two items and read them simultaneously. Interestingly enough, the emerald earring belonged to the man!

Doc's final demonstration hailed from his days as a spiritualist. He instructed the audience to rest their hands lightly on the tables. "In the old days of spiritualism, people would attempt to communicate with the dead through a phenomenon known as table-tilting. Several people would sit around a table, hands resting lightly on the surface, and ask for a sign from the spirit world. Believe it or not, sometimes the table responded by tilting up on two legs. People soon discovered that the table could even answer questions: one rap for yes, two for no."

Doc told about a group of magicians who, at the turn of the century, decided to hold their own table-tilting séance. Their curiosity spurred by reports from the spiritualists, the magicians wanted to see if it were possible to make a table move without the aid of wires or other tricks.

According to Doc, eight magicians sat around a solid oak table that weighed almost 150 pounds. They placed their hands on it, concentrated mightily, and nothing happened. Not so much as a tremble. The magicians took a break and discussed their failure. It turned out there was a high degree of skepticism in the group, so they agreed to try it again with open minds. This time, the results were spectacular. Within five minutes the table shook, gyrated, and then flipped over, cracking in half.

"The power of belief at work," he continued. "The magicians were correct when they believed the table wouldn't move. But, as events proved, they were equally correct when they believed it would. Nothing changed about the experiment except their attitude. Bear that in mind as we attempt to recreate this experience. Just rest your fingertips on the table and concentrate on moving the table with your mind. Try to make it rotate in a clockwise direction. Concentrate . . . concentrate . . . believe it can happen, and it will . . ."

Doc's voice droned on, encouraging the audience to try to make the table move with their thoughts. Some brows furrowed with concentration, other people laughed and obviously didn't take the experiment seriously.

"Oh!" a woman's voice cried out near the front of the room. "It moved!"

I stood up and looked over the heads of the crowd. Sure enough, the table had tilted over onto two legs. The people sitting at the mischievous table shared identical expressions of blank amazement.

Within minutes, most of the tables were gyrating. I heard shouts of amazement as one table became temporarily airborne! It landed back onto the floor with a loud thump.

Before long, pandemonium ruled the Country Club. The tapping and squeaking of table legs blended with cries and gasps. Some of the tables had minds of their own, seemingly trying to flee while their sitters chased after them. After several minutes of this activity, Doc took the stage again.

"Ladies and Gentlemen, I now suggest to you that the tables are slowing down. The movement becomes fainter and fainter, weaker . . . weaker . . . and gone. I hope you enjoyed your little visit with the spirits!"

Doc bowed and the audience rose to their feet, cheering and clapping.

■ ■ ■

"What's eating you?" he asked me as we were packing up. "Didn't you enjoy the show?"

"Yeah, of course I did. You were great. I liked the way you handled the woman who tried to mess you up."

He smiled. "Ah yes. She thought I'd fallen off the truck yesterday. As though nobody ever tried to mess me up before. Of course she lied about her word. What she wasn't expecting was for me to boldly ask her to tell me out loud. Most people who try to play this trick on me never think to have a backup word handy, so they'll look around the room and name the first thing they see—like a glass, or a chair. Or a pocketbook." He looked at me closely. "So what's wrong? Mad at me for putting you on the spot?"

"That too," I replied with a grin to show I wasn't serious. "I'm just trying to figure out what happened to my locket."

He looked at me. "It's missing?"

I nodded. "I wanted to bring it along today but I can't find it."

Doc stroked his chin. "Did you try using a dowsing stick?"

"No." I imagined my family looking on in horror as I dashed around the house holding a vibrating twig. I almost laughed. "It didn't occur to me."

"Then I can also assume you didn't ask the pendulum where it is?"

I nodded again.

"Well, that only leaves one recourse." He patted the surface of the small end table he'd used to hold his props. "Ask the table."

"What?"

"Table tilting wasn't always an amusing trick. Not so long ago, it was considered a direct conduit between this world and the next. I think that, like the pendulum or the Ouija board, it's another way to tap into the subconscious mind. Give it a try. What can it hurt?"

I shrugged. "What do I do?"

Doc pulled the small table closer. "Place your hands on the top, just like this," he illustrated with his own hands, "and let your mind become blank and receptive."

I complied, trying not to think of anything as I listened to Doc's voice. The cobra ring he wore arrested my gaze. Its ruby eyes glinted mockingly. *What are you doing, boy?* it seemed to ask. *What if someone walked in right about now and saw how foolish you look?*

The table twitched under my hands. "Wow!"

"Don't break contact," Doc admonished. "Now, concentrate on your locket, what it looks like, its weight in your hands . . . ask the table questions. Remember, one rap for yes, two raps for no. Try to narrow down the location."

The table vibrated under my hands like a living thing. I wet my lips and said in a low voice, "Did Brian lose my locket?"

The table tilted on two legs and fell back, twice: *No.*

"Did I lose it?"

Yes.

"Is it in my room?"

Two raps. *No.*

"Is it in the living room?"

Yes.

I looked at Doc. "Continue," he urged.

"Is it under something?"

Yes.

"The couch?"

Two raps.

"Dad's chair?"

Yes!

I looked up at Doc. "I was watching a show about the powers of the mind on television last night . . . I bet I had the locket with me and it slipped between the cushions!"

The table rapped once in agreement. I felt exhilarated. I probably would have remembered where the locket was eventually, but Doc always knew ways to make the simplest problems magical.

"The table agrees with you," Doc said dryly.

I didn't have a clue what he meant. I looked down and my exhilaration turned to astonishment.

The table floated about six inches off the floor!

I snatched my hands away and the table dropped back to the floor with a loud thump. I looked at Doc for an explanation.

He stuck a cigar in his mouth and shrugged. "It happens," he said.

■ ■ ■

When Doc dropped me off at my house he handed me his bag of props. I quizzed him with my eyes and he winked. "Today was my last performance. The show is yours now, Craig."

"But—"

"No hurry. When you're ready, you'll know."

He honked twice and drove away.

■ ■ ■

Do I need to say it? The locket was exactly where the table (or my subconscious) said it was.

CHAPTER TEN

Yandee

JUST BEFORE I STARTED SCHOOL Dad presented me with a new watch: a "grown-up" gift. Eighth grade occupied most of my time for the next couple of weeks, so I didn't see Doc very often. There was a lot to think about: classes, new and interesting subjects, extracurricular activities . . . girls. Especially girls. I felt full of life and very adult. I examined my face in the mirror every morning looking for signs of facial hair.

One day I was sitting in English class, daydreaming about my down-the-block neighbor Rebecca Simmons (who had matured remarkably during the summer), picturing her as my assistant as we toured the world performing shows. It occurred to me that I hadn't seen Doc and May in a while. Because of a teacher's meeting we had only half a day of school, and I could catch the bus into town and pay them a surprise visit. Dad could pick me up on his way home from work. It was the perfect plan, and I thought it would be a nice surprise. After school I called Mom and got permission.

The bus dropped me off downtown and I walked across the bridge, enjoying the view of the Ohio River and the foothills. The afternoon was beautiful. Autumn was creeping in, and the colors of the trees were just starting to turn; a red, gold, and magenta splendor that made the foothills appear to be on fire. A few tattered clouds floated above the trees like gigantic birds.

I heard the commotion before I saw it.

Angry shouts, muttering, voices lifted in indignation. I quickened my steps, wondering what was going on. Whatever it was, it didn't sound good.

Five cars sprawled at the mouth of the driveway, hastily parked at every angle. My intuition warned me something was wrong. Perhaps Doc or May was hurt! By the time I reached Doc's yard I was running. I stopped, breath hot in my chest, when I saw the crowd gathered outside Doc's yard. At first I felt relief. I thought Doc and May were having a party. But then I noticed a car parked on the edge of the front yard, crushing May's irises and bee's balm. No guest would have done such an inconsiderate thing. Everyone knew how much May loved her garden.

I stopped short. About twenty people milled around Doc's porch, angry and shouting. It didn't look like a party. It looked like a lynch mob. Cries of "Warlock!" and "Witch!" rang through the air.

I worried about Doc and May. After all, they were two elderly people, living alone. "Let me by!" I yelled, pushing around the mob.

A middle-aged woman grabbed my elbow. "Don't go in there, boy! He does the devil's work!" With a shock I recognized Beatrice, the woman who'd tried to mess up Doc during his show at the country club.

"Leave me alone," I muttered, jerking away. I shoved through the crowd, making my way to the porch.

Doc appeared, wearing his red dressing gown. He looked tired, face pale, dark rings under his eyes. He saw me, and his voice soared above the jabbering. "Let him through!" I made it to the porch, and he took me by the arm and pushed me behind him. "What is the meaning of this?" he demanded.

A tall, extremely thin man stepped to the front of the crowd. He was about Doc's age, I guessed, with a long nose and a bald head that (except for black horn-rimmed glasses) made him resemble an angry bird of prey. Judging by the way the crowd deferred to him and fell silent, it was obvious he was their leader. "You know why we're here, Alain DeLyle," the man sneered. "Or should I say 'Alan Green.'"

The crowd stirred. "He hides behind a false name," someone muttered. "No honest man would fear to use his own name." Of course, I knew Doc had changed his name years ago to spare his family embarrassment, but the angry mob had no way of knowing this. Nor, from the looks of things, would they care if they did know.

Doc removed a cigar from his pocket and stuck it in his mouth. He lit it, puffed, and smiled. "Hello, Steven. Good to see you again. You obviously have something on your mind. Would you like to come in and talk about it?"

Steven drew himself up to his full height. "I would rather die than enter the abode of one who flouts God's Law."

"Your choice." Doc laughed. "So you finally worked up the nerve to confront the wizard in his den. I guess it's a marginal improvement over anonymously vandalizing my house and car. But *this*," he gestured at the crowd, "this is beneath even you, Steven—or should I call you *Yandee*, as we did in the old days? Do your disciples know you once trod the stage under the billing of 'High Priest of the Occult?'"

The man raised his head. "That was long ago, DeLyle. I saw the error of my ways and followed the path to God."

"So was it God who told you to vandalize my car? And send me hate letters in the mail?" More muttering. A few faces in the crowd reflected guilt and embarrassment. "I save them by the way, Steven—makes very amusing reading, although you should encourage your flock to practice proper spelling and grammar in formal correspondence. For your information, 'damnation,' is spelled with one *M* and two *N*'s, not the other way around."

Steven shook his fist. "You can mock us all you want, Wizard. But you can't mock God!" The crowd roared their agreement.

Doc shrugged. "So much for common courtesy," he remarked to me under his breath. He puffed his cigar. "All right then, Steven. What do you want from me?"

Steven looked amazed. "You know what we want! We want you out. Your evil activities are corrupting our citizens. Get out of our city with your witchcraft. Pack up and go back where you came from!"

"And if I don't?" Doc asked coolly.

Steven glared at him. "Then things could get ugly." He turned to his followers. "Brothers and sisters, it's only a matter of time before this man's wickedness brings the wrath of God down on us! Why should we have to pay for his sins? We want him out!"

"Out! Out! Out!" chanted the crowd. "Get out, Wizard!" I looked at Doc, truly scared.

But Doc was calm, his shoulders straight and square. "Steven, I know it's no use trying to reason with you, but I owe it to the memory of our past friendship to try. You claim to be doing God's work. Didn't God teach love and tolerance? Where did all this hate and anger come from? Do you truly expect me to think it's from a loving God?"

"God's righteous anger—"

"Oh please." Doc cut him off with a gesture. "Just because I encourage people to think for themselves and practice control over their own lives, you think I'm the devil's right-hand man? Do you really think God's nose gets out of joint whenever I read somebody's palm? Doesn't Paul say that of all the gifts of the spirit, the greatest is the gift of prophecy? All spiritual gifts come from God. Stop using the Scriptures as a justification for your own hate. Quit using the Cross for a sword. You're a wolf in lamb's clothing! Wouldn't your time be better spent helping the poor?" Doc ignored Steven's shouting and tried to talk to the crowd. "Think about it, folks: what are you so upset about?"

"Black magic!" "Telling of fortunes and casting spells!" "Don't listen to him!" "Suffer not a witch to live!" someone shouted. At that last, icewater ran through my veins. Where were the police?

Doc sighed. "I'm not a sorcerer, I don't practice black magic, nor do I worship evil spirits."

"Lies!" Steven screamed. "Close your ears to his witchcraft! He has the power to enchant you."

Doc raised his hands over his head. The crowd fell quiet. He spoke. "I will pray for you. Please leave now."

Well, that did it. The mob became furious. "*You* will pray for *us?*" was the general outcry. They screamed, moaned in disbelief, choked in outrage. "God will punish you!"

Doc pinched the base of his nose and sighed. "Come on in, Craig."

He placed his hand on my back. It was firm and steady, although I was shaking like a leaf. We walked together toward the front door.

A rock about the size of an egg hit Doc in the back.

He spun around, eyes blazing, and for the first time in our acquaintance I saw his temper rise to the surface. "Who did that?" he roared. Another rock whirred through the air, Doc caught it in mid-flight and hurled it to the ground. I stepped in front of Doc to prevent him from tearing into the crowd with his bare hands. I felt strong tendons swell in his arms and wondered if he actually could take them all on. A part of me wanted to see him try.

I don't think I'd better mention this to Mom and Dad, I thought.

Steven grinned. "Come on, DeLyle. Show us what you got." Several people nodded—they couldn't wait to get their hands on the wizard! A few people bent down and picked up rocks from the driveway, never taking their eyes away from Doc. My head swam in disbelief. Were they going to *stone* him, like something from the Old Testament?

Doc growled, and I knew I couldn't stop him even if I tried my best. Nor could I stand by and watch him take on a mob by himself. I looked around for a weapon of some kind, a stick or axe handle, with which to back him up.

Why doesn't Aunt May call the police?

Just then, as though in answer to my thought, the window next to the door shot open. Aunt May leaned out, a double-barreled shotgun balanced across her arm. She aimed it at Steven. The man's mouth dropped open. If the situation hadn't been so serious it would have looked comical.

May certainly wasn't joking. "Stevie, you have until I count to ten to get the hell out, and take your friends with you. I won't have this disturbance at my home! One . . . two . . ."

Steven turned even paler. "You married him!" he shouted. "I loved you, and you married this . . . this . . . *witch doctor!*"

My eyes felt like they were about to pop out of my skull. *So that's what this was all about. A love triangle!*

May gazed along the length of the gun barrel. "Four . . . *five* . . ."

Doc had regained his composure. "She'll do it, Steven," he said with a smile. His eyes glittered. "She's not as tolerant as I, as you know full well. When she finds out what you did to her garden, I wouldn't want to be in your shoes."

May looked shocked by Doc's words, disappeared from the window, and ran out to the porch. She looked at her ruined garden in dismay. Her face clouded. "My irises! You son of a bitch." She cocked the hammers and pointed the gun at Steven. "You're dead."

He backed into the arms of the crowd. "Somebody call the police—you'll go to jail!"

May's voice was cold. "You assaulted my husband on our own property. You're trespassing and threatening my family. I don't think the police will arrest me for shooting a hostile trespasser—*me*, a helpless old woman. If you truly know any prayers, you'd better say them quick!"

Steven stared at Doc and May for several seconds, then broke the gaze. "Let's go," he muttered to his congregation. "We'll be back."

"No," May said. "You won't." She lifted the shotgun into the air and fired.

The crowd broke and ran down the driveway, casting terrified glances over their shoulders. Soon there was no evidence (with the exception of May's ruined garden) that the entire incident ever happened. Doc looked at May, and she looked back solemnly. "You shot the bird feeder out of the apple tree," Doc said. They both burst out laughing, and Doc gave her a noisy kiss on the lips.

■ ■ ■

"Steven Slade," Doc said, sipping a cup of steaming Irish coffee. "Also known as Yandee, High Priest of the Occult. Years ago, he was my brightest pupil—and my best friend. He performed with us in our vaudeville show for a couple of years."

"I never trusted him," May commented. "He always seemed too slick to be completely honest. I tried to warn you."

Doc nodded. "You were right, my dear—as usual. Craig, Yandee was one of the best mentalists I've ever seen, but he began believing in his own powers too much. He learned that there was no limit to the number of people looking for leaders to guide them, and he let his own power corrupt him. He stepped from the stage and into the pulpit."

He sighed. "Taking a great deal of our money with him to start his church. After our falling out he wanted May to join him. She refused, and after we were married Yandee never forgave either one of us."

May snorted. "He claims to serve God. All he serves is his own ego."

Doc looked mildly disapproving. "Now, May, we have to be loving. After all, I consider Steven part of the family. We still have to hold out hope that we can help him."

May answered, "You hope all you want. I gave up on him years ago. If he comes here again, I'll part his hair with my shotgun. My poor, poor irises." She disappeared into the kitchen.

Doc chuckled. "She always was a stubborn girl. One thing you never want to do, Craig, is get on her bad side."

I smiled. "I've already figured that out." I grew more serious as I realized this was the perfect time to ask Doc something that had been on my mind of late.

Doc glanced at me. "Spill it."

"What do you mean?"

"You have that wide-eyed expression you get when you want to ask me something but you don't exactly know where to begin."

"Well . . . it's about God and everything . . . I don't know where to begin . . ."

Doc laughed. "That's what I just said. Try beginning at the beginning."

I tried to gather my thoughts, but I guess I was still a little rattled from finding my uncle in the middle of a confrontation with a religious cult. "Well, I've learned a lot about the powers of the mind, and of belief. I've learned that miracles aren't supernatural at all, but perfectly natural if you look at them the right way. I guess I was just wondering . . ."

Doc's eyes were bright. "You were wondering if there is really a God at all—or is there only the mind?"

Tension ebbed out of my body like air from a deflating balloon. "Exactly!"

Doc looked delighted. "Craig, you've come a long way. I was twice your age before I began to wonder if what I'd been told about God was the truth, or just a comforting fiction. Questioning the existence of God is the first step in understanding God. There's something inside each of us that asks 'Is there more to life than this?' We dimly sense that there's something bigger than us, something perfect and grand and infinitely loving. We instinctively know there is a *Source* from which all things arise and to which all things must eventually return. We don't know what that something is, so we call it 'God.' We create a symbol in our minds, a benevolent old man, or a stern but loving parent. Or whatever. First of all, we have to decide what it is we're looking for. Is God just a symbol, a concept created by the mind? Or is God real and understandable?"

"I don't know," I said. "That's why I asked." What brought the question to mind was a discussion I overheard between my mother and some of her friends. A heated controversy rocked the community (and indeed, the entire country) about whether to teach creationism or evolution in the classroom. Battle lines formed. Each side claimed to know the truth, and each side had compelling arguments for their position. I was confused. I'd always assumed that God made us—but the evidence for evolution seemed logical and scientific. Where did God fit in all this scientific rationalism? I mentioned this to Doc.

Doc sipped from his cup. "Yes, indeed. When seeking God, science can't help us much. Logic is a sort of window through which the scientist sees the world. If a phenomenon doesn't fall into the logical window, too bad for the phenomenon. God, like psychic powers, the human soul, and even consciousness itself, is intangible and improvable. Illogical."

"Science doesn't accept the idea of God," I said.

He agreed. "Since we can't directly observe God through our telescopes or microscopes, it's easy to assume that what we can't see or touch or measure with instruments doesn't exist. Yet the scientist pays homage to God as he or she studies God's work. The search for ultimate truth is a sacred quest. But we make a mistake when we speak of the scientist 'discovering' things when he or she comes across one of God's creations. It's sheer arrogance to ever claim we 'discover' anything. It would be more correct to say that we finally noticed what was under our noses all along."

"But what about evolution? Where does God fit in there?"

He paused, reflected. "Perhaps evolution is God's process for improving on His own creation. I believe life on earth is a giant, complex jigsaw puzzle. Every living thing on the planet, from the smallest to the highest, has its own special place in the puzzle. Nothing living, no matter how small, is insignificant to the whole. In my opinion, it's a mistake to assume that evolution just happened by accident. I can't believe that the random dance of molecules at the beginning of time led to this moment, with the two of us sitting in this den trying to unscrew the inscrutable. I don't feel like an unlikely mishap, do you?"

I grinned. "No—but sometimes I wonder about Brian."

Doc winked. "I understand. I had brothers, too. Craig, I think God exists, but it's up to each of us to find this out for ourselves."

I considered it. "How?"

Doc laughed. "You ask tough questions, my young pilgrim. There's no *one* path that leads to enlightenment. All religions claim to know the *truth* about God. Each preaches a certain aspect, point of view, or system of worship to communicate with the Higher Being. I don't think there is any one *true* religion; all sincere people who honor compassion praise God in his or her own way. You find God by keeping an open mind. Remember when I said that logic is like a window through which you view the world? If you open the window and wait patiently, eventually a warm breeze will blow through. You don't command that breeze, you don't summon it. It comes when you patiently wait for it. That warm breeze, so to speak, is God. The open mind is like an open window, allowing all possibilities to enter. God is the sum of all possibilities."

"The sum of all possibilities . . . ," I repeated. I liked the way it sounded.

"What is God to you, Craig?"

The abruptness of the question startled me, and I couldn't answer for a moment. "God is the Father, the Son, and the Holy Spirit."

"Answered like a good Catholic boy. He is all that, and much more. God is gratitude, and every loving relationship, and all acts of compassion. What I'm trying to say is that God isn't hard to find. He isn't hiding out there somewhere." Doc pointed up and to the right, indicating some far-off point of the universe. "He's here—," Doc tapped his chest, "—and here." He reached across and drew a circle around my heart with his forefinger. "When you help someone less fortunate than yourself, or you try to make the world a better place, you've found God. When you put aside your own selfishness and try to ease another's pain, God is there. But when you act out of hate or anger or resentment, God is *not*. Do you understand?"

"I think so."

"God is a *verb*, Craig, not a static concept or symbol. Faith and belief aren't just words, but actions. God speaks through love. Have you ever noticed that hate is loud, but love is quiet?"

I thought about it, then shook my head. "I don't get it."

"Love is action, not words. Love isn't expressed in shouts of anger, or violence or arguments. Love happens when you hold your beloved's hand and watch the sunset, or when you pet your dog, or sometimes when you just look at each other and let your hearts speak what the lips cannot. Keeping a loved one's memory alive in your heart after they've passed away is perhaps the greatest love of all." He waved his hand in the air. "What Steven and his followers have is not love, nor is it God. It isn't God they follow, but their own hate. They worship anger, and use the Scriptures to justify their own prejudices. This angers me."

Doc cracked his knuckles and stood up, stretching. "I'm an old man, Craig, and I've seen a lot of suffering in my lifetime—more than we could possibly eliminate in a thousand lifetimes. It's easy to believe that man is incapable of achieving perfection. But the fact that we keep *trying* is sheer proof that we're more than our animal nature. Always show your love, Craig. Don't wait until it's too late. Let the people you love know how you feel. Be kind and considerate to everybody. Love your little brother even though he drives you crazy—*especially* when he drives you crazy. Do this and you'll find God." His eyes twinkled. "In fact, you'll realize that you never lost Him."

May stuck her head into the den. "Craig, your father called to let you know he has to work late. He'll be by to pick you up after dinner."

"I don't want to impose . . ."

"Oh nonsense. You know there's plenty. Dinner's ready."

Doc rubbed his hands together. "Enough theology for now. Let's eat!"

Dinner was, of course, excellent, but my mind still reeled with questions—which I fired at Doc all through the meal. He laughed. "No one really has all the answers. For every mystery we can explain, there's a hundred that we can't. God set the world into motion and it's up to us to sort it out. All I can tell you is what I believe, take it or leave it."

I grinned at him. "I'm all ears."

"You're getting to be all lip. Too big for your britches." He winked to show me he was just kidding, and I laughed.

Doc tapped his chin, thinking. "I don't believe in fate or destiny. That's why I'm not a fortune-teller, as Steven would have me. I believe futures are *built*, not predicted or preordained. We have free will, and sometimes that seems more like a curse than a blessing. I don't believe God interferes much with our comings and goings. But He's always there with us, lending us strength and guidance. Pass the potatoes."

I said that with the daily news programs airing footage of the horrible suffering in Vietnam, not to mention the recent earthquake in Los Angeles (a so-called "act of God" that injured almost a thousand people, some fatally) it seemed that God wasn't responding to the prayers my church sent up for Him to look out for and protect the world. "Do you think prayers do any good? Is anyone listening?"

To my surprise, it was May who answered. "Certainly. But you have to pray for the right things. I've seen the devout pray that their team win the Super Bowl while there are starving children in faraway places who've never even been exposed to the concept of God. Would God help the Steelers win a football game because someone asked, while thousands of children starve to death because none of them knew how to pray? I don't think so, nor do I think God takes sides in a war. That wouldn't be very compassionate, and I have to believe God is compassion. You have to pray for strength, and for healing and for horrible things to end."

Doc applauded. "Well put, my dear. The power of prayer is the power of the group mind at work."

I was confused. "But isn't that still just the mind, like the time we healed my leg?"

He shook his head impatiently. "You're confusing your brain with your mind. The brain is the organ of thought, just as the eye is the organ of vision. Without the mind to operate it, the brain is just a lump of clay or a vehicle without a driver. Your mind is more than just a collection of brain cells. It is the interface between your spirit and the Divine."

I must have looked puzzled because he said, "I've made it sound too complicated, when it's really very simple. God created your mind so that you can understand Him. God created prayer so that you can share your thoughts with Him. While prayer is directed thought, it's also much more than that. Our minds are small reflections of God's mind. Our powers are tiny imitations of God's powers, and our creativity is our soul's desire to emulate our Maker. Is it any wonder that we yearn for reunion with the Source? God gave us a tremendous gift, a mind capable of examining His universe, and we should always remember where this gift originated."

May said, "I think he's wondering about church, dear. If there's any point in it."

Doc satirically smacked his forehead with the palm of his hand. "It's all our fault, May. We've set a bad example with our pagan ways, and our irreverent love for sleeping late on Sundays! Craig, church is a good place to be with people of like mind. God doesn't need a house to live in. The entire universe is His home, but when a number of sincere people form a Group Mind and act with loving intent—and that's the key—concentrating on a specific goal that will help others, miracles can happen. Miracles do happen. Don't underestimate the power of prayer. But remember, as you celebrate Mass, don't allow the rituals to lose their meaning through complacency. Also take care to respect others' beliefs, no matter how different they are from yours. Nobody holds a monopoly on Truth. Never pray for selfish reasons. The most sincere prayer is when you thank God for your life. Right, May?"

May nodded. "I thank Her every day."

I goggled at her. "Huh?"

"I thank Her for my life."

"Her who?"

She smiled. "Goddess, the Great Mother, who gave birth to us all."

I was shocked! Today, with the advent of the New Age, the idea that God has a feminine aspect may not seem all that shocking. But in 1971, to a young Catholic boy, the concept seemed close to heresy.

Doc nudged my elbow. "Close your mouth, son, something might fly in there. May, you caught him off guard."

She smiled mischievously, saying nothing.

Doc shook his head good-naturedly. "Craig, remember God is the sum of all possibilities—*all* of them. Call Him or Her God, or the Great Spirit, Father, Grandfather, Mother, whatever, God is still God: the ultimate consciousness of the universe. As I've said, the main thing is to act from compassion and from love."

"But how do you *know?* I know the sun rises, and I know I have two brothers, but how do I know if I'm doing the right thing or not?"

"Good question," May commented. I got the strong impression that she was enjoying watching me grill Doc.

Doc harrumphed. "Listen to your heart. Your heart knows right from wrong. It all comes down to a question of faith. And faith is a curious thing. I had a friend once, a confirmed atheist, who suddenly learned to pray to the God he didn't believe in with all his heart and soul when he thought he was going to die. On the other hand, my uncle, a devout, born-again Christian, wept in fear when he found out he was dying. That puzzled me. If your faith is strong, wouldn't you welcome death? To die and be with God?"

I nodded. "I guess so. I don't like to think about it."

He raised his bushy eyebrows. "Why not?"

"Death is scary."

He touched my hand. "Death is nothing to fear, Craig. Personally, I'm looking forward to solving this last mystery. I believe it's going to be a great and wondrous adventure!"

May left the table, returning with a fragrant dish. "Ready for dessert?" she asked.

"Yes dear." Doc grinned. "You want to experience the Divine, Craig? Wait 'til you taste your Aunt May's apple pie!"

CHAPTER ELEVEN

Halloween

HALLOWEEN OF 1971 marked a point of passage for me: it was the first Halloween I didn't go trick-or-treating. Instead, I went to a guy-and-girl party at the CYO, with dancing and drinking (well, punch and soda) and a minimum of chaperones. Although a little bit of necking occurred here and there, it wasn't a very wild party; as it turned out I got home before Brian did.

Around 10:00 P.M. he banged open the door, dressed as the Lone Ranger, with his treat bag brimming with goodies. "Ha, ha," he gloated, clutching the bag like it was a lover. "You missed out on all the treats!"

I grinned. "Yeah, but it looks like you have enough for both of us." I lunged at him, and he ran screaming from the room. I caught up with him in the bedroom, tackled him, and gave him a noogie until he laughed so hard he begged for mercy. I helped myself to a candy bar and an apple from his bag (ransom) and returned to the living room.

We were playing the new video game Pong when the doorbell rang. "I'll get it!" Brian yelled. He zoomed across the hall and I heard him throw open the door.

The next couple of seconds happened quickly. I heard the door open, then saw a blur shooting back through the living room like a rocket. The blur was Brian, screaming at the top of his lungs, "Ahhh-h-h-h! Monsters!" Brian disappeared into our bedroom, slammed the door and locked it.

Curious, I went into the living room to investigate. Standing in the doorway were a petite witch and a stocky vampire. It took me a couple of seconds to recognize them.

"Hi, Doc," I said. "Hi, May. Nice costumes."

May looked concerned, an expression that seemed out of place on a green-faced, warty (possibly child-eating) witch. "I think we scared Brian half to death."

"He'll get over it. Come on in."

Mom came in and greeted our guests. "Was that Brian I heard whooping through the house just then?"

Doc smiled, showing extremely realistic fangs. "I'm afraid we gave him a bit of a turn."

Brian cracked open his door, checked to see if the coast was clear, then strutted out with cocky dignity. "I wasn't really afraid," he said. "I was just pretending. I knew it was you."

Dad came in and chuckled at Doc's and May's attire. "A little old for trick-or-treating, aren't you?"

Doc bared his fangs. "You're never too old to have fun. We came by to commemorate the season by telling the boys an appropriately scary ghost tale. It's traditional, you know."

"Come on, Dad, it'll be fun," I said. We gathered in the living room, Dad turned out the lights, and I lit several candles. Brian sprawled on the floor, hands under his chin.

Doc stood in the candlelight and began his tale.

"A long, long time ago I had the opportunity to see a bit of the world. I traveled to Egypt, where I spent the night in the burial chamber of a pharaoh. From there I went to the United Kingdom to gather information about the infamous Druids, whose mystic monuments remain a puzzle to this day. I was traveling through Scotland when a sudden storm forced me to stop for the night. I was far, far out in the country, and there weren't any houses or stores, or anywhere a stranger could ask for directions. I kept driving, and eventually came upon an old castle, far away from civilization of any sort. It wasn't the ideal place to spend a chilly, wet night, but I didn't have much choice. I was afraid to try to drive any further on the slippery roads. The castle was nothing but a shell, large and rundown, although in its time it was probably something to see. Now, with the stone weathered away and covered with green moss and the roof sagging and groaning in the middle, it looked more like a haunted house.

"Which, as it turned out—it was."

Doc sipped from his drink (for dramatic effect, I suspect), then continued. "I found a small chamber that was relatively dry and rolled out a few blankets on the hard floor. Oddly enough, there was a large key in the door and I was able to lock the room. Outside, the wind moaned and groaned, and from my window the interlocking branches whipped about in the wind and seemed to want to reach in and grab me!"

Doc lunged out with his hands and Brian let out a yell. After the laughter had subsided Doc raised his hand for silence. "Eventually, I slipped into a troubled doze. My dreams were haunted, however, by hideous visions of specters and dark shadows lurking in every corner. I didn't know the history of the castle, but I began to suspect it was a bloody one indeed. There was an oppressive feeling of wrongness about the place.

"Suddenly, I was awakened by a fitful scratching noise, like a cat or dog, worrying at the rotten wooden door. Only it wasn't an ordinary cat or dog scratching at the door. Judging from the sound, and the alarming way the door shivered and rattled in its frame, whatever was trying to get in must have weighed about two hundred pounds! I thanked God that the door was locked, and that three inches of solid oak stood between me and It."

Doc took another sip from his drink. "But then, the key began to turn in the lock."

Brian watched Doc with eyes as round as umbrellas. "What happened then, Uncle Doc, what happened?"

"Well, Brian, I'll admit I was scared. In fact, I was terrified! I sat on that cold, dank floor and watched as the key turned slowly . . . slowly in the keyhole. I tried to move; I couldn't. I was literally paralyzed with fear. And then I heard the beast chuckle, a low, rumbling sound of total cruelty. You cannot possibly imagine the depth of evil expressed in that sound.

"Then, the door slowly creaked open. Outlined against the dark hallway was a huge, bulky creature the likes of which was never meant to exist on a sane earth. It was covered with hair, its eyes burned with green fire, and on its horned head was a tattered red stocking cap. As it moved into the moonlight its fur gleamed black, then blue, and then a color that I cannot describe. The only sound in the room was the beast's respiration, a noise like the rubbing of a rope against a tree. And the clicking of its claws, as the creature's hands twitched in anticipation. Its eyes—but to describe those flaming, hungry yellow orbs would be to invite madness. It reached for me, tongue rasping across its jagged teeth, and then began to enter the room. Escape was impossible; the window was far too small to allow a means of fleeing the awful thing. I covered my face with my hands and huddled in the corner, thinking that I was surely dead. The creature had me trapped. It giggled, drool dripping from the corners of its fanged mouth."

"Did it kill you?" Brian asked, and then looked surprised when we all laughed.

Doc managed to maintain a perfectly straight face. "Then a very strange thing happened. I felt a slight tug at my sleeve and heard a tiny voice. I looked up, and standing next to me was a young girl about eight years old. 'The key,' she whispered. 'You must get the key. It's the only way to stop Redcap!' Then I noticed that I could see the window right through the girl, as though she were made of smoked glass. Well, it's always been my policy never to argue with spirits, so I tried to think of a way to get around the creature to get the key. Apparently, I had inadvertently summoned the monster when I turned the key in the door before retiring for the night. As though reading my intentions, the creature took a step forward, crouched, and then sprang right at me!

"I threw myself aside, barely escaping the beast's—Redcap's—claws. My nostrils burned with the monster's foul smell. I rolled to a sitting position and bumped my head against something hard. I looked around and saw that I had come up against a very old, very large mirror. This gave me an idea. Redcap was climbing to its feet, shaking its head and sneezing in a most hideous way from the dust in its nose. It looked at me, and murder was in its eyes. I rolled the mirror over so that the first thing the creature would see was its own re-flection.

"When Redcap gazed upon its own terrible countenance, it raised a howl of agony so shrill and horrible that it sounded like a soul howl-ing from the depths of Hades. I took advantage of the moment to run to the door, close it, and remove the key from the slot.

"'Throw it at him!' my little friend urged, and I complied. I wound up like Nolan Ryan and hurled the key with all my might. Redcap saw it coming, and raised another one of those ear-splitting howls. Then the key hit it, there was a great flash of fire, the smell of rancid fur burning—and the creature vanished into whatever portal of Hell had originally spawned it."

Brian and I watched Doc with fascination as he continued.

"By the next day, I'd convinced myself that the whole experience had been a particularly vivid nightmare brought about by exhaustion and the spooky atmosphere of the abandoned castle. I drove into town, looking for breakfast and, perhaps, someone who could give me direc-tions. I stopped at a small pub near the English border where both my needs were satisfied. 'Where ye be coming from, then?' the pub owner, a plump, ruddy woman asked. 'There's not anyplace to stay for miles and miles, and surely ye didn't spend the night out in the storm?' I told her I'd spent the night at an old castle, near the moors.

"She looked at me in amazement. 'You spent the night in Her-mitage Castle?' she asked.

"'Yes,' I replied. 'I suppose I did, although I didn't know that was its name. Why? Is it against the law to trespass there?'

"She wiped her face with her apron and said, 'It's against the laws of God and common sense to set foot in that cursed place. D'ye know that eight hundred years ago it was the home of William de Soulis, the evil wizard, and his spirit still haunts the place?' The woman went on to tell me the history of Hermitage Castle.

"In the twelfth century it was inhabited by the evil sorcerer William de Soulis, who used to kidnap children from the village and murder them in the castle, sacrificing them to his evil masters. It was said that the bodies of the poor children were still in the dungeon, and that their spirits still walked the halls. When I heard this, I couldn't help but think about the little girl I saw—or thought I saw—the night before. But the worst thing was that William had sold his soul to an evil creature called Robin Redcap, so named because he wore a cap made from the skins of children. The villagers finally killed William de Soulis by wrapping him in a lead sheet and boiling him alive. Now his spirit returns every seven years to the castle, accompanied by Robin Redcap, who owns William's soul, but is held in check by the spirits of the children he had murdered. Even the foulest darkness cannot withstand the purity and innocence of a child's inner light."

Doc paused. Brian yelled, "Did that really happen?"

Dad laughed. "Of course not, Brian, it's just a story."

Doc ignored them. "I thought that I might encounter a bit of skepticism, so I brought along a souvenir of the experience. It seems that in my haste to leave the castle, I'd accidentally put the magic key in my pocket. Here it is." Doc removed a large, apparently ancient skeleton key from his pocket and held it out on the palm of his hand. "It's said that the key is haunted by the spirit of Robin Redcap, and that every seven years the creature goes out in search of its property."

May interrupted, "Doc, if I'm not mistaken, this is a seventh year!"

Doc looked thoughtful. "My dear, I believe you're right . . ."

As Doc spoke, the key began to turn in his hand! I was fascinated, but Brian ran screaming from his spot on the rug and hid behind the couch. Even Dad was a bit startled by the key's eerie movement. The key turned a complete revolution, and Doc closed his hand around it. "But of course," he said, "it was just a bad dream." He opened his hand, and the key had vanished. "Well, it's getting late, boys. May and I should be leaving so you can get some sleep." He paused at the door. "I hope you fellows won't have any bad dreams tonight because of my little anecdote?"

"No problem, Doc," I said. "Thanks for the story. It was great, wasn't it Brian?"

"Y-yeah," Brian agreed. "G-great."

After Doc left, Dad laughed. "I swear, that guy is really full of it. He's a helluva storyteller though. That key trick was all right. Now you boys go to bed and don't let that story cause you to have nightmares."

I had trouble sleeping, but not because of Doc's story. I was laughing at my little brother Brian, who burrowed under the covers, where he stayed completely buried for the rest of the night like a bug under a rock. However, I'll admit that every time the wind sent a tree limb scraping across the house, I jumped. I didn't really believe in monsters, of course, but after all, you never know . . .

CHAPTER TWELVE

The Old Victoria

BY EARLY NOVEMBER I was completely acclimated to life at the top of the ladder at St. Vincent's and feeling a bit cocky. My classmates noticed a difference in me. My habitual shyness had evaporated during the summer under Doc's tutelage, and I felt more confident and self-assured than I ever had in my life. I visited Doc two or three times a week, continuing my training. He taught me how to memorize long lists of information at a glance, how to perform complex mathematical operations in my head, and how to remember the names and telephone numbers of everyone I met. These skills not only helped my studies, but came in handy in my social life as well. Everyone thought I was a genius. Everyone except Robert Davis, that is, who accused me of being a mutant.

One Saturday afternoon I asked Doc what brain-stretching activities he had planned for us. To my surprise, Doc told me we were going to play hooky and go into town to see a movie. In fact, it was a James Bond double feature: *Goldfinger* and *Dr. No.* Knowing Doc as I did, I suspected these movies contained some esoteric lesson for my benefit. But even with the veiled threat of education lurking beneath the surface, it still sounded like fun.

May drove us downtown in the big Jaguar and dropped us off near the old Victoria Theater, a vaudeville house built in 1904 that had been converted into a movie theater. Doc paid for our tickets, and we went inside.

The Victoria had certainly seen better days. Paint flaked from every wall, the gilded arabesques were tarnished, curtains and backdrops tattered and moth-eaten. It smelled like popcorn and mildew. "A shame," Doc said. "This place used to be beautiful."

I couldn't imagine it. Everyone knew the old theater was falling apart. As though to emphasize this point, when I asked if we could sit in the balcony, we were refused. "Unsafe for use," the usher told us. "Condemned."

About a handful of people were in the theater. We made our way to the center section and settled in to watch the double feature. Doc seemed to enjoy himself thoroughly. I munched popcorn and carefully watched each movie looking for hidden messages. I found none, but I can honestly say that I've never paid more attention to any film in my life! I thought it was cool that the big Oriental guy could kill people with his hat. Maybe that was the lesson: never underestimate the power of a chapeau.

When the credits began to roll, the theater quickly emptied, but Doc didn't seem to be in a hurry to leave. He gazed around the theater and sighed. "I guess I just wanted to take one more look at the old girl before they decide to tear her down. I wish you could have seen this place in its prime, Craig. Absolutely beautiful. We housed the big show here. We rehearsed all summer, then debuted our production each season on that very stage. The management loved us and treated us like royalty." A mouse ran across Doc's foot, but he didn't seem to notice. "Magnificent. The best stage any performer ever trod."

I yawned. The fast-paced double feature had made me tired. "You performed here?" I asked.

He nodded. "Oh yes, many times. Back in the '40s we were quite an attraction. Broke all box office records." His eyes drifted around the room as though seeing through time—a better time for the old theater. "After I moved to Wheeling from New York I always began every tour in this theater. 'From the Victoria to the world,' was my motto."

I rubbed my eyes. "I wish I could have seen it." I yawned again, so hard my jaws cracked.

"Why can't you?"

I was startled by the question. "Well, I can't, that's why."

His eyes glittered. "You can."

"I can? How?"

"Just imagine it. Relax, concentrate . . . stop the flow of time."

Of its own accord, my head drooped.

"Slowing, slowing . . . stop. Now reverse the flow and allow your mind to travel back in time . . . back . . . the year is 1940 . . . the theater is packed to capacity; the lights go down . . . down . . ."

My eyelids slid closed.

"Over there is the orchestra pit, see it? The conductor raises his arms. Oriental music begins to play; the curtains part to reveal an opulently decorated stage. In those days we combined Oriental mystique with pompous-sounding lectures. Can you see it?"

"Yes," I muttered, and I *could* see it. Large woven tapestries adorned the back wall, behind a stage full of intriguing props. In the center of the stage perched a curious tripod supporting a large glass bowl. Incense fumes tickled my nostrils.

Doc's voice, low and soothing: "A strange device dominates the right side of the stage: The Hindu Torture Couch, its spikes polished to gleaming brilliance." I nodded. I could see it clearly. It was the same odd contrivance I'd noticed rusting away in the corner of Doc's den. This daydream, or whatever it was, was unusually powerful. I could actually see the lights gleaming from the couch's pointed spikes. So compelling was Doc's suggestion that I thought I heard the murmurs of a large audience, waiting for the show to begin.

And then, suddenly I could hear the orchestra playing!

With a start, I opened my eyes and looked to the left and right. The formerly empty theater was packed with people from all walks of life: well-dressed gentry, merchants, common laborers. I craned my neck around, not believing what I saw. The old Victoria, completely restored to its former glory, a shining, bright piece of fine jewelry!

Doc said, "The old lady looks good with her make-up on, doesn't she?"

He'd been sitting right next to me, but when I turned to ask him what was going on, a large middle-aged man who looked like a banker had replaced him. Doc was nowhere to be found. *Damn him!* I thought. *He's hypnotized me again!*

I wondered what was going to happen next, when a stocky, well-built man strode out to center stage. His black hair swirled back from his broad forehead like a dark wave on the ocean; his eyes stabbed out into the audience. With a shock I recognized Doc, at least thirty years younger.

He bowed with old-fashioned formality. "Ladies and gentlemen, my name is Dr. Alain DeLyle. Good evening. Since the dawn of civilization, man has sought to improve his vision—his vision of his immediate surroundings, of things distant, and visions of things in the future. Each step forward in the occult sciences was heralded by the public with awe, admiration . . . and yes, even damnation. Cries of fraud, evil spirits, and even witchcraft filled the air, and yet today, the fascination of ordinary people toward *those who see* continues unabated. In the past, anyone with special ability was put on the rack and the stake. Entire bloodlines of gifted psychics were exterminated in the Middle Ages. Even today, misguided individuals see the gift of prophecy as the work of the Infernal. And yet my friends, the gifted ones are still among us. You will see them tonight!"

Doc was really laying it on thick. His overblown delivery reminded me of the guy from the *Wizard of Oz*. By now I'd figured out that I was in the middle of a hypnotic dream. Doc's old-fashioned spiel was enough to convince me of that. However, it was the most powerful dream I ever had. I could smell the perfume of the woman sitting in front of me and feel the weight of the portly gentleman's arm pressing against my elbow. My senses were hyperactive; I heard the music from the orchestra pit and the soft sounds of the silk costumes of the dancing girls sliding against smooth skin.

The audience applauded again. Doc was working them!

"Now I would like to introduce to you a man whose mental powers eclipse any who have ever lived. He will penetrate your minds, reveal your innermost thoughts, and answer your unspoken questions in a manner that is nothing short of miraculous. Ladies and gentlemen, I give you Yandee, High Priest of the Occult!"

I gasped. *Yandee! Steven Slade, Doc's arch-enemy!*

But then I remembered this was before their falling out. This was the year 1940, not 1971, and Yandee was still Doc's best friend.

Yandee, a handsome, mustachioed man, dressed in robes and turban, took the stage. His dusky skin and penetrating gaze hinted of desert mysteries and the Riddle of the Sphinx. He simply oozed charm and charisma. It was hard to reconcile this smiling young man, no more than twenty years old, with the embittered fanatic he became.

In a deep, lightly accented voice Yandee asked the audience to pass forward the sealed envelopes they had brought from home. Scantily clad dancing girls appeared from the wings to collect the envelopes. I sat up and took notice, my interest suddenly renewed. Wherever this dream was taking me, as long as it provided sexy dancing girls I was willing to go along for the ride.

I heard Doc's voice in my mind: *"Watch closely. Yandee was the best in the business. Each envelope contains a private question of a personal nature that the audience members hope Yandee will answer. Watch the crowd; see how they react."* By now, the envelopes had been gathered by the dancing girls and brought to center stage.

At a nod from Yandee, the assistants dropped the envelopes into the glass bowl on the tripod. Yandee gestured toward the bowl. Gasps from the audience as the envelopes burst into flames! Yandee's eyes rolled back in his head until only the whites showed. He muttered and chanted as he passed his hands through the fire, oblivious to the heat, entering a trance state.

I kept my eyes on the dancing assistants, weaving around the stage. The extremely well-built blonde attracted my attention. She was absolutely gorgeous—and more than a little familiar.

Doc's voice chuckled in my mind. *"Your Aunt May. She was quite a looker, eh?"*

I blushed and turned my attention to Yandee.

The High Priest of the Occult had plenty of material to work with. By my rough guess, over six hundred sealed questions were tossed into the mammoth glass bowl and burned before the eyes of the amazed spectators. Yandee spoke in a loud voice. "I see the initials C.B. . . . Charles something? Charles B., please stand up."

"Here I am!"

"Charles, I see that you are considering going into business with your brother-in-law. Beware. His intentions are not honorable. Bring your own legal advisor to the meeting. Now the vibration is changing, and I see a young woman, her name is Lisa. She's thinking about marrying a young man named James . . ."

"That's me!"

"Lisa, I see that you have truly met your soulmate. I predict a long and happy marriage, with one, two . . . no, *three* children. Two boys and a girl. Congratulations!"

I took Doc's advice and studied the audience. Everyone was mesmerized by this display of mental prowess. How could he know all that information? Cheating seemed impossible; after all, the questions were incinerated right before our eyes! The audience watched, tense and intrigued. It was obvious that time wouldn't permit him to answer all the questions, but everyone hoped they would be next. If the present-day Yandee—Steven Slade—had retained one-half of the charisma of his younger self, it was no wonder his followers adored him.

One answer in particular brought the house down: "S. B., you ask me 'is she faithful?' Yes, she is—but you are not!" As the audience howled, a man two seats down from me jumped to his feet and ran from the theater.

For fifteen minutes, Yandee answered questions about love, health, marriage, who was faithful and who was not; what trips certain people were going to make for business or pleasure; matters of commerce, politics, and finance. It was more than just a performance; it was a sensation.

Suddenly, the High Priest of the Occult emerged from the trance, eyes blinking rapidly. Exhausted, he gave a weak smile and toppled over backward into the arms of the two dancing girls (Aunt May and a tall redhead), who helped him offstage to a mixture of wild applause and disappointed groans. I don't know if the groans were caused by the departure of Yandee or of the two beautiful young women.

Dr. DeLyle took the stage once again and waited until the applause died down. "We now stand on the threshold of a wonderful new vision," he said, "the technology of television, created by a vision that began in the mind of man. Who can say that the next step will not be magic of the mind; our ability to see and forecast events, to peer inside each other's thoughts, and to communicate with those no longer living amongst us? Sounds unbelievable, doesn't it? But tonight, my friends, you will see things you have never seen before, and you will believe. Yes, you will believe."

Doc raised his hand, and two enormous slate blackboards, suspended from red silken ropes, lowered from the wings. They looked exactly like two children's slates, except each measured about four feet wide by six feet high. "It's long been man's quest to communicate with the dear departed. Is it possible to move aside the diaphanous veil that separates the world of the living from the realm of the dead? Perhaps. It's been said that the line between life and death is thin as a razor's edge. Tonight, we will attempt to test that fragile barrier."

Aunt May and the redhead came out and turned the slates front and back. "These blackboards, as you can see, are completely clean. Place them face-to-face, please." Aunt May and the other assistant complied, latching the two slates together with large brass hasps. Just before they closed, Doc dropped a large chunk of chalk, about the size of a baseball, between them. He turned his attention toward the audience. "I need a volunteer, please."

A middle-aged man made his way to the stage and Doc handed him a large, leather-bound book. "Please concentrate on the name of someone you hold dear to your heart, who has passed away," Doc instructed.

The man closed his eyes for a moment, then opened them, nodding at Doc. "Got it."

Doc raised his hands to his temples, concentrating, and then took the large leather book from the volunteer. He raised the book over his head. "Spirits from beyond, hear me. Send us a message, a confirmation that life doesn't end at the moment of death, but continues forever after. Hear my plea, Spirits, and communicate with us. Reveal this man's thoughts!"

Suddenly the suspended slates began to vibrate, as though buffeted about by spirit winds. Scraping sounds emerged from within, the sound of chalk moving across the rough slate surfaces. "Yes!" Doc yelled in triumph. He turned to the volunteer, who had backed away from the gyrating blackboards. He waited until the eerie commotion stopped, then asked, "Who are you thinking about, sir? What departed soul is in your heart and mind?"

The middle-aged gentleman wet his lips nervously.

"D-David," he said. "He was my cousin."

"Open the slates!"

May and the redhead unlatched the slates. The audience gasped and cried out in disbelief. The chunk of chalk dropped to the stage in a small cloud of dust, reduced to about half its former size. The reason for the reduction was obvious: Chalk dust completely covered the two inner surfaces of the slates. On the left slate, standing out in black against chalky white (as though scrawled in the dust by a giant, clammy finger) was the name *David*. On the right slate, the word *believe*. The audience went wild. One or two people got up and left, muttering about pacts with the devil.

Next Doc introduced the Hindu Torture Couch. "This item of furniture, Ladies and Gentlemen, is a glittering crystal settee pierced with over eleven hundred razor-sharp spikes—an uncomfortable repose indeed. It was said that this awful device was constructed by Aga Baba two centuries ago to punish one of his wives for infidelity." Doc touched one of the spikes and held up his finger to show a drop of blood. "A cruel conception from a crueler time. Imagine the effect of those razor spikes on young and delicate flesh."

Doc gestured toward the conductor, and the orchestra began a light, hypnotic melody. Aunt May and the redhead returned to the stage. My eyes popped out when I saw the redhead's outfit: a couple of silken wisps that barely covered her at all. Doc waved his hand in front of the redhead's eyes and she went rigid, then fell back into May's arms. She was hypnotized, out cold. All this occurred without speaking, to the ethereal music.

Doc and May conveyed the sleeping woman to the Hindu Torture Couch and gently placed her on the spikes. She lay there peacefully, as comfortable as if she were in her own bed at home. Doc and May stepped away, and the audience 'oohed' and 'ahhed.' Doc stood perfectly still for a moment, arms outstretched; the orchestra fell silent. Everyone in the audience held his or her breath.

Then Doc did an unbelievable thing. He quickly stepped up on the couch, paused a moment to gain his balance, then stood on the bare stomach of the hypnotized assistant. The audience was thunderstruck. "Unbelievable!" "Impossible!"

Doc raised his voice over the commotion. "The legend goes on to say that when the palace guards forced her to lie on the bed, she did so without harm! Even the weight of a fully-grown man couldn't force the spikes into her innocent flesh. Such is the power of belief, ladies and gentlemen. The power of conviction. Aga Baba, convinced of his wife's innocence, released her and elevated her to the position of his favorite. Her accuser, revealed as a liar, suffered the fate that had been decreed for her—but less successfully. It was said that the screams of the false witness could be heard for miles."

The orchestra struck up the tune again and Doc jumped down, waving his hands to tell the audience to hold their applause. He and May helped the redhead from the couch of glittering spikes and to her feet. He snapped his fingers in front of her eyes; she blinked a couple of times and smiled. Doc turned to face the audience and the two took a bow. The clapping and shouting shook the rafters!

This is a great theater. Doc was right: it's a shame it's been so neglected.

I remembered how, at the beginning of summer, I daydreamed about performing a magic show on just such a grand stage before a packed house. How one day I—the Amazing Craig—would inspire those sounds of amazement.

Maybe someday I'll perform here? I considered it. *Nah, by the time I'm good enough, this place will be nothing more than another parking lot.*

Now Doc rolled forward an upright, golden coffin. It was made of thick metal and solidly riveted at the joints. On either side of the coffin were two unlit altar candles in large metal holders. I settled in to watch the finale.

"In this experiment, we will prove the existence of the Astral Body. I would like to invite a committee from the audience to step up and examine the Golden Casket." Approximately twenty people rose from their seats and hurried to the stage. The metal coffin was scrutinized, thumped, examined, and finally pronounced free of any type of chicanery.

Doc spoke for a while about how certain Eastern mystics had learned to project their spirits out of their bodies, leaving their physical forms behind in a trance state. While free from the body, Doc asserted, the mystic's spirit—or Astral Being—was capable of superhuman accomplishments. "Tonight, we will see this miracle for ourselves!" He clapped his hands twice, and Aunt May stepped from the wings, dressed in a black, floor-length evening gown. Doc hypnotized her and led her to the golden coffin, where she rested against the silk cushions, apparently in a deep trance.

Two men helped Doc replace the lid on the coffin and securely bind it with several leather straps. There appeared to be no way for May to escape the casket, at least not without significant help from the outside. Doc covered the coffin with a large, black velvet cloth and turned his attention to the onstage committee.

He asked one committee member to set his watch to a random time. A second volunteer selected a playing card. Yet another chose a poem from a book. One man wrote his address down on a slip of paper and sealed it in an envelope. Doc placed the book of poems, the deck of cards, the envelope, and the watch on a small table. He gestured toward the draped coffin, and the altar candles on either side suddenly burst into flame. A chorus of amazed sounds—that chorus I so longed to inspire someday—came from the audience. Doc whipped aside the black cloth and there stood Aunt May, pale and ephemeral, her black dress now a diaphanous white, still deeply entranced. She looked scary and unreal; no tint to her skin at all, like a black-and-white photograph somehow superimposed onto the world of color and sunshine. Under the bright spotlights she was slightly iridescent, like pale starlight.

Doc turned to the audience. "What you are seeing is this young woman's Astral Body, what some call the soul. Her physical body still rests quietly within the safety of the coffin. Watch . . . learn . . ."

Slowly, May (or was it her spirit?) glided over to the table and picked up the pack of playing cards. She removed one without looking and handed it, face-down, to the man who had selected the card earlier. He seemed reluctant to accept it.

"What was your card?" Doc demanded.

"The Queen of Spades."

"Ah, the Dark Lady. Look at the card in your hand."

The man showed it to the audience. It was, indeed, the Queen of Spades!

Next, May walked over to a blackboard and drew a large clock face, filling in the hands at 4:45. It matched the time randomly selected by the audience member.

May approached the man who had written down his address and took his hand. The man looked suddenly startled.

"What's the matter?" Doc asked.

"H-her hand . . . it's ice cold . . ." The audience shifted and murmured.

Doc said in a reassuring voice, "The Astral Body has no need of warmth—it basks in the radiance of the Almighty. Don't be afraid. In this spiritual form, she will not harm you. Concentrate on your address, where you live. Try to imagine your house in full detail."

May turned to the audience and spoke. Her voice was high and clear; bell-like, yet strangely hollow. "This mortal lives at 89 Poplar Avenue. He lives in a large brick house with twelve rooms. He has a den, where he often retires to rejuvenate his spirit by reading books about the Civil War. I also see several golf trophies . . ."

"Is this correct?" Doc asked the startled man.

"Yes," he whispered. Then in a louder voice, "Yes. Every bit of it!"

May went on to describe the man's residence and family in detail, her voice ringing through the silence that had fallen within the theater. I wondered why there was no reaction from the audience. One look around answered my question: The audience was literally too stunned to applaud. They sat bolt upright in their seats as though they were the ones who were entranced.

Finally, May walked over to the table and picked up the book of poetry. She held it lovingly for a moment, opened it to a page and smiled. Showing the book to the person who selected the poem earlier, she asked, "Is this your poem?"

The man nodded.

"A very good selection," May replied.

> *"Do not pursue the past.*
> *Do not lose yourself in the future.*
> *The past is no longer.*
> *The future has not yet come.*
> *Look deeply at life as it is*
> *In the very here and now,*
> *This is the source of all stability and freedom.*
> *Be a bud sitting quietly on the hedge.*
> *Be a smile, one part of wondrous existence.*
> *Stand here. There is no need to depart."*

The man stood with a look of awe on his face. The meaning of the verse wasn't lost on the audience, and at last the silence broke. They clapped and cheered as though released from a spell. Beaming, Doc dismissed the committee and took a bow, while May gazed haughtily upon the crowd like a supernatural empress from another world. When the applause began to die down, Doc covered May with the black cloth. The dark velvet was a striking contrast to her stark paleness. Doc ran over to the coffin. It was the work of a few seconds to unstrap the coffin and raise the lid. The cheering renewed when everyone realized the coffin was completely empty.

Doc ran back to the covered form, tore away the black cloth and there stood May, no longer a pale specter but smiling and pretty, warm, alive, rosy-cheeked, her black evening gown setting off the diamonds at her ears and throat. Her body had flown from the coffin to reunite with her Astral Being. The crowd went wild. They had witnessed an escape from the clutches of Death Itself!

■ ■ ■

I opened my eyes.

"You hypnotized me, didn't you?"

The Victoria had returned to its familiar, smelly, tattered, and dirty self. After seeing it (or thinking I saw it) in its glory, the return to reality was depressing.

This hand-painted window card was used to promote
Alain "Doc" DeLyle's largest theatrical tour that featured
"The Girl in the Golden Casket"—better known to
Craig Karges as his Aunt May!

ALAIN DeLYLE

THIS REMARKABLE MAN WILL TELL YOU THE TRUTH. STOP! THINK!

Get your bearings before you go on in darkness. Don't be afraid of the Truth. LEARN THE TRUTH NOW— Before it is too late.

Is the one you love sincere? Are persons you trust deceiving you?

SPECIAL LOW FEE—Consultation 50c and $1.00.

There are so-called advisers who make great claims of what they can do for you when upon investigation their surroundings and every action would convince any sensible person that they are incapable of helping themselves.

There are counterfeit dollars, imitations of the genuine, there are good doctors and bad ones; just so with Psychologists. There are a few genuine, and a great many imitations. "Judge me by my work," my extensive patronage and great success are the envy of all competitors. I am never idle. My motto is "Work and Win." I help my patrons to succeed in attaining their various ambitions. That's why I have so many of them and each recommends me to friends.

Information Clear, Concise and to the point. I have helped thousands to attain happiness and success in life. Why not You?

Hours—1 P. M. to 8 P. M. Closed Friday and Sunday. Remember REV. ALAIN DeLYLE can be seen only at his office during the above mentioned hours. Permanently Located. Private Parlors. BRING THIS CARD

Alain "Doc" DeLyle possessed many of the secrets of the ages—
including self-promotion as evidenced by this direct mail card!

Doc shook his head. "No, you hypnotized yourself. All hypnosis is self-hypnosis, Craig. No one can be hypnotized against their will. You made a wish, and I helped you get it the best way I knew: by summoning your imagination."

I relented. "It was an excellent show. I have to say it was better than the movies."

"Yes, it was." Doc laughed. "Nothing today can touch it. Before we leave, do you have any other wishes?"

I didn't even have to think about it. "I'd like to do my show here, at the Victoria. Not as it is now, but as I saw it in my dream. New, restored. Without the awful smell." I raised my eyebrows at him. "If you can make that happen, I'll be really impressed."

Doc laughed again. "I say again that I can't make anything happen. But you can. You have your entire life ahead of you. Believe in your dream, and perhaps one day it will come true. I have faith in you." He stood up and stretched, then sat back down. "I'll show you a little trick that will help you. It's called creating an affirmation. You ever hear of it?"

"No."

"Affirmations are simply encouraging statements, positive declarations we can use to implant the seeds of self-fulfillment in our brain. What you think about most of the time, you eventually become."

"The power of the mind again."

"The power of the mind. Try this: close your eyes, take a deep breath—"

I pointed my finger at him. "No funny business now. I've had enough hypnosis for one day."

He laughed. "Nope. It's all up to you. Now, imagine clearly what it is that you want. In this case, you want to perform your show here at the Victoria. See it."

I closed my eyes and did as he asked.

"Repeat after me: I have total control over my life."

I opened my eyes and looked at him. "You mean just say it out loud?"

He nodded.

I shrugged. "I have total control over my life."

"I can make my life anything I want."

I repeated it, feeling a bit foolish.

Doc looked at me intently, as motionless as one of the Buddhas in his office. "Now, state your objective out loud."

I sighed, resigned to follow this exercise to its conclusion. "I want to perform at the Victoria someday."

Doc shook his head. "No, you have to be more positive. Not, 'I want to,' but 'I WILL.' Try again."

"I WILL perform at the Victoria someday."

"You will! Say it like you mean it."

"I WILL PERFORM AT THE VICTORIA! I will!"

Doc beamed. "I think you will." He thumped me on the shoulder. "Craig, I know it seems a little silly, but affirmations *work*. It's like training your mind, both the conscious and subconscious, to align themselves toward your goals. A simple trick, but like most simple tricks, it's both powerful and effective. Just do it every day, and see what happens. It's the mental equivalent of tying your shoelaces; after you've done it a while it becomes automatic. You don't even have to think about it. Will you do that?"

I told him I would.

He stood up. "Good. Let's go. May will be here soon to pick us up."

■ ■ ■

It never occurred to me to wonder why May was driving us around. I was too tired, and too preoccupied with thinking about the wonderful magic show I had apparently created within my own mind. If I could imagine such a magnificent show, wasn't it possible that somehow, someday, given enough experience and practice, I might actually perform it? Doc was right. The mind can create anything; it was the source and the solution to all our problems. Maybe I would try that affirmation trick on other things too.

On the way home, May asked Doc if he was feeling all right. Doc grunted. "I'm okay. A little tired, that's all." I could relate. I was completely exhausted too. As it turned out, I was coming down with the flu and had a mild fever.

When they let me out in front of my house, Doc shook my hand and gave me a hug. "Remember the Victoria, Craig. All things are possible." He and May drove off. I think he waved at me through the window, but it was getting dark and I wasn't sure.

CHAPTER THIRTEEN

Doc's Final Bow

THAT NIGHT, I had a dream:

It starts out commonplace enough. I'm sitting on Doc's pier, looking out over the Ohio River. It's mid-morning and the air has a pinkish quality that illuminates every detail of the water and the sprawling green hills. Although it's early November to the rest of the world, bleak and cold, on my dream island it is summer. Here, it's always summer.

As I drift deeper into sleep, Doc's voice calls my name from a distance. I get up and wander into the woods to look for him.

I find him sitting crossed-legged in a sunny glade, under the shade of a huge oak tree. I have to grin. He's dressed in a loose white outfit like David Carradine in Kung-Fu: a guru's mantle. He smiles when he sees me. "I'm going on a trip in a little while, and there are a few things I want to tell you before I go." With a flourish, Doc shows me a large owl's feather. "Watch!"

He carefully balances the feather on the palm of his left hand, in a vertical position. He's absolutely motionless for a few seconds, then takes away his right hand. The feather remains balanced on its quill in an upright position!

"Concentration. Focus. That's the key. Remember this, Craig." A breeze makes the precariously balanced feather wobble; Doc moves his hand slightly to prevent it from toppling over. "The forces that govern your life are as pre-

cisely balanced as this feather—love, passion, duty, honor, security—and each require attention lest one try to gain dominance. Do not let your passions rule you, son. You must tend them with a firm hand. But never, ever let the fire die out."

Now I notice that the woods behind him are on fire. The air fills with smoke, and I'm reminded of another dream, one of Blennerhassett Island.

"When you find something to live for, you've found purpose—but when you find something worth dying for, you've found passion. Death, passion; just two sides of the same coin. Whatever you choose to do in life, don't do it halfway. You'll hear a lot of people tell you to do all things in moderation. Hah! Can you love only halfway? Can you live life halfway? Anything you do, do it all the way. Burn, Craig, burn—let your passion and love blaze like a beacon. Incinerate the world with your power; ignite the human soul with your vision. Become an arsonist of love. Drink kerosene and piss flame! When you tread the stage, let the audience know you mean it!"

The fire is almost upon us. Withering heat blasts my face and hands, the smoke chokes me. Doc tosses the feather aside, snugs his Panama hat on his head, and rises to his feet in one fluid motion.

"Walk with me," he says, and I follow.

We wind our way through the burning woods toward the river. A fog has rolled in; or maybe it's the smoke from the fire. At any rate, it's now impossible to see even halfway across the water.

Doc rests his arm around my shoulders as we walk. "Our time on earth seems like forever, Craig, but to the spirit one hundred years is just one strand in a spider's web. A brief moment of discomfort, like when you go to the doctor and get your finger pricked: a moment of pain, and then it's over. Shakespeare was right: life is nothing more than a stage. The show must go on, but every good showman knows when it's time to leave the stage and make room for the next act."

He looks out over the Ohio River as the fog creeps in toward the bank. I eye the fog uneasily; something about it disturbs me. For the first time I notice the River Shaman floating at the end of the small pier. Doc and I walk over to her, and he gets in. I start to follow. The fog frightens me, but I trust Doc.

He raises a hand to stop me. "Not this time, Craig," he says with a gentle smile. "This trip I go it alone."

I'm scared. The fog seems so thick and gloomy. But a faint light begins to break through the gloom, the sun, I think.

Doc throws off the moorings and climbs behind the wheel of his beloved boat. At the touch of the key, the engine roars to life. "I'm not going far, Craig. I'll be here if you need me. We'll see each other again. Remember, the lessons haven't ended." He laughs. "Oh no—by no means have the lessons ended!" He looks off into the fog, toward the pale light. "I have to go. Someone's waiting for me over there. Au revoir, son. I really enjoyed this summer. Thanks for showing me a good time." He turns away, pauses, and turns back around. "Oh yeah, I almost forgot." He tosses a small object to me. A glint of gold in the air; I catch it without really looking at it, entranced by the fog. The light on the other side is definitely brighter. "That's for you."

"Thank you, Doc," I say, watching him putter away from the pier. I really don't know what else to say. I put the cold, metallic object in my pocket.

I stand on the bank, between fire and water, and he waves at me, and from the distance a trick of light and shadow makes it look like his hair is black instead of silver, his face unlined and beaming with a strange joy. He cups his hands around his mouth and yells, "Remember!" I hear his voice as a whisper in my ear.

The fog swallows him up, and soon even the sound of the engine fades away.

When I awakened, my pillow was wet, my face hot and flushed with fever. I brought my hand up to wipe away sweat and something hard tapped my forehead. It was Doc's ring, the one fashioned in the likeness of a cobra with ruby eyes that we'd found on Blennerhassett Island. I hadn't noticed it when I retired for the night, but then again I'd been bone-tired—and apparently sick. Had Doc slipped it on my finger while I was hypnotized at the Victoria? I didn't have time to think about it, for at that moment Mom tapped at my door and entered. Her fingers worried away at a piece of facial tissue. It was obvious that she was upset.

"What is it?" I asked. But a part of me, deep down, already knew.

"Oh, Craig, it's your uncle . . ." —Doc had passed away quietly in his sleep.

I didn't cry then, nor during his funeral. I think Doc would have been proud of me.

After the funeral, we drove back home across the bridge and I looked out over the Ohio River, the rocky shore a lacy fringe against dark velvet waters. The storm had passed; the evening sky was a pale blue marble.

"Well, that's that," my Dad said. Just another one of those meaningless phrases people use to fill awkward silences. "Think May will be all right?" he asked my Mom.

Mom nodded. "I think so. May always was pretty tough."

I thought about May peering along the barrel of her shotgun the time she routed Steven Slade. *You don't know the half of it, Mom.*

1971 was a year I'd never forget; Charles Manson led a group of his followers on a killing spree in California; the beginnings of the national disgrace that came to be known as Watergate; the height of the war in Vietnam and the My Lai massacres. It was the year of *All in the Family*, *Clockwork Orange*, the Twenty-sixth Amendment and—later that year—a first kiss. In 1971, magic happened in the world.

In 1971, a wizard died.

As the sun went down past the river, bleeding red into the water, I thought about my uncle, Doc DeLyle, the wisest and best man I had ever known. He was a true wizard, in every sense of the word. I reached into my pocket and touched the folded piece of magenta stationary, Doc's last message.

Craig—believe in real magic.

The first tear of many formed in the corner of my eye.
I'll try, Doc. I'll surely try.

PART II
Tales of
the Wizard

What appears to be the end may really be
a new beginning.

CHAPTER FOURTEEN

Doc Reappears

It's the day before my fortieth birthday, and I'm on an airplane, preparing to depart for New York. I'm scheduled to appear on a syndicated talk show in a few hours. Afterward, I have a business meeting with my manager, and then it's off to Dallas for an after-dinner appearance for a large corporate meeting. It's a typical day. I'm used to this kind of schedule.

So why do I feel so tired?

I lean back in the seat of the airplane, strategically place a pillow against the window and shut my eyes for a quick, much needed power nap. The man in the seat next to me continually wakes me to ask questions. This is typical too. Some people seem to think that if your eyes are closed, it actually means you're dying to talk to somebody, and for some reason, I seem to attract these kinds of people.

"You travel much?" my seatmate asks.

"Some," I say. "Work-related, mostly."

"Whatcha do for a living?" he asks.

"I'm a mind reader."

He looks at me for a moment to see if I'm serious. Apparently he decides I am, because he responds with the most common reaction to this claim. He asks, "Can you read my mind?"

Sighing, I have him write his birth date on one of my business cards and fold it into quarters. I touch it for a moment, look him in the eyes and say, "March 5th, 1953."

He's stunned for a moment, then breaks into a smile. "That's good. That's really good." He begins telling me about his dreams and all the paranormal events he'd ever witnessed or heard of. Apparently, his sister has some psychic abilities. "She knows when things are going to happen. Well, not anything useful, and they don't always happen. Sometimes they do, but not like she said they would." He seems eager to discuss the topic. Also typical; there aren't many people you can really talk to about supernatural occurrences without them thinking you're a little wacky.

I give up on the idea of sleep and remove my day-timer from the briefcase. My schedule is packed: over 170 personal appearances lined up this year alone on university campuses, for corporate groups, and in theaters and performing arts centers around the country. Add to these the occasional television spot and it makes for a busy life. It's always been that way. I made my debut as a stage magician in the eighth grade variety show in 1972, the spring after Doc passed away. The transition to mentalist came a couple of years later, when, at the age of sixteen, I performed for the local Shriner's Club. One thing led to another, and when I was ready for college, I paid my tuition by performing, while my friends pumped gas and waited tables. In my last year of school, I met Charlotte, the love of my life. We were married shortly after graduation; I hit the road with her by my side and never looked back.

Life's been good. Though hardly a household name, I have been able to carve out a nice little niche in the entertainment world. I've been halfway around the world with my show, from the Hawaiian Islands to Egypt and Saudi Arabia. I've even appeared on *Leno* and *Larry King*.

As my seatmate drones on, I stare out the window and watch as the last of the bags are loaded. I remember the thrill (mixed with a lot of anxiety, I'll admit) of performing magic in front of a large audience for the first time. It seems like it was a hundred years ago.

■ ■ ■

I wore a black suit with a ruffled shirt and bow tie, the typical magician's garb. I produced silk handkerchiefs and a glass of Kool Aid from a small, flat trifold screen; covered my arm with a gaudy tube and shoved a flaming candle through it. My magic was fairly standard, amateur-quality stuff, but in my mind I had arrived—I was performing a show!

I included a tribute to Tony Curtis' *Houdini*, the movie that started me on the long road to Magicdom. I asked a person to write their first name on a piece of paper, which was then burned. Chanting magical words, I rubbed the ashes on my arm. Mysteriously, the name appeared on my forearm in smudgy letters. As a finale, I escaped from a locked trunk after being handcuffed, chained, and thrown inside.

The applause tasted wonderful. I learned then that the collective sound made by a roomful of amazed people could become addictive.

The variety show ran Thursday through Saturday night. Sunday, after Mass, I asked Dad to drive me out to the cemetery where Doc was buried. I wanted to tell Doc of my success.

While Mom, Dad, and Brian tended to the family plots, I went over the hill to see Doc. I was glad to see that the headstone was in place. It hadn't been ready at the time of his funeral. The inscription read: *Alain DeLyle 1887–1971* . . . 1887! I whistled between my teeth. A quick calculation told me that Doc had been eighty-four years old at the time of his death. It hardly seemed possible.

I told Doc about my success (very quietly; I didn't want anyone to think I was weird) and went back to rejoin my family. On the way home I told Mom and Dad about finding out about Doc's true age. Dad was amazed. "He held up pretty good for someone that old."

Mom said, "I always assumed he and May were about the same age. In fact, there was some speculation in the family that May had married a younger man . . ."

Dad harrumphed. "Maybe the date is wrong. Could be a mistake."

But later that day Mom phoned Aunt May in California.

"No, that's the correct date," May confirmed. "He was a bit older than he looked. Doc took care of himself, you know."

Mom commented, "I only wish I look half as good as he did when I'm his age! He could have passed for a man twenty-five years younger."

Doc was full of surprises, even in death.

■ ■ ■

The flight attendant's voice brings me back to reality. "We are beginning our descent to LaGuardia. Please return your seat backs to the upright position, raise your tray tables, remain seated, and fasten your seat belts for the duration of the flight. Welcome to New York."

I look around, blinking. I must have dozed off after all. For one vertiginous moment I thought I was still dreaming, then I saw my day-timer and briefcase spread across my lap. I quickly return the day-timer to the briefcase and do a double take. There's something else there, something I didn't notice before, an old, musty leather book.

I pick it up and riffle through it, frowning. At first I don't recognize it, then I turn to the flyleaf.

It's one of Doc's notebooks.

I have no idea how it got there. Until a few minutes ago it had been years since I last thought of my great-uncle. As they say, time marches on. A lot had happened since 1971. I went through high school, college, marriage. There was a career to build. Bills to pay.

Doc's notebook seems to look back at me, accusingly. I return it to the briefcase and close the lid.

Did I put it there? I can't remember. In fact, I can't remember much at all about the last few days. I wipe a hand across my face.

I must be getting old.

The plane lands with a thud at LaGuardia Airport, and I'm off and running.

■ ■ ■

"You're not getting old," Charlotte, my wife, said. She sat at her dresser and prepared for bed. "Forty isn't old."

As I washed my face, I looked closely in the mirror at the wrinkles near the corners of my eyes. "I feel old. I can't remember anything."

"You're trying to do too much. You looked tired on TV yesterday. You need to slow down."

"Hmmph." She probably had a point. The last week had been grueling. I finished washing up and returned to the bedroom, holding the small leather book. "Did you put this in my briefcase?"

"No. What is it?"

"One of Doc's notebooks."

She looked surprised. "Maybe you did it without knowing it. You've been walking around in a fog lately."

I considered it. "Nah. I think I'd remember bringing this down from the attic. In fact, I don't remember even seeing this one before. I don't know where it came from."

"Let me see it?" She took the book and riffled through it, studying it front to back. She tapped it, sniffed it, and rubbed it between her hands. "I know where it came from," she said.

I smiled at her. "I thought I was the mind reader around here."

"No, I mean it. I know exactly where it came from."

I crossed my arms and looked at her. "I'm listening."

Charlotte is an antique dealer and frequently buys boxes of books dirt-cheap to resell to some of her wealthier clients, who enjoy filling the shelves of their opulent libraries with old, leather-bound books. "Not that they ever read them," she informed me. "It's purely decorative." She had recently bought six boxes of old books, which were currently in our garage. She was sure the notebook had been among them. "I know I saw this in an old box of books I got at an estate sale. I think there's some more of them too. Let's go check!"

I was skeptical, and more than a little tired. But once Charlotte's curiosity is piqued, there's no standing in her way. She insisted we go out to the garage and check the other boxes. Sure enough, after several minutes of rummaging around in Charlotte's stock, we came up with a dozen of Doc's old notebooks.

Charlotte sat on the floor, streaks of dust on her face, looking puzzled. "How is this possible?"

I turned the old books over and over in my hands, thinking about it. "Simple. After Doc passed away I kept most of his memorabilia, and only about ten of his notebooks. My parents sold the rest." I could almost hear my mother's voice in my mind. *We don't have room for all of Alain's belongings. Where would you store it all? You can't just keep every-*

thing. Besides, Aunt May needs the money to help her move to California. "This guy must have bought them."

"But that was what—twenty-seven years ago? And now they found their way back to you . . ." Charlotte grabbed my arm. "There's no telling how many others may be out there, moldering away on bookshelves. Or in attics." She tapped the small leather book. "What did he write about?"

I shrugged. "I don't know."

She looked at me in amazement. "You never read his notebooks?"

I shook my head. "Well, not all of them. There are so many I could never find the time. I know I've never read *this* one before."

In the months following Doc's death, I occasionally rummaged through the boxes of his effects to see what I could find. Mostly, I looked at the playbills and program notes for his vaudeville show. I always meant to look at his notebooks, but Doc had been a compulsive scribbler. The prospect of rummaging through volumes of tight, margin-to-margin handwriting never appealed to me. Besides, from what I saw, the notebooks mostly discussed doing readings for people, and I'd decided long ago that I didn't want to go that route. For weeks after Doc's death, people came by his house looking for him. When Aunt May told them Doc had passed away, most of his former clients looked lost and confused, and I wasn't interested in having anybody depending on me for guidance.

Eventually, I had lost interest. I was a kid, and after Doc died I got on with my life. He became a fond memory, taken out every now and then with affectionate recollection, but high school and college were more important. Reality, as my Dad would say, is pretty insistent.

"Craig?" Charlotte asked.

"Um-hmm?"

"Maybe it's a message."

I looked at her, bleary-eyed from the dust. "Maybe. What message?"

"Finding Doc's notebooks like this. Maybe he's trying to tell you something."

I thought at first she was joking, but her expression was serious. "If it's a message, why did it take twenty-seven years to arrive? Even the post office is faster than that."

She punched me on the arm. "I'm serious. Maybe Doc's trying to get your attention. Haven't you ever wondered if he was still around? His spirit, I mean. Looking out for you? Have you had any signs?"

I shook my head. "Just a few dreams, I guess. Or an occasional flash of insight. Sometimes I think I feel his guidance. Maybe it's just wishful thinking."

She looked at me in that charming, cunning way that still holds sway over me after more than twenty years of marriage. "Maybe it's time you practice what you preach. You're always telling people to focus their attention and be aware of the miracles in their lives. You should focus on Doc and see what comes from it."

Sighing, I got into bed, opened the notebook and began to read. Charlotte fell asleep within minutes, and I envied her. I was exhausted but, too restless to sleep, I thumbed through the notebook and the dusty smell of years of neglect came from the pages. Was it my imagination, or was there the faint whiff of cigar smoke, too?

I never really knew very much about Doc's early life. He was extremely private and didn't talk much about his past. However, he apparently wrote about it, and in great detail. I was still reading when the sun came up.

Twenty-seven years after his death, Doc had hooked me again.

C H A P T E R   F I F T E E N

The Transformation of Alan Green

DOC HAD BEEN BORN ALAN GREEN on July 24th, 1887, in San Francisco. In spite of Doc's customary vagueness about his past, I knew this for fact. Years ago, Aunt May had sent me a photocopy of his birth certificate to prove Doc was as old as his gravestone indicated. By one of those accidents of birth that seem to prove the universe has a sense of humor, he was born into a tightly conservative religious family. According to Doc's notes, his psychic abilities asserted themselves at an early age. In an early journal he wrote about how, when he was three years old, he always knew when someone was coming to visit the family, even when nobody else was expecting company. Apparently his father disapproved of this talent. Alan's mother advised him to keep his visions to himself so as not to upset his father, so young Alan learned to hide his light under a bushel. He wrote, "I think Mother was psychic, too, but had learned to keep her insights to herself. She was right; it wasn't wise to upset Father." Alan's father believed strongly in the Biblical injunction "Spare the rod and spoil the child" and often put his belief into practice.

Alan Green had three brothers—a jeweler, a lumber salesman, and a minister—all conservative, realistic, down-to-earth fellows with no use for mysticism. Evidently, none of his family knew what to think of Alan's fascination with spirits and the occult. He was a wild card in a deck of deuces, a free-thinker in a family in the stranglehold of fundamentalism. He learned to keep a low profile.

Young Alan had another interest, one that vied for first place in the pantheon of his father's disapproval. At the age of twelve, while on a trip into town with his mother, Alan saw a troupe of street performers. One of the performers was a magician who performed mind-reading tricks. Later, Alan wrote, "While his techniques were crude by modern standards, his performance was sufficient to hopelessly ensnare me." In other words, he was hooked. He found what books he could on magic and hypnotism and studied them avidly.

San Francisco was on the vaudeville circuit, and any time a magician or mind reader appeared in the local theater, Alan would sneak off to see the show. Often, he'd stick around afterward and try to meet the theatrical folks. The serious, lonely young man impressed some of the performers, and Alan (always charming and persuasive, even in his youth) talked his way into their circle. As he got older he took lessons, worked behind the scenes, and learned the ropes of show business. Alan's father, as you can imagine, was less than enchanted. The gulf between father and son widened.

As Rudyard Kipling wrote, "San Francisco is a mad city—inhabited for the most part by perfectly insane people whose women are of a remarkable beauty." And by now, Alan knew he could never live up to his father's standards. Stifled by his family's conservatism, Alan craved a taste of the fruits of the "mad city." In the face of his family's hostility toward his psychic propensities and his great love for theater, at the age of seventeen Alan moved out on his own, opening an office in the downtown area for the purpose of giving readings. "I found I had a talent for quickly sizing people up and delivering information that they found useful," he wrote. He parlayed his knowledge of palmistry, astrology, and human nature into a small but loyal clientele and managed to make enough money to squeak by.

Things went smoothly for a while. Although Alan's family had all but disowned him, he remained in touch with his mother and for a while there seemed to be hope for reconciliation with his father. But

Alan couldn't seem to keep out of trouble. Before long, there was another source of shame for the family Green. It seems that Alan was what was known in those days as a "hot ticket," a lady's man, and when he got involved with a local preacher's daughter, a huge scandal ensued. I don't *think* he got her "in a family way," but it was possible. From the description in his diary, all the necessary requirements had been met—frequently, and with mutual enthusiasm. "I found," he wrote, "that I had extremely strong appetites, which would in all probability be my downfall if I gave them free rein."

It was during this scandal that he decided to change his name to Alain DeLyle, to spare the family further embarrassment.

■ ■ ■

Not everyone came to Alain for advice with a problem or a message from the departed. Quite often, he received clients who wanted help with unethical, immoral, or even illegal activities. One day an obviously well-to-do gentleman showed up for a reading. The man, a large, red-faced individual, waited impatiently as Alain related various events concerning his childhood, hidden talents, and a tendency to want everything exactly his way. Finally, the man interrupted. "Enough with the gypsy stuff, Mr. DeLyle. I'm not some grieving widow seeking solace from happy-happy land. They say you can help people make things happen in their lives. You helped my cousin save his business from certain bankruptcy. They say you can do magic."

In spite of the man's rudeness, Alain's voice was mild. "I helped him help himself. The turnaround of his business was a result of eliminating certain negative elements in his life."

The man grinned and nodded. "That's exactly why I'm here! I need your help ridding myself of a negative influence. Something that's standing between myself and happiness."

Alain suddenly realized he was dealing with a totally unscrupulous man. "What is this . . . 'negative influence,'" he asked in a cold voice.

"My wife."

Alain stroked his chin. "Ah . . ."

"You see," the man continued, "my wife and I don't get along. Well, actually, we hate each other. But I can't divorce her or she'll ruin me.

My business was built from her money, and my attorneys assure me she'll get it all back. Every cent. I can't stand to live with her anymore, but I don't want to lose my business either. You see my dilemma."

Alain only nodded, encouraging the man to continue.

"This is all confidential, right?" the man asked.

Alain nodded again.

"You see, I met this, this girl. She works in a nearby factory. I'm quite in love with her, and I want to be with her—"

"You're already 'with her,'" Alain interrupted. "Several times a week, in fact."

The man was unimpressed. "Yeah, yeah. But what I want to say is that I have a business proposition for you."

"Oh?"

The man laid his briefcase on the table. "If you can do what they say you can do, and if you can help me with my little problem, well . . . I can make it worth your while."

The man snapped the briefcase open. It was full of money. "This is ten thousand dollars. If you can make something happen to my wife, it's yours. No questions asked."

In 1905, ten thousand dollars was a great deal of money. Alain wrote, "I felt as though I'd been dipped in ice-cold wax. I'd never imagined seeing so much money in my life, and it was all mine, if I complied with the gentleman's wishes. It was an incredible amount of cash, but I guess the going rate for having your wife murdered was pretty steep."

Alain and the man stared at each other. Finally, Alain broke the silence. "Please tell me you're not suggesting what I think you're suggesting?"

The man shrugged. "Accidents happen, so do illnesses."

Alain's voice was arctic. "Nothing good can come from what you're planning to do. I urge you to abandon this course of action. Your plans will backfire. You'll end up losing everything."

The man remained unimpressed. He waved a chubby, well-manicured hand in the air. "Don't worry about that. I got all the angles covered. Maybe you can cast a mojo; perhaps you have an herb or tonic that can do the job. I've got it! Maybe you can hypnotize her and make her walk out in front of a train or jump off a pier! I'll take care of the rest. What do you say?"

Alain sighed and lowered his head. "Get out."

The man didn't budge. "What?"

Alain raised his head and said in a louder voice, "I said take your goddamned money and get the hell out." He pushed the briefcase toward the man. "What part of this simple statement eludes your comprehension?"

The man stood up and glared at Alain. His eyes were awful, the embodiment of frustrated rage. He shook a finger at him. "You don't know who you're screwing with."

Alain gave a quiet laugh. "Oh yes I do. I know exactly whom I'm dealing with. I've seen your kind before."

The man looked at Alain for several long moments, grabbed up his money, turned and left.

A few months later, Alain saw the man's picture in the newspaper. *Ruined Industrialist Takes Own Life*, the headline read. The man had gone into a downward spiral after trying to hire Alain to kill his wife. After writing a tell-all letter to his wife, the industrialist's girlfriend committed suicide. When his wife found out about the affair, she divorced him, leaving the man destitute. Alain clipped the newspaper article and pasted it in his notebook. Under the man's picture he'd written, "He had everything anyone could want—everything, that is, except the capacity to love. Without love, the cars, money, property meant nothing. I wonder what drove him to such greediness? I tried to warn him."

■ ■ ■

Alain's reputation continued to grow. A major turning point in his career came in February 1906, when a reporter from the *San Francisco Chronicle* interviewed Alain and was somewhat impressed by the young psychic's prowess. The reporter asked Alain if he had any "prognostications" for San Franciscans during the coming year. Alain looked into his crystal ball and announced that the salmon industry was in danger of closing as a result of overfishing the harbor. The reporter scoffed. After all, the ocean was full of fish (as it turned out, San Francisco's last salmon cannery closed down in 1920 because of overfishing. But Alain wasn't there to enjoy his success, as we will see). "Tell me something impressive," the reporter challenged. "Something to get the people talking. What do you see happening in the stock market?"

Alain peered into his crystal ball again. "I see an earthquake that will cost the railroads a great deal of money. An upheaval of the earth, fire. Union Pacific Railroad will be ruined."

The reporter wasn't all that impressed. After all, this *was* California. Earthquakes happened all the time; the city was well prepared to deal with them. The resulting article was a bit lukewarm. A spokesperson for Union Pacific Railroad scoffed at Alain's prediction. "An earthquake would have to lay low the entire city to hurt us," he boasted.

But Alain was convinced that a very costly disaster was waiting in the wings. He advised his clients to sell their Union Pacific Railroad stock at a loss, although the company was on extremely firm financial ground. Or so it seemed.

Two months later, on April 18th, 1906, San Francisco was practically destroyed by what came to be known as the Great Earthquake. Thousands of lives were lost when the ground liquefied beneath the tenements and businesses. Uncontrollable fires raged throughout the city, taking thousands more lives. The damage was estimated in excess of $500 million in 1906 dollars. The final death toll was more than three thousand people. And, as Alain predicted, miles of Union Pacific Railroad track and tons of equipment were destroyed, and the company's stock plummeted.

Alain's conscience was tortured at the thought of all the lives lost, but to make matters worse, one of the fatalities was his father's nephew! Needless to say, this mishap served to further alienate Alain's family. Alain's father believed the earthquake had been a judgment from God. Only by returning to a holy way of life, the senior Green asserted, would the city be spared further and more drastic judgment. He therefore cut all ties with Alain until his errant son was ready to renounce the ways of the devil. Even Alain's mother wrote him, saying, "Why, oh why, if you knew this terrible accident was going to occur, didn't you at least make the simplest effort to protect us from it?" It did no good to explain that he had no way of knowing when or where the earthquake

Know Thyself!

KNOW THE TRUTH!
KNOW IN TIME!

When In Trouble, Doubt, or
Suspense, Consult DeLYLE

"THE MAN WHO KNOWS"

DeLyle is not a mere mindreader
or fortune-teller, but is a qualified PSYCHOLOGIST, PSYCHO-
ANALYST and METAPHYSI-
CIAN, who can and will help you
solve your most perplexing personal problems now and without
delay. What he tells you of your
past and present proves his
power to help your future.

LOVE, COURTSHIP, MARRIAGE

I will tell you the one who is
sincere and the one that is fooling
you. If affairs of the heart and
emotions of love interest you. I
give the exact and truthful revelations of all love affairs, settle
lovers' quarrels, enable you to
win the esteem and affection of
anyone you desire. I tell if the
one you love is true, also date of
marriage restore lost affection,
peace and confidence in lovers
and discorded families. Give you
the full secret how to control,
fascinate and charm the one you
love, also those you meet, and
how to make a person at a distance think of you.

If you knew what I could do
for you, you would go many a
mile to see me.

— INTERVIEW —
Hours: Daily 1 o'clock to 8 o'clock
P. M. Closed Friday and Sunday

"THE MAN WHO KNOWS"
NO LETTERS ANSWERED

Throughout his life Alain "Doc"
DeLyle hung out his shingle as a
psychic advisor and promoted
himself in local newspapers as
"The Man Who Knows."

would occur, or even if it would happen or not. Alain's faith in his own powers was shaky. No one was more appalled than he that his prediction had come true.

Alain was learning a lesson that would serve him well in the future: Sometimes it doesn't pay to be *too* right. The name Alain DeLyle became linked to the disaster in the public's mind. Instead of applause, Alain's reward was public outrage. As the city struggled to rebuild itself, the reporter who had interviewed him before wrote a scathing editorial blaming the young psychic for not doing anything to alleviate the horrendous effects of the disaster. People stopped Alain on the streets, demanding to know why he didn't warn anybody. He received letters from those few family members who would still talk to him, wondering why he didn't at least try to save his own kin.

Rocks were thrown through his office window; threatening letters were almost a daily occurrence. Alain was accosted on the street. San Francisco was still wild in the beginning of the century. And lynchings were not exactly unheard of, Alain thought uneasily.

Alain DeLyle decided it was time to move on. He wrote a final letter to his mother (which was never answered), closed his office, took his savings and a few belongings and disappeared. The year was 1906; he was nineteen years old. Still young, but a lot wiser.

CHAPTER SIXTEEN

The Man Who Lost His Harmonica and Other Stories

UNFORTUNATELY, THE NOTEBOOKS for the years spanning 1906–1914 are missing and I have no information concerning Alain's activities during this period. As far as I can tell, he just vanished from the face of the earth for seven years.

The next notebook begins with an article from the *Chicago American*, dated August 25th, 1914, folded up between two pages of the notebook. The article dealt with two psychics who were working in Chicago at the time. One article mentions a "mystic" whose custom was to invite his attractive female clients to lie down on a bed of roses. The purpose of the roses, the article said, was to mask the smell of whatever the "mystic" used to render his female clients unconscious! Once they were in a trance, the article lasciviously hinted, God only knew what was done to them. I was relieved to see that this scandalous mystic was not my great-uncle.

However, the second article was about "The King of the Clairvoyants." The tone of this write-up was much more respectful than the first. The reporter had come to Alain's Chicago office to scoff, but left extremely impressed. Alain's comments in his notebook are quite pithy on this subject: "The *Chicago American* is one of those all-too-common periodicals that rely on scandal and innuendo to garner sales. The term 'yellow journalism' was coined to describe rags of this variety . . . for me to glean such a favorable review from this scandal-sheet is a bright feather in my cap indeed."

When World War I began in 1914, Alain became inundated with new clients. His records show that he saw people fourteen hours a day, every day. Most of his clients wanted news about relatives who were fighting the war overseas. Unlike the spiritualists of his time, who produced spooky manifestations under cover of darkness, Alain delivered his "spirit messages" in a normal tone of voice, in broad daylight. He avoided the supernatural trappings of his peers, who used them, he believed, to give their shoddy performances a dramatic edge. Alain saw himself as a messenger or interpreter of the subtle impressions he received. He charged very little for his readings (indeed, he refused to accept payment from war widows or grieving parents) yet he managed to save quite a bit of money and continue his interrupted education. It was at this time he earned his first doctorate, in herbalism. "Doc" De-Lyle was born!

Chicago seemed to be a profitable place for Doc, providing him with the opportunities to develop both his image and his skills. He displayed a knack for courting the press and apparently received a great deal of coverage through the performance of various publicity stunts that he learned from his vaudeville pals. Often garnering front-page headlines by driving blindfolded through the downtown area (the sight of Doc behind the wheel of a Model-T Ford with his head swathed in bandages must have been quite impressive!) or predicting the outcome of horse races, the young psychic was soon the talk of the town.

Doc also apparently appeared on the vaudeville stage a few times during this period, although his show wasn't as big or as spectacular as his later productions. Several radio stations offered him airtime exposure, but he declined. For some reason he didn't like radio, just as in later years he declined to appear on television. However, Doc loved newspaper exposure. He made an arrangement with the *Chicago American* to predict the outcome of various events, including the horse races and other sporting events. He refrained from making predictions concerning big disasters. He'd learned his lesson in San Francisco.

■ ■ ■

A few months after Doc established his office in Chicago, a man whom Doc calls William C. came for advice concerning a sudden, ongoing depression he'd been suffering. Doc's notes describe an attractive man in his mid-forties, in good health and circumstances, but with a puzzling dilemma.

The problem had been going on for about two months. One day, while William was riding the trolly home from work, he suddenly burst into tears. "I had no idea why," he told Doc. "One minute I was thinking about what to get the kids for Christmas—we've had a good year at the plant, and I wanted to do something special for them—and the next I was bawling my eyes out."

Doc was intrigued. "Is there any reason why the thought of Christmas would make you sad?"

William shook his head. "Nope. Always liked Christmas."

"Has it happened again? The crying?"

William shifted in his chair. "Yes. A lot lately. I just have this sad feeling come over me, like I'm about to die or something." He laughed. "That's why I came to see you. Can you look at my lifeline and tell me if something awful is going to happen to me or my family?"

"Let me see your hands," Doc said.

William extended his palms for Doc to examine. Doc saw that William was an intelligent, sensitive man with many creative talents and an almost limitless energy. His success came as no surprise, as Doc realized William was gifted with a great many talents; one, in particular stood out. Doc asked, "Are you doing anything with your musical abilities?"

William laughed. "Nah. I can't carry a tune in a bucket."

"You may want to consider taking music lessons sometime. You have a lot of potential there."

William shrugged. "Never interested me," was his curt response.

Doc finished the reading. He told William he needed some time to think about his case, and made an appointment for him to come back in a week.

"I'm at a loss to explain his deep melancholy," Doc wrote. "He seems to have everything a man could desire—a beautiful wife, children, a satisfying career—and yet, he suffers from a profound lack of satisfaction. Something is missing from his life. Could it be something so tiny and insignificant that I'm overlooking it? Something from his childhood, perhaps?" Doc believed that everyone had an "original wound," a trauma that happened when the person was very young, usually long forgotten and yet still affecting the person's actions in adulthood. Doc believed that some people continued to relive this original trauma again and again, "like your tongue worrying at a sore spot in your mouth" until the traumatic incident is recognized and confronted. Doc saw this phenomenon in action time and again, to such extent that he felt he'd stumbled across a common psychological principle. "What," he wondered, "was William's original wound?"

The following week, Doc queried William about his upbringing. "Was your childhood difficult? Did your parents neglect or mistreat you in any way?"

William shook his head. "No, I had a pretty good life. My parents were firm but fair. I got punished only when I deserved it."

Doc pursued this meager clue. "What do you mean, when you deserved it?"

"You know, when I was bad."

"Give me an example."

William laughed. "Well, when I was about eight, I was playing ball with my friend. I hit the ball a good lick and it broke out Miz Thompson's parlor window. It was just an accident, but I should have been more careful."

"How were you punished?" Doc asked.

"Daddy took away my ball and bat and threw them away."

"How did this make you feel?"

William shrugged. "I cried, but I got over it."

Over time, Doc saw a pattern emerging. William's parents (especially his father) punished him by taking things away from him. Doc wrote, "Of course, this gave Mr C. a sense of powerlessness as a child, but it wasn't enough to explain his depression. I began to search for the one incident that was the source of Mr. C.'s apathy, what I call 'the original wound.' I was sure that the answer was hidden in his early childhood."

Doc's intuition insisted that William's latent musical ability was at the source of the problem. "When you were a child, did you ever have a toy instrument, a horn or a drum?"

William shook his head. "No, my Daddy worked nights and I wasn't supposed to make any noise—"

A look of surprise appeared on William's face.

"What is it?" Doc asked.

"When I was six years old . . . my uncle gave me a harmonica for my birthday."

"Go on."

"I loved that thing. Played it all the time." William laughed. "I even learned to pick out *You Are My Sunshine* on it, after a fashion. I was pretty good, for a kid."

"Why did you quit?"

"My Daddy made me. One day I was marching around, tootling away. I guess I wasn't thinking. Daddy was asleep. It was his night off, but, well, Daddy liked to drink sometimes. Anyway, he came out of his room like a bear, mad as the devil. 'I told you not to play that damned thing while I'm trying to sleep,' he yelled at me. He took my harmonica and threw it away."

"Did you cry?"

William thought about it. "I don't remember. I don't think so."

Doc agreed to see William one more time. "Come back next week if the problem doesn't get any better." He was sure he had the answer.

Doc believed that the quickest way to break the chains of the original wound was by getting rid of the sense of powerlessness all children feel. After all, children know that their safety and security are in the hands of adults. Children aren't allowed to do anything without parental permission. Doc believed that many people go to their graves seeking permission and approval from parents long dead. All William needed, Doc theorized, was permission to be a child again.

The following week, William showed up punctually, as always. Doc showed him into his office and asked him to take a seat. "Mr C., do you believe in magic?"

William looked at Doc like he was crazy. "Magic? I can't say that I ever thought about it."

Doc smiled. "Do you believe that certain objects have magic powers? That our spirits can be healed just by coming in contact with an inanimate object?"

William rubbed his chin. "Seems kinda farfetched."

Doc handed him a small box. "This is for you."

William shook the box suspiciously. "What's in there?"

"Magic."

William opened the box. It contained a brand-new Hohner harmonica. Doc wrote, "He looked at the instrument, then at me, then at the instrument again, and I knew I had reached him. His lips trembled; tears welled in his eyes. Then he emitted a howl of such pain and loss that it hurt my heart to hear it. I rushed to him and held him as he poured out all the grief he'd kept prisoner for thirty-four years; it poured out of him like infection from a lanced wound."

When William calmed down, Doc took him by the shoulders and spoke to the man in his soothing, hypnotic voice. "Mr C.—William. Listen to me. You're a grown man, not a six-year-old child, and things that could hurt you when you were small can't hurt you today. Your father can't take anything away from you now. You learned at an early age a very discouraging lesson: that if you loved something, you would lose it. Over time, you became afraid to love *anything* with all your heart. This is the source of your problem. Just remember this, and believe it: your father can't take away your harmonica anymore." Doc handed William a handkerchief. "Do you feel better?"

William nodded. He tapped the harmonica. "Is this really mine?"

"Of course it is."

William got up, wiped his eyes, and shook Doc's hand. "Sir, I don't know how to thank you. I feel so much better."

Doc said, "I should thank you. I've learned something here myself."

William and Doc continued to stay in touch. Tucked away in the notebook, I found a letter from William C. It read in part:

"I still have the harmonica you gave me, and I play it fairly well these days. Whenever things get too stressful at the plant, or I feel a little down and out, I just rip out a few bars of *You Are My Sunshine* and everything's okay again. Who knows, maybe when I retire I'll join a band."

At the bottom of the letter, in Doc's sprawling handwriting, was the comment: "I sent William *The Wonderful Power*, but he really didn't need it. He found what he needed. Maybe all *any* of us needs to be happy is to find our own lost harmonica." I wondered what Doc meant by the phrase *The Wonderful Power*. He'd never mentioned it to me during my apprenticeship. Or if he did, I'd forgotten about it. I figured I'd eventually run across it in one of the other notebooks.

"We must learn to give ourselves permission to do what makes us happy," he wrote. "We must become both parent and child to ourselves. Simple in concept, but often the hardest thing in the world to achieve." At the bottom of the page, Doc had written the Chinese saying, "The child is the parent of the man." Doc was convinced that the happiest people he met were those who had succeeded in realizing their childhood dream. "Often, they faced strenuous—often bitter—opposition from their families to go into a 'sensible' field of employment, but those who held steadfast to their childhood vision seem to be the most blessed. Could it be that we all have a calling, and the straightest, surest path to happiness is to follow that inner urge of the soul—no matter how unlikely or unrealistic it seems to other people? One trait I've noticed that most happy people have in common: they all have a strong sense of 'rightness;' that what they do is the best and correct path for them.

"They've learned not to worry about the opinions and criticisms of others and to listen for an inner, quiet voice that provides them a sense of guidance and direction. Needless guilt and shame have no power over them. They firmly believe they are the sole masters of their fate; that they can achieve anything they desire, with determined effort. They possess an almost childlike sense of enthusiasm, a willingness to live in the present, unburdened by the past or by worries about the future, and an eagerness to try out new experiences. Most of all, they believe in magic. To them, everything is a miracle. They do not let the light go out; it burns within them, fueled by passion and the sheer joy of life and discovery."

That last rang a bell. I remembered that Doc had told me the very same thing when I was thirteen. "Make me a promise, Craig," he asked me. "Never let the light go out." I also remembered that I promised him I would try my best to keep it burning. Had I kept this promise? I truly didn't know.

■ ■ ■

Why Doc had to leave Chicago is an interesting story in itself. Business was good; Doc saw clients from dawn to dusk. His publicity stunts, especially the ones involving the horse races, garnered much publicity. It was a great reputation-maker. However, Doc hadn't foreseen the consequences of establishing a proven track record at predicting the outcome of gambling events. A very popular form of public betting at the time was the *pari-mutuel* (French for "mutual stake") system, which originated in France. It consists of a pool of betting moneys. Those who correctly predict winners of the first three places in a race share the total moneys minus a percentage for track management. In this case, however, Chicago's gangsters owned the entire pool! Once Doc's accuracy was taken for granted, a lot of people began betting large sums of money on the races. When one of the horses Doc predicted to win broke its leg coming around the bend, it was more than just a failed publicity stunt: it involved the loss of a huge amount of money by one of Chicago's most notorious crime syndicates.

The gangsters, convinced they'd been set up as part of an elaborate con game, sent a few of their "boys" to talk things over with Doc. The result of this conversation, we can speculate, would have ended in broken bones for Doc or perhaps a quick ride to the nearest body of water for a rather long swim. Fortunately Doc, relaxing with a cigar between clients, heard them coming and threw the heavy bolts on the door. He wrote in his journal, "I didn't need my intuition to tell me they were trouble. I could hear their loud cursing a mile away." By the time the thugs broke down his office door, Doc, clutching a small bag of personal belongings, had climbed through the bathroom window and was several blocks away. He laid low until sunset, caught the first train out of town and disappeared over the horizon.

Doc watched telegraph poles tick by, waiting for his heart to slow down. He casually looked around the train, ready to bolt at the first glimpse of any hostile face. No sign of the gangsters. Sighing, he relaxed and lit a cigar.

"Where are we going?" he asked the porter.

"New York City, sir," was the reply.

Doc shrugged. It was as good a place as any.

CHAPTER SEVENTEEN

More on the Power of Affirmation

MORE THAN TWO-AND-A-HALF DECADES AGO in the decaying shell of the Victoria Theater, Doc taught me that anything the mind can imagine can be achieved. Doc firmly believed in the life-changing power of controlled thinking, or, as he put it, affirmation. Under Doc's encouragement, I constructed an affirmation that I would become a professional mentalist. This affirmation stayed with me into adulthood, giving me the strength and determination to juggle both college and a budding career, and to deal with the many setbacks and challenges inherent in climbing the show-business ladder.

Doc told me he had discovered the concept of self-affirmation during his studies of Eastern mysticism in New York. Oriental mystics would sit for hours intoning a mantra (a phrase or sound said to activate the spirit), training their minds to exist in peace and serenity. Doc decided that anything could serve as a mantra, any thought repeated often enough would tend to manifest itself in the person's life.

Today we understand that the brain is, in many ways, like an incredibly complicated and advanced computer, programmed by the way we think. Although there were no such things as computers in Doc's youth (even in the wildest speculation of fantasy and science fiction tales, which Doc loved to read), nevertheless Doc realized that the brain could be trained to think in certain ways. He was fond of a saying by Charles Darwin: "The highest possible stage in moral culture is when we recognize that we ought to control our thoughts."

Doc realized that a person was not only the sum of their experiences, but—more importantly—how they *chose to react* to their experiences. Some people suffered horrendous childhoods, yet grew up to become happy and well-adjusted adults. Others, who had it much easier, became sour and bitter. Attitude was everything, Doc decided. He wrote, "The difference between heaven and hell is one of attitude. And attitude depends on how one chooses to see the world." Obviously, if a person sees the world as a threatening and violent place, teeming with hidden dangers, he or she will focus on the events that prove this perception. But those who see the world as full of opportunities for happiness and fulfillment will tend to focus on the more positive aspects of life.

The bottom line, Doc decided, was that none of us are helpless victims of circumstances. We *choose* how we react to the world, and by extension, we are in total control of our fate. "It's almost like casting magic spells," he wrote. "The spoken word becomes reality. If you think positive thoughts, you seem to attract more positive things into your life. If you think negative thoughts, you chase positive things away. Remarkable!"

A powerful example of the healing power of proper affirmation is exemplified by one of Doc's New York cases. In 1920, Doc was visited by a woman who had a terrible condition. She was extremely overweight, so much so that she couldn't leave the house without assistance from her family. The woman's parents brought her to Doc as a last-ditch effort to save their daughter from killing herself with her own appetite. Doctors had tried everything they knew to curb the woman's voracious appetite, including a new technique that had been used with some success in Vienna: hypnotherapy. Nothing seemed to help. At twenty-nine, the unfortunate young woman was literally a prisoner of her own body.

Doc watched in pity as the young woman, with the help of her parents, squeezed through the door of his office. She was so large she had to enter the room sideways. The young woman—Serena—wheezed and gasped under the exertion of the simple task of making her way to the sofa and plopping down. Rivulets of sweat ran down her face while her parents fluttered about solicitously.

Doc brought Serena a glass of water and handed it over.

"Thank you," Serena gasped, and drank it down.

Serena's parents lost no time in bringing Doc up to date on the efforts they'd made on their daughter's behalf. "We've spared no expense, Dr. DeLyle," the mother said. "We've had her to the finest doctors in the country. Nobody can help her." The mother burst into tears while her husband comforted her. "There's something wrong with her glands, and she can't help it!"

Doc made a few notes in his book. "Is this what the doctors told you?"

The mother became defensive. "No, but isn't it obvious?"

Doc studied the girl's medical records and questioned the family, requesting some background on Serena's condition. Apparently, Serena had been a 'delicate' child (as the mother put it) and as a result she wasn't allowed to play with other children. "Her health was fragile, Dr. DeLyle," Serena's mother told him. "We had to watch her and make sure she didn't overexert herself." She dabbed at her eyes. "We had to protect her." Serena's parents had exhausted every available medical solution; obviously, they expected him to perform some sort of magic or witchcraft to return their daughter to a healthy state.

Doc wrote in his notebook, "There's no indication of any medical condition causing Serena's obesity, but the problem here is obvious." Doc saw that Serena was the center of her mother's existence; taking care of her afflicted daughter gave the mother's life meaning and purpose. Serena's mother didn't really want her daughter to get better; but to maintain the image of a doting parent, she took Serena to various doctors and healers. Doc had seen this pattern before: parents who wanted their child 'fixed,' but who were unwilling to change anything about themselves.

"I'd like to talk to Serena now. You two can wait out in the parlor." Serena's parents reluctantly left and Doc shut the door behind them. He took Serena's hands in his. Her hands were remarkably small and delicate, so out of place on such a large body. He looked into the young woman's eyes. "Serena, do you want to be well? Are you ready to regain your natural health, return to your natural weight and learn to enjoy life?"

"Yes sir," Serena said. Her eyes avoided Doc's.

"Look at me, Serena," Doc said.

Serena raised her eyes from her hands and looked at Doc.

"You must listen to me, and believe what I say. You don't have to live like this anymore. Starting today—right this second—you can be free from your condition. It's totally up to you. You chose to gain all this weight, and only you have the power to get rid of it."

"I can't," Serena said. "It's my glands. Mommy said . . ."

Doc shook his head firmly. "No. Doctors have examined you and they have found nothing wrong. You are a young lady in remarkably good health, except for one thing: your weight. And I'll tell you again, you are in complete control of that. Do you want to be free? Do you want to live your life happily, or be trapped in your body for the rest of your days?" He looked at her intently. "What do you want, Serena?"

A tear trickled down Serena's face. "I want to be able to date boys. I want to go to shows and dances. I want to get married and have a family." A look of total misery appeared on her face. "I don't want to live like this anymore. I want to die."

Doc nodded. His heart was breaking for this poor girl, who had been trained by her parents to isolate herself from the rest of the world with layers of fat—a victim of her mother's negative affirmations. "Serena, I say to you that you can have anything you want in life; you can decide to get rid of as much weight as you want. But, most importantly, you can decide to be free from your parents."

She looked up sharply, as though he'd slapped her. "My parents? Why would I want to be rid of them? I love my parents!"

Doc took her hands again. "Serena, just bear with me. Answer a few questions, and answer them honestly. Will you do that?"

"Okay," she muttered.

"First question: Who told you that you were sick?"

"My mommy. She said—"

Doc held up his hand. "We'll get into that later. Now, who decided that you were too, as your parents say, 'delicate' to play with other children?"

"Mommy," Serena said. "She said I would get hurt if I roughhoused with other kids."

"Um hmm . . . Serena, I have one last question: Who prepares your meals and serves them to you?"

Serena sank her face into her hands. "Mommy."

Doc let the young woman cry for a while, then took her by the hand. "You've made the first step. Now the rest will come easier. You must be brave, and you must be strong. All your life you've allowed your mother to make you believe things about yourself that aren't true. She's kept you in the helpless state of a small child, completely dependent on her for your most basic needs. But I think you have it in you to overcome this negative mentality and change your life for the better."

Doc taught Serena to use affirmations to help her control her appetite. "Always include the words 'I' or 'me,' to make the affirmation as personal as possible. You must repeat to yourself, 'I don't need this extra weight. I can live without it.' Always phrase your affirmations in the present time. It does no good to say you'll drop weight next week or next month—you must say, 'I'm attaining my goal weight *right now!*'" Doc also taught Serena visualization techniques. "See yourself becoming slender, begin to think of yourself as slim and attractive. Stand erect and proud, with your head held high."

Later, he taught her to loosen her parent's smothering hold. "Your mother is going to fret that you're not eating enough, or that you're too 'delicate' to exercise," Doc warned. "She'll try every trick in her repertoire to keep you an invalid. But you must try to do some light physical activity each day. Even if it's just walking up and down the hall a couple of times. Be prepared—you're mother is going to have a fit. This is where you must be brave. You have to learn to tell your mother 'No!'"

Doc explained that Serena had to phrase all of her affirmations in a positive light. She mustn't think of her weight reduction as "losing weight," for example, because people hate to lose things! "When we lose the key to our house, or we lose our wallet, we grieve for it. By thinking of weight reduction as a loss, we're already preparing ourselves to fail. We want back what we've lost! You must think of getting rid of your excess weight as a *positive* action. You're setting it aside, you're getting rid of it, you're throwing it away—you don't need it anymore."

Over time, Doc gave Serena further affirmations: "I am in control of my feelings and thoughts. I choose how to react to events in my life. My parents cannot control me with guilt. I only eat when I'm hungry, not to alleviate stress or sadness."

Over time, Serena managed to drop a significant amount of weight. Predictably, Serena's mother became nervous, cried a lot, and eventually pitched temper tantrums. When Serena took her daily walks, her mother warned her that she'd fall and break her hip. But Serena remained steadfast in her determination to change her life.

"It wasn't easy, and there were several setbacks, but a year and a half later Serena moved out on her own. She'd found a job as a seamstress, and soon was happily making dresses of her own design. She'd dropped more than one hundred pounds!"

Doc also worked with Serena's mother, trying to free the woman from her obsessive desire to control every situation. Serena's mother eventually found an outlet for her need to care for others by volunteering at the local charity hospital. Two years after Doc undertook the healing of an overweight, unhappy young woman, he considered the case closed.

Did Serena ever meet her prince and raise a family? Doc's journal doesn't say. His final remarks concerning Serena: "I've tried to teach Serena to become her own best therapist. My job was easy: she already had the Wonderful Power but didn't realize it. All I did was help her rediscover it. Now the rest of her fate is between Serena and her Creator."

While Doc possessed many tools that enabled him to help people from all walks of life with many different problems, I don't want to give the impression that he was able to help everyone, or that he possessed a magic wand he could wave over people and make their problems evaporate like magic. Doc knew that people had to take responsibility for their problems, and he defined his job as providing people with the tools they needed to help them heal themselves. His success rate was remarkable, but there were some things even Doc couldn't fix.

One day, a man brought his sixteen-year-old daughter into Doc's office for a reading. It was just a lark, the man said; the two were spending the day together doing whatever the daughter wished to do. Doc asked the young lady what kind of reading she wanted.

"Read the tarot cards," the girl said. "I've always wondered what they would say about me."

Doc smiled and bowed his head. "Very well, my dear."

Doc laid the cards out in a standard formation known to students of the tarot as the Celtic Cross. Interestingly enough, the cards spelled out the girl's past in great detail—so great that the father sat there with his mouth hanging open. But the cards said nothing about the girl's future.

"This is quite unprecedented," Doc said. "The cards aren't telling me anything about your future. There's nothing there." When the girl's father glowered at Doc, he knew he'd made a terrible mistake. Suddenly, he understood the girl's situation. Doc decided to follow the compassionate course and lie to the girl. He dealt out a few more cards. "Ah there," he beamed. "Much better! It all looks good, my dear. I see years of happiness ahead of you. You're going to travel and meet very interesting people along the way. I see you living a full life, in superb health." He looked over the cards one last time, embellishing the fictitious reading. "Any questions?"

Doc answered a few inquiries from the girl about her future husband, how many children she was going to have, etc. All the time, the girl's father looked as though his heart was breaking. At the end of the reading, Doc said to the young lady, "My dear, will you wait out in the parlor while I have a word with your father? There's a few things I must speak with him about."

She stood up and kissed her father's cheek. "Don't be too long, Poppy," she said. "You promised we'd go see a motion picture!"

"Yes, Pumpkin," the father said in a tired voice. As soon as the door closed, the man turned to Doc. "What did you mean when you said the cards predicted no future for her?"

Doc touched the man's hand. "I'm not sure what it means," he said. "But from the look on your face when I said it—you do."

The man gave a shuddering sigh. "She's sick. The doctors say she has less than six months to live. You see, there's something growing in her brain—," the man tapped his forehead, "—and she doesn't know that it's killing her. She wanted to see a fortune-teller, and I brought her here because I thought that fortune-tellers told people what they wanted to hear; you know, good stuff. I wanted her to hear happy news. But you—you're spooky."

Doc poured the man a brandy and handed it over. "As soon as I realized what was going on, I told her nothing but good news. I saw no point in telling her what you've decided to keep from her."

"Thanks," the man said. "You're really good at what you do. You were spot on about her childhood. My wife and I just adore her." He smiled. "I think we spoiled her rotten. Thanks for telling her she'll live a long and happy life."

Doc chewed the ends of his mustache. "Is there nothing to be done for her?"

"No."

"I'm terribly sorry. I wish I could do more."

The man finished his brandy and stood up. "You helped her by painting such a wonderful picture of her future. You'll never know how much I appreciate that." He removed his wallet. "How much?"

Doc waved it away. "No charge."

"But—"

Doc rummaged around in his desk for a moment, coming up with a sealed envelope. "Take your daughter someplace special." Doc grasped the man's hand and placed the envelope in it. The man didn't know it at the time, but the envelope contained five hundred dollars.

"Don't open that until you get home," Doc said. "It's a little surprise for your daughter. Sir, I firmly believe that life isn't measured in years alone, but by quality of experiences. Make what time she has left so rich and so full of experiences that it will seem to be an entire lifetime. Take her places; show her the world. Care for her. And yourself. God bless you."

"But where will I get the money?"

Doc smiled. "It will come. Trust God. This prediction I know will come true."

The man stammered more words of thanks and left.

Doc sat in his office for a long time, smoking a cigar and thinking. Finally, he rose, went through the parlor and stood outside his office, locking the door behind him. He hung a sign on the door: CLOSED FOR THE REMAINDER OF THE DAY.

Doc walked up to the highest hill in town, sat on the grass, and watched the sun set. That night he wrote, "Even the power of affirmation cannot conquer death. But perhaps it can make what life we're apportioned worth living."

CHAPTER EIGHTEEN

Missing Pieces

THE TIME DOC SPENT IN NEW YORK gave him plenty of opportunity to pursue (if only vicariously) his other great love, show business. Whenever he wasn't working, he took every chance to go to the Hippodrome Theater and watch the shows.

Vaudeville shows comprised several individual acts, such as acrobats, musicians, and comedians, working in a continuous circuit. Such notables as W. C. Fields, Mae West, Houdini, Eddie Cantor, and William "Bojangles" Robinson got their start in vaudeville. Theaters could be found in almost every major city of the United States. Before the rise of motion pictures, vaudeville was the most popular form of entertainment during the early twentieth century.

Doc lost no time making himself known to the top mentalists and magicians who came through New York on the vaudeville circuit. He met Alexander—*The Man Who Knows* (C. Alexander Conlin, the greatest crystal ball reader in history), Joseph Dunninger (inventor of the famous Dunninger challenge box!), and Harry Houdini. Doc's impressions of the famous escapologist are enlightening:

"Mr. Houdini is undoubtedly one of the greatest showmen of our time—and one of the most egocentric. He can't stand the thought of anyone getting one over on him, or of anyone receiving more attention. When Houdini is in the room, no other magicians are allowed! Some of the boys were showing each other a few tricks at Martinka's (the preeminent magic shop in New York at that time) and Houdini insisted on dominating the session. Tommy Downs would do a trick— Houdini would shout 'Give me the deck!' and try to outdo him. Flosso would do a bit, and Houdini would grab the deck and hold forth for all he was worth, constantly reminding us he was known 'back in the old days' on the Keith vaudeville circuit as *The King of Kards*.

"Finally, I did a bit I came up with years ago, where an individual thinks of a card and I find it. Houdini was completely astounded—although he didn't admit it. He insisted I do it again and again, while he watched me from every angle trying to spot the 'gaff.' Finally, he pretended to catch me and shouted, with a knowing wink to the boys, 'Ah. It's just as I thought!' and proceeded to give a totally bogus explanation involving cards with shaved edges. I declined to correct him. I had had a busy day and was too tired to wrangle."

Doc learned a lot from his show-business friends, all of which he recorded in his journals against the day he would realize his childhood dream of touring with a show of his own. In the meantime, he continued to work with his clients.

One of Doc's most remarkable New York cases involved an encounter with a skeptical reporter. The reporter (whom we will call Mr. Scott) specialized in that style of writing we refer to today as "investigative journalism"—in other words; muckraking. Mr. Scott decided to turn his attention to the psychic scene in New York. In an article entitled "No Two Fortune-Tellers Give Same Answers," he lambasted the various fakes and frauds he encountered:

> One told me I liked children. The other told me I get nervous around children. I've been punching moppets and giving candy to the neighbor's children ever since. I found out I was artistic and think deep thoughts because I'm a Sagittarius. I assume all you other Sagittarians out there do the same. Maybe we should form a club. None of the palmists and soothsayers was particularly original, though. For a while, it looked like a pretty colorless day.
>
> But that was before I met The Great One.

(The Great One, if you haven't realized by now, was my great-uncle Alain DeLyle!)

The Great One's consultation room was remarkable. Around the wall were diplomas attesting The Great One's proficiency in herbalism, physical culture, secret sciences, and sundry other arts. All in all, it was not what you would call a natural room. But when The Great One entered, there was nothing unnatural about the bottle in his hand. It was good old American rye.

He took a seat behind the desk and introduced himself, caching the bottle somewhere along the way. The consultation room is better imagined than described. It was foreign, and it was filled with a conglomeration of artifacts from around the globe. It had Buddhas: gold, silver, and plain. It had trinkets and jewelry, and tapestries hanging from the walls. There were glass cases filled with little vials that couldn't have held anything less important than bath salts for Arabian princesses. There were lights, mirrors, and candles. The lights came from every direction and were of every color.

The Great One not only told me, he showed me. I thought of a word from a book. He stroked his chin, looked into my eyes for a moment and told me what I was thinking! I totaled up a series of random numbers, he told me the answer. "You must have a mental blackboard," I said. He smiled. "I prefer to call it telepathy."

Forty-five minutes later I left with my faith in the occult restored. The Great One told me things that nobody else, outside my family, could know. He said I came from a broken family. This was true. My sisters and I were orphans, and for years we had been trying to locate a long missing brother, who was an infant when we were separated. I asked The Great One (somewhat skeptically, I admit) "Where can I find my missing brother?"

The Great One reflected, rubbing his chin. I was a bit disappointed. No crystal balls or occult mumbo-jumbo? What kind of seer was this? Then he lit a cigar, leaned back in his chair, and spoke.

"I believe your brother is alive and well. I see the name Oscar, and the initial M . . . the rest is blurred by time. It appears he has something wrong with his hands; scars or burns perhaps."

Now I was really interested, because my sisters and I had all been born with what the doctors call 'double little fingers,' which had been removed at birth. No one outside of our family knew this, though. The Great One urged me to make inquiries to the postmaster of Campus, Illinois, and everything would become clear.

The bottom line? I left The Great One's office very impressed, and I intend to contact the Postmaster of Campus, Illinois. Will this shed light on the mystery of my missing brother? I don't know. But for five dollars, I can say that I got more than my money's worth!

Doc's notebook doesn't say if the reporter ever found his missing sibling, but Aunt May was able to shed some light on the matter. She told me that Mr. Scott had found out the name of the Postmaster was Oscar Morgan, and that he had the tell-tale scars on his hands from the childhood surgery. General resemblance and shared family memories (not to mention the identical scars) convinced Mr. Scott and his family that they had indeed, found their little brother!

This wasn't the first missing person Doc helped locate. During the first World War, he'd helped find a soldier who was reported missing in action and presumed dead. The parents were convinced their son was still alive, and brought his picture to Doc to see if he could help them. After concentrating deeply, he told them to have the army make a search of the hospitals for a young man missing a leg and who was suffering from amnesia caused by a head injury. The parents complied, and found their missing son in a Virginia Veteran's hospital. Eventually, his memory came back to him and he returned home.

"War," Doc wrote, "makes no sense to me. If we spent half the money, time, and energy learning to heal people that we spend on learning to kill them, mankind could create a Paradise on earth." He breathed a sigh of relief when World War I ended, although he suspected that the silence the world hoped was final peace was actually the calm before a much bigger storm.

"My job, as I see it," Doc wrote, "is to help people locate the missing pieces of their lives."

One day a middle-aged woman came to see him out of sheer desperation. She had been abandoned by her husband a year previously and had four children to support. She had no family to help her. What she wanted, she told Doc, was the number to a winning lottery ticket!

"Let me see your hands, my dear," Doc said.

Doc held the woman's hands, shaking his head in sympathy at the work-hardened calluses on her fingers and palms. Her work ethic was superb. She was intelligent, resourceful, and determined. However, none of these gifts helped her put food on the table. He searched for something—anything—to give the woman hope. Doc knew that the lottery was a sucker bet. With its astronomical odds, the woman's chance of winning was approximately that of getting struck by lightning while waltzing at the Apollo Ballroom.

It was time, Doc decided, for her to experience a taste of *The Wonderful Power*.

"I see you enjoy cooking," he said. "Are you currently employed as a chef?"

"I work in a bakery. Long hours. I make pies and cakes."

"From your own recipes?"

She smiled, showing dimples. "I make a mean Devil's Food cake. I'm hard pressed to keep up with the orders." The woman sighed. "The problem is, I'm getting too old to work double shifts much longer. And I want to spend more time with my kids. Can you help me?"

Doc rubbed his chin. "Why don't you start your own business?" he asked.

She laughed as though the suggestion was the most ridiculous she had ever heard. "Me? I have no head for business. Besides, I could never be successful at something like that."

Doc saw that the woman's interest in cooking was more than just a skill. It was her passion. However, she was working herself to death with little compensation, all because she didn't believe in herself. In the meantime, her employers were getting rich from her creative talent. "You have more power than you think," he told her. "Here—come with me!" Doc led her to his back office and sat her in a comfortable chair. "Have you ever been hypnotized before?"

She blinked, slightly nervous. "I don't think so."

Doc removed his shiny pocket watch. "Just keep your eyes on the watch . . . you're getting sleepy, very relaxed . . ."

During the next thirty minutes the woman performed a series of remarkable feats designed to reveal her hidden power. She broke a thick board with her bare hands. Doc led her barefoot across a box of broken glass. Finally, she reclined on Doc's Hindu Torture Couch, and he broke a large rock from her stomach with a sledgehammer. Incredibly, she emerged from these grueling tests unharmed! The woman was elated.

"See?" Doc told her. "You can do things you didn't think possible." He removed a scrap of paper (I assume his trademark magenta stationery), wrote down a number, and handed it to her. "Take this."

She peered at the scrap of paper. "Is this the winning lottery number?"

Doc laughed. "It's a winning number, all right—at least I hope so. I'm not so good with random numbers, my dear. My specialty is reading people and events, and helping folks find their own, inner jackpot. This isn't a lottery number, it's the telephone number of an acquaintance of mine, a man who recently started a company devoted to the manufacture and distribution of what he calls 'snack cakes.' He's currently collecting choice recipes for pies and other confections. Why don't you give him a call and tell him I referred you to him? Take him one of your cakes. See what happens."

The woman left, uncertain that the phone call would do any good. The upshot of this odd story is that the woman and Doc's "acquaintance" hit it off superbly. The two formed a partnership and the company soon became quite successful. They began by selling desserts to upscale New York restaurants, and from there went on to the frozen pastry market. The woman remarried (her partner's older brother!) and, as they say, lived happily ever after. And, while I can't divulge the identities of any of the players in this drama, or even the company they created, I can tell you this: if you're a person who indulges in the occasional delicious over-the-counter snack cake, you've probably enjoyed one of the woman's recipes.

The years passed quickly for Doc, as he continued to study and develop his craft. It was during this time that he earned several of his impressive degrees. He was an inveterate and voracious reader, eager to expand his horizons in any directions that would increase his knowledge. According to his notes he published a manuscript called *The Wonderful Power* in 1929, which, I assumed, explained what this Wonderful Power was. Unfortunately, I couldn't find a copy of the manuscript, either in the notebooks or in the boxes of Doc's memorabilia stored in the attic, although I did find an advertising flier, couched in the sensationalist style of the time, that only served to pique my curiosity even further:

THE WONDERFUL POWER

How to use it to gain Health, Happiness, Success, Prosperity, Love, Money and the Realization of all your Legitimate Desires! A complete course of instruction in three inspiring lessons by the mastermind of mental science Professor Alain DeLyle, D.P.A.- M.H. - D.P.C. - P.Pg.C. - Ms.D.

YOU HAVE POWER: LEARN HOW TO USE IT!

BE WISE! LEARN HOW TO USE IT NOW!

Arise! Throw off your shackles, exchange sorrow for joy, darkness for light, be the master of your own destiny.

Where there is a will there is a way.

This course of lessons is particularly designed to point the pathway to supreme success.

Soul inspiration will be administered personally by Professor Alain DeLyle at the conclusion of each and every lesson. None are too young; none are too old to benefit from The Wonderful Power.

ENROLL NOW; TODAY—DON'T WAIT. BE HAPPY EVERMORE.

A tall promise, I thought, for only three lessons. I wondered why Doc never mentioned any of this to me? Frustrating! The flamboyant description that followed the above proclamation didn't help much either—except to increase the mystery!

"It is the power that is above and beyond both good and evil. It is that which embraces the golden light of wisdom, the blue flame of truth and the purifying force of the violet lightning. It may be used for either good or evil, as it is directed it can either create or destroy. It can make you sick or well, it can kill or it can cure, it produces either life or death. It can be accumulated, concentrated, transported and projected into the most remote regions of sidereal space, and more rapidly than the twinkling of an eye! It was known to the ancient Christians as the Holy Ghost, to the American Indians, the Great Spirit. It is the Grand Architect of the Masons and the Hindus called it Brahma. The Yogis designated it Prana, it is the Buddha of the Buddhists, the Allah of the Mohammedans, and the Ahura Mazda of the Zoroastrians. In the psychological realm it is the power of suggestion, the power of visualization, the power of concentrated thought, and all the powers of the mentality combined. When this Wonderful Power is used for good and helpful purposes it is called White Magic. When it is used for evil, it is called Black Magic or Voodoo. It is omnipotent, omniscient, omnipresent and illuminating."

All this—and more—was available to Doc's clients for the price of only five dollars!

According to Doc's notes, *The Wonderful Power* sold well, he was busy and successful, but he felt something was missing. He'd helped countless others find fulfillment in their lives; now he felt the time was approaching when he should seek his own. He knew he wasn't ready to marry and settle down, nor was he willing to abandon his reading practice to become a full-time performer. On his birthday in 1932, Doc figured out what was missing from his life. He realized to his amazement that he was forty-five years old and had never been outside the United States. "Most of my travel," he wrote, "has been from necessity."

He took stock of his financial situation. In spite of his somewhat impulsive generosity, Doc had saved enough money to do what he pleased. He had no responsibilities keeping him in New York, nor had he planted his roots there very deeply. New York was always supposed to be a temporary stop—he'd wound up staying years longer than he'd intended. Doc drew up an itinerary of places he wanted to see and began making plans. Closing his office, he booked passage on a ship and set out to see the world. First stop: Egypt!

CHAPTER NINETEEN

A Psychic Abroad

"MAN'S CONSTITUTION WASN'T DESIGNED BY NATURE TO TOLERATE SEA TRAVEL," Doc complained in his journal. "I've never been so sick in my life. I've always told my clients that death is a blessing; that we go to a better place where suffering is ended. Now, more than ever, I feel the truth of this policy to the depth of my soul." In spite of his bout with seasickness, Doc managed to stay on his feet long enough to entertain the passengers on more than one occasion. The captain gave him a letter testifying how much the passengers had enjoyed the performances. Doc wryly noted, "I wish I could remember what I did."

Doc wasn't alone on this trip. He makes reference to a certain Juliana, whom he describes as a "lovely, budding theatrical ingénue." Apparently, she came to him for a reading in New York, and the two hit it off. Juliana accompanied Doc on his journeys, although he doesn't go into details concerning their relationship. One can only speculate. It was hard for me to imagine Doc with anyone other than Aunt May. When I was thirteen, it seemed to me that the two of them had been together forever.

In Egypt, Doc found a land where mystery was not only alive and vital, but also as common as the shifting sands. The pyramids fascinated him, ancient monuments to the afterlife. Who made them, he wondered, and for what purpose? Doc rented a small house in Cairo and spent several weeks studying the Great Pyramid firsthand while Juliana roamed the marketplaces. His quest for knowledge was relentless; he hobnobbed with shamans, peddlers, and storytellers, spending money freely in exchange for information. He even claimed to have been led by a guide one moonless night through some of the pyramid's inner labyrinths.

From a resident archeologist with the unlikely name of Wittinger he learned that there were no less than three schools of thought about the purpose of the Great Pyramid of Cheops. The first—and most common—held that the dimensions of the pyramid were archetypical measures of length and time; a gigantic yardstick of sorts. "Of course," the archaeologist told Doc, "it seems unlikely that a construction of such scope was intended for so simple a purpose."

The second school maintained that the pyramid was a universal sundial and astronomical observatory. The proponents of this theory believed that the ancient builders knew a great deal more about astronomy and the earth's dimensions than previously suspected. French scholars under Napoleon made careful measurements of the pyramids that yielded an astonishing fact: the dimensions of the Great Pyramid were directly related to the size of the planet. The conclusion was obvious. The ancient architects knew the circumference of the earth! Some of the more speculative scholars maintained that this knowledge came from Atlantis, or even from other worlds.

It was the third school of thought, however, that intrigued Doc. Doc's new friend believed the shape of the pyramid concentrated natural forces within its walls. The archaeologist, Wittinger, had constructed scale models of the Great Pyramid and discovered that when the bodies of dead animals were placed inside the models, they became mummified within a matter of days. Fruit placed beneath the pyramid stayed fresh longer, and even razor blades regained their edge!

"This discovery could revolutionize science as we know it," Doc's friend Mr. Wittinger told him. "Imagine if we could learn to harness this energy!"

Doc was skeptical that modern science would ever accept his friend's somewhat bold conjectures, but wished him the best of luck with his studies. For Doc, the Great Pyramid represented the union of body, mind, and spirit. "The triangle is the most stable form in nature," he wrote. "The Egyptians recognized this and built their monuments to the human spirit in the form of a triangle squared, just as a person consists of three elements: body, mind, and spirit. The precise measurements of the pyramids confirm their belief that perfect balance is essential. A lopsided pyramid wouldn't last very long! Likewise, no single element of the body/mind/spirit pyramid can be neglected. All three elements must be developed for a person to operate at fullest potential. Neglect any one of these elements and the whole system is weakened. The triangle collapses, from bad health, bad attitude, or bad thinking. The fact that this shape focuses an inner energy or light proves that Egyptians certainly knew about The Wonderful Power."

He spent several weeks in Egypt, collecting artifacts, trinkets, and information. He spent one night near the Great Pyramid and wrote that he thought he heard "whispering, phantom voices." But as much as Egypt fascinated Doc, Juliana was getting bored. He learned a great deal in Egypt (including a delightful method of telling fortunes from the residue left in a cup of strong coffee) but he decided to move on, making a mental note to return sometime and continue his studies.

From Egypt he went to the United Kingdom to gather information about the Druids. While in Scotland (the land that Sydney Smith described as "that garret of the earth—that knuckle-end of England—that land of Calvin, oat-cakes and sulfur"), he got lost and spent the night in a ruined castle, that, I was delighted to realize, must have been the scene of the ghost story he told Brian and me on that distant Halloween so many years ago. There's no mention of his being attacked by a shaggy beast in his journal, but I did find a yellowed article from a British magazine that related the entire story of William de Soulis and Robin Redcap. Doc hadn't been as "full of it" as my Dad had thought, although I have serious doubts if the entire story, as Doc told it, was true!

Nor was there any mention of the Loch Ness monster, but I did discover the story behind Doc's getting lost. Apparently, Juliana had traveled ahead to London to meet with friends while Doc did his research in Scotland. Left to his own devices, Doc couldn't seem to stay out of trouble. It seemed he had been drinking in a pub when he became involved in a back-room poker game with some of the locals. He won a small sum of money from them—by fair means, we assume—but apparently the locals were sore losers. A group of angry roughnecks followed Doc as he left the pub and attacked him. Doc defended himself, but he'd had a lot to drink and was outnumbered. The toughs beat and robbed him, taking his wallet and the pouch containing all his travel information. Doc had stashed a little money in his belt so he wasn't totally broke, but he was in no shape to drive the hundred miles or so to the nearest town. Hence, his night spent in the ruins of Hermitage Castle.

In Scotland, Doc found a land where psychic abilities were not only accepted, but considered commonplace. Doc believed that the character of a people could be estimated by the richness of their folklore, and in this respect, he wrote, "Scotland is a land of enormous wealth." Practically every Scottish family had a witch or psychic among them. In one of his books, Doc found an odd quote by German physicist and philosopher G. C. Lichtenberg: "The second sight possessed by the Highlanders in Scotland is actually a foreknowledge of future events. I believe they possess this gift because they don't wear trousers. That is also why in all countries women are more prone to utter prophecies." After reading this, Doc briefly considered the idea of doing readings in his underwear, or perhaps while wearing one of Juliana's sparkling evening gowns. "Nah," he decided. "My legs are too hairy."

In Edinburgh, Doc spent some time with an old gypsy and his wife, who taught him a great deal about the art of reading palms. Doc wrote that it was a shame the gypsies were so persecuted that they had to practice fortune-telling as a scam in order to survive. He believed the gypsies were the last great practitioners of palmistry in Europe.

Doc caught up with Juliana in London and spent several weeks resting, seeing the sights, and recovering from the drubbing he'd received outside the Scottish pub. Juliana had professional contacts in London and she and Doc were invited to several parties. Doc usually was called upon to perform—"paying for his supper," as he put it. They had a wonderful time. Doc loved England and the English people.

On Doc's last night in London he was attending a party in the manor of a friend of Juliana's, one Lord Featherstone, who held a minor governmental position. The party was well attended by some of England's most important people. Doc, of course, was his usual charming self and acted as though he was quite accustomed to hobnobbing with the elite. During the course of the evening, he was called upon to do some readings. "He's really quite clever, for a Yank," Lady Featherstone said.

The crowd encouraged him, and Doc complied. "I can never say no to a lady," he commented—a trait that landed him in trouble more than once. However, on this occasion he outdid himself, amazing the lords and ladies with his uncanny and humorous readings. The partygoers gathered around while Doc delivered his prognostications, oohing and ahhing at appropriate moments. Doc noticed a short, stocky middle-aged gentleman watching the proceedings with sad eyes and the hint of a smile on his lips. Doc wondered about the melancholy gentleman. He seemed a bit out of place among the festive crowd.

Suddenly, a large, red-faced man grabbed Doc's arm. "Do a reading for the Chancellor, Mate. He loves this hocus-pocus stuff. Come on, Chancellor,"—the red-faced man waved at the sad-eyed gentleman—"Come face the music, there's the good lad!"

Lord Featherstone laughed. "Didn't you know? The Chancellor's mum was a gypsy!"

Lady Featherstone tapped him with her handbag. "Oh, she was not!"

The stocky, middle-aged man bore these sallies with a patient smile while he finished his drink and his smoke. Like Doc, he apparently had a fondness for neat Scotch and fine cigars. The Chancellor of the Exchequer made his way through the small crowd with a good-natured wave of his hand. He sat down next to Doc and held out a pudgy hand. "What can you tell me, then, sir?" He watched Doc with a speculative, challenging expression.

Doc took the man's hand, gazed at it for a while, then gave a sad smile. "Mr. Chancellor, you have the hand of a born leader. However, I see you've had some very serious disappointments and setbacks in the past. I see you were forced to resign a position for reasons that were not entirely your fault. Never fear; you'll regain your lost prestige and climb even higher. You have a well-developed sense of humor that helps see you through strenuous times. I'm afraid you will call upon this wonderful gift very shortly, in the difficult times ahead."

The crowd fell silent. The somber tone of this discourse was a stark contrast to the light-hearted readings Doc had been delivering. The Chancellor looked at Doc and pursed his lips. "Difficult times?"

Doc hesitated. "Sir, I must warn you about something. There is a great storm building in Europe, and you will be caught in the thick of it. You'll rise to leadership and distinguish yourself in service, but you'll see sights that will break your heart. You'll write books and re- ceive recognition as an author; your name will be well-known. I pre- dict you'll be Prime Minister one day, but the burden will be heavy."

"Prime Minister Chamberlain will be sorry to hear that!" Lord Featherstone laughed. "That old boy plans to sit in the chair until he dies."

The Chancellor peered at Doc with his large, sad eyes, eyes that Doc swore could see right through a person. "Dr. DeLyle, you're a man of prodigious talent and insight. I would consider it an honor if you would join me for a couple of drinks while we discuss this 'storm' of which you speak. I have some cigars whose excellence I can per- sonally attest to."

Doc bowed. "Sir, I am the one who is honored." Doc followed the Chancellor into an anteroom, where they spoke long into the night.

What the two men talked about is not revealed in Doc's journal, but the anecdote concludes with a very telling comment: "The Chancel- lor is a man on whose shoulders hard Fate is resting. If the responsi- bility of the job doesn't break him, he will achieve immortality. I sus- pect we'll be hearing a lot more about Mr. Winston Leonard Spencer Churchill."

The next morning, he and Juliana left London for the small coun- try where Doc finally got the break that put the missing piece of his own life in his grasp.

Monte Carlo is a small Mediterranean country off the French Riv- iera, known primarily for its casinos and the Monte Carlo automobile rally. Doc wanted to see the famous casino (which had been designed by Charles Garnier, who also designed the Paris Opera House), not only to appreciate the remarkable architecture, but also to try his hand at some of the games of chance. Doc checked in at the Grand Hotel (evidently, he'd saved a fairly sizable bankroll) and he and Juliana prepared to take in the sights.

After attending the opera and enjoying a wonderful dinner, Doc and Juliana made their way to the casino. Doc played against the roulette wheel and the craps table with moderate success, finally settling in at the baccarat table. There, he found his niche.

Baccarat is a game similar to blackjack, where the winner is the player holding two or three cards totaling closest to nine. Certain mathematical principles govern the game, and Doc, with his unique abilities to carry running totals in his head (not to mention his skill in reading the reactions and thoughts of others), found himself quite at home. He watched the play for a couple of hours, testing his intuition against the fall of the cards, then nodded to Juliana.

"I'm going to try my hand at it," he told her.

Doc bet lightly at first, winning some hands and losing others. Soon, he had figured out the mathematical principles of the game and began making bolder wagers.

By 3:00 A.M. Doc had won eight hundred thousand francs—about twenty thousand dollars American!

"Juliana had long since given up on me and retired for the night. Yet I was winning, and I couldn't stop. I understood then that gambling was a fever; an insane drive that could ruin a person. I'd probably still be there, and quite poor, if I hadn't been interrupted."

Doc was interrupted by a slight brushing sensation against his back. He turned around to confront two extremely large gentlemen. Both had extremely large bulges under their jackets.

"Excuse us, *Monsieur*," the larger of the two men said smoothly. "We regrettably must ask you to leave."

Doc was bewildered. "Why?"

"We are devastated with remorse, *Monsieur*, but you must leave. Please do not make a scene. Take your winnings and go."

Doc realized they thought he'd been cheating! His reckless wagering and unprecedented winning streak had aroused the Pit Boss's suspicions. Doc opened his mouth to explain, but the expressions on the two gentlemen's faces convinced him to close his mouth, nod, collect his winnings, and leave hastily.

The next day, Doc and Juliana checked out of the Grand Hotel, cutting their vacation short, and booked passage back to New York. An idea had occurred to him in the wee hours between dusk and dawn, that period of time belonging to the tellers of tales and the makers of mystery. He was twenty-four thousand dollars richer. Plenty of capital, he thought, for launching his own theatrical show!

CHAPTER TWENTY

On the Road
with Ramazon

DOC SOON LEARNED that show business consisted of two parts: *show* and *business*. He had the show part down pat; it was the business end he had to learn.

Doc entered show business a little too late to take full advantage of the vaudeville circuits. By the late 1930s, motion pictures had pretty much spelled the end of the old-time theatrical revues. People seemed to prefer the dark anonymity of the movie theater to the live performances of the vaudeville house. By this time, motion pictures had achieved a high degree of art, and audiences could travel vicariously to remote lands, see a man turn into a werewolf under the full moon, and enjoy watching their favorite books come to life on the screen.

However, live entertainment wasn't quite dead. Theater chains would often hire a live attraction to play for an hour in between the showings of films, and a great many traveling performers practiced what the old-timers call "four-walling." Basically, they would rent a hall, print up advertisements, and hope people showed up for the show. Some troupes made a lot of money this way. Others lost their shirts.

Doc's little group fell somewhere in between, living a hand-to-mouth existence as they toured the East Coast.

Ramazon and His Hypnotic Zombies toured up and down the East Coast for several years. The "Zombies" were hypnotized assistants who wandered among the audience in a trance state. He also worked occasionally as *Zebara*, and *DeLyle: Supernormalist Supreme*. His partners included Juliana, who was billed as *The Mental Radio Girl*. She specialized in playing on the piano any song audience members thought of. Juliana wasn't really telepathic, however, so Doc worked out a simple code to clue to her what song the audience member selected from a list. The act was a great hit. Another member of the troupe was *The Great Milton*, a hypnotist who, unfortunately, had a drinking problem. One night Milton was performing the bit where he hypnotized an audience member, laid her on Doc's Couch of a Thousand Spikes (the ancestor of The Hindu Torture Couch) and prepared to break a rock on her belly with a sledgehammer. From the wings, Doc saw that the rock was too small to absorb the force of the sledgehammer—and Milton was too intoxicated to hit it squarely anyway. Doc intervened, avoiding disaster.

And there was *Prince Shah Babar*, an Indian seer who was a friend of Doc's from New Jersey. The Prince answered sealed questions from the audience (apparently Steven Slade—Yandee—learned the act from Prince Babar). Shah Babar's wife, Marie, an accomplished violinist, played in the background as he answered the sealed questions in a dramatic manner. One night Doc was in the audience and wrote: "Am I going to get a drink after the show, and if so, where?" Prince Babar answered the question from the stage, naming a local bar. After the show, he took Doc out for a drink at the very bar he mentioned from the stage, proving the accuracy of his prediction.

It was an anxious time, an uncertain life as Doc and his band of gypsies made their way from theater to theater. Often, they didn't have enough money to rent a place to sleep. Sometimes, they missed meals. Doc was never happier.

The reviews became steadily more enthusiastic. *"Amazing . . . astounding!"* shouts one yellowed clipping, while another attests, *"Ramazon's show is the finest of its kind available anywhere. Even the most skepti-*

cal will emerge from the theater with the belief he has seen a truly remarkable performance. Ramazon takes psychic phenomena from the spiritualist's darkroom and performs it under the bright footlights."

Doc, ever analytical, explained the success of his show as follows: "Since mankind's infancy we have looked at the vast universe and wondered what may be out there. With my stage production I attempt to rekindle that sense of wonder at the mystery of the universe . . . my intention is not to trick the audience or fool them, but to raise their level of consciousness by evoking a sense of wonder. The wonders of the show are only reminders that there are all kinds of enigmas and extraordinary happenings around us, if we only paid attention. The production reflects the universal desire of man to reach beyond the boundaries of the possible . . . Theater goers may enjoy a musical act, a dramatic reading, a comedian or a lecturer, but no matter how entertaining or informative these presentations are, the patron doesn't leave the theater questioning the nature of reality itself. That is the desired effect of my show. I use every means possible to make my audiences feel they have stepped outside normal reality into a world where anything is possible. My goal is to entertain my audiences through the creation of mystery, and to encourage them to open their minds to greater possibilities. Hence, the skeptical spectator—the one who is only interested in figuring out 'how it is done'—misses out on the whole point of the experience. Stage magic provides the ultimate paradox between the old adage 'seeing is believing' and the mind's reaction that 'this is clearly impossible.' Within this paradox, we discover that magic is more than just illusion and trickery; it becomes a metaphor for the impossible made possible . . . perhaps the art of magic may contribute to unlocking the mysteries of the mind; the discovery of the wonders of the past, and future wonders yet to be."

Before long, Doc's troupe was garnering ever more enthusiastic reviews and showing a considerable profit, and between his thriving reading practice and his theatrical tour, his life seemed complete.

But then everything hit the fan. About one year into the tour, Doc (apparently trying to repeat his Monte Carlo coup) lost a great deal of money at the craps table in a local gambling house. Doc packed his bags and moved to Wheeling, West Virginia, apparently two steps ahead of his creditors. Shortly thereafter, Juliana left the show. Since Doc never mentions her again, I assume their parting wasn't completely amicable. I wondered why, of all the places in the world, Doc decided to relocate to a small town in West Virginia? No explanations were given for Doc's sudden move or his breakup with Juliana. It appeared to be a sore subject.

He writes that he had fallen in love with Wheeling after a sold-out appearance at the Victoria Theater. He comments that the beauty and serenity of Wheeling was a refreshing change from the bustling sophistication of New York, and the cost of living was much more affordable. Plus, he absolutely adored the Victoria Theater and wanted to live closer to it. For whatever reason, Doc had found his home. He lived the rest of his life in Wheeling. Doc made arrangements with the manager of the Victoria to hold rehearsals there, and he once told me that he always launched each new theatrical tour from the Vic. This all sounded logical, but I couldn't help but think there had to be more to the story than Doc's love of an old theater. What, exactly, motivated him to leave New York and settle in Wheeling?

Interestingly enough, I had already received the answer from Aunt May several years ago! After Doc's death, Aunt May had moved to Southern California to live with her brother and sister. May outlasted them all and was living alone when Charlotte and I visited her in a small California bungalow in the mid-80s. She still had her cats, and got around quite well in a motorized wheelchair. A big fluffy Persian was her constant companion, resting on her lap. During our visit, I expressed curiosity about how she had met Doc. May didn't answer, but gave me a handwritten document, a short story entitled *My Romance with a Clairvoyant*. I reproduce it here in its entirety.

My Romance with a Clairvoyant

It is now some three years since I first met him, and yet I shall never forget the impression he made upon my mind. A mutual friend, one of his admirers, introduced him to me. I was spellbound by his spiritual appearance, which hardly seemed human at the time. I found him quiet, reserved, and difficult to bring into conversation. As he sat under the moon, a soft light playing about his ethereal face, I imagined that he was a being from another world, who had descended to our globe to spread the laws of spirit and teach an erring humanity a better way to think and act. I have always looked back upon that eventful meeting as one of the greatest events in my life. The man I refer to was a clairvoyant of unusual powers, who had amazed and enlightened the public for many years. He had a great contempt for the average medium and kept to himself, rarely conversing with strangers, save as they came to him in the course of human events. When strangers did come to him, the average was an open book. He was a handsome man with a fine profile, and as I looked at him, I determined to know this man better, to somehow creep into his life and fathom the mystery of his true and inner nature. The conversation soon turned upon psychic subjects, and there he found that I had an intense interest. The extent to which he discussed hypnotism and occult phenomena fascinated me beyond description. The evening sped by all too soon, and before he left he offered to teach me some of his mystic knowledge, if I would call at his studio the following afternoon. I gladly promised to do so, as I am frank to say that he truly enchanted me, and I could not wait to see him again.

Let me try and describe the experience as I walked into his Sanctum the following day. The place was richly decorated with oriental rugs and hangings, incense fumes hung heavily in the air, mysterious pictures and ancient statues were placed here and there about the room, and on the recesses of corners silence reigned supreme. After waiting for some minutes, I was ushered into his private study, and he sat there, clad in a rich embroidered robe, bending over a huge chart upon which were drawn the signs of the zodiac. He was engaged in drawing up a horoscope for a client and seemed engrossed in his work. He motioned me to a chair, and I sat for minutes in silence before he spoke and addressed me.

"So my little student has come to see me," he said with a smile, the first one I had ever seen him offer. "Well, we shall see what we can do for you. Sit here. Please let me see your hands.

Yes, take your glove off, that's right." I gave him my hand and he closed his eyes in thought. For some moments we sat there in silence, then he began to speak. I cannot tell here what he said to me, but he gave me a most remarkable reading. He told me the chief events of my life, the troubles that surrounded me, and predicted events in the future many of which have since come true. I was amazed, dumbfounded and frankly told him so. He seemed pleased with the success of his reading and the conversation then took a more personal turn. I was frankly attracted by his magnetic personality and he seemed interested in me too. He seemed delighted by my unusual views of life and my outspoken way of expressing what I thought. When I left him that day, I was, I must admit, in love with him and could hardly wait until the next day, when I was to see him again.

In the course of the next few weeks, I saw much of him and our association soon turned into a real romance. I accompanied him on his travels all over the world, and the experiences we had during that time would fill a book. Upon our return to this country, I joined his traveling theatrical group and soon became an integral part of his show. As we traveled from town to town I performed upon the stage and he always made himself available for readings after each show. It became apparent that he knew every detail of the business in which he was engaged. He had given readings for many celebrities and his knowledge of human nature was profound. We were together for nearly a year when he informed me that he was leaving New York and going to a small town in West Virginia—of all places! I thought that my heart would break when he told me the news, and I told him that I could not live without him. He promised that he would send for me as soon as he became established there and, sure enough, within a few days I received a letter and money asking me to join him. I could hardly wait to get my things packed, and I was on my way west by the very first train I could catch. He met me at the station, and we were together constantly after that, closely associated together personally and in a business way for about another year—a year which I have always looked back upon as perhaps the happiest in my life, despite the difficulties and hardships which I had to put up with.

His interesting and unusual personality never ceased to attract me, throughout this long period of time, and I never fully succeeded in penetrating the depths of his mysterious self. I never even succeeded in learning his true name! I was very much in love with him and I think he was with me too. We were happy together, and I learned more of life and human nature from him than I have ever dreamed possible. His stage performances were remarkable, but what interested me especially was his readings, the remarkable things he did, the mystic powers he seemed to possess and the extraordinary cures he frequently effected. Many a time and often I have seen sick persons come to him for advice and treatment. He would place his hands upon them, close his eyes and concentrate. He would make passes over the diseased parts, give them simple herbs to drink and some hygienic advice. Some of these cures were really remarkable. I feel sure that he did a great deal of good for sick persons by these curious methods of treatment, whatever they were.

This strange man did not believe in spirits or any other alleged psychic powers said to be possessed by ordinary psychics at all. He said that he had a sort of "sixth sense" and that was what he depended upon in his readings coupled with his vast knowledge of human nature. While it's true that many so-called clairvoyants are merely fakes, who obtain information about their prospective sitters and palm it off on them when they come for their readings, such was not the case here. He never wished to know anything in advance about his sitter, and if anyone desired to tell him anything, he had to wait until after the reading was finished. Sitters who are easy, who believe everything and give money freely are known as "suckers" in the clairvoyant profession, or "38's," a curious expression which seems to be in common use.

But it must not be thought that all clairvoyants are frauds, charlatans and blackmailers. No doubt some of them are, but I am convinced that many of them are not. Many clairvoyants help people who come to them for advice, and often do a great deal of good in the world. I have seen this over and over again. The people who come for the sittings are often more to blame than the clairvoyant is for problems in their lives. They are the ones who have wrong, even criminal thoughts in their minds, and are willing to pay to have them carried out. These people will come again and again and beg for help. It is hard to keep such people away. They keep coming back, and they are willing to pay large sums for any advice or assistance they can obtain. The seamy side of human nature, which can thus be discovered in a very short period of time, is astonishing.

One of the most remarkable things I noticed during my stay with this mysterious man was the curious attraction that he seemed to exercise over the opposite sex without consciously exerting himself. Many and many a time I have seen women come into his office to consult with him regarding some affair of the heart. Usually, she no longer loved her husband and wished to attract and secure the love of some other man. She already made up her mind to do so willingly and only wanted to see how this could best be accomplished. In instance after instance I have seen these women leave his office madly in love. The mysterious power that he possessed cast a spell of glamour over these women and made them forget all else. Of course, some of these women were willing, even anxious, to develop love affairs with the "Professor" and admitted they were his, body and soul, for the asking. I have seen this happen not only to ignorant and superstitious women, but also to cultivated and highly intelligent women.

Naturally, under the circumstances, I was seen as the deadly rival, and I have no doubt that a great deal of jealous hatred was directed against me in the various towns and cities we visited. Here I was, closely associated with the man of their heart, whom they could not seem to capture. I am not saying that he did not respond to any of these overtures, for he did, and many were the unhappy hours that I spent in consequence because of my naturally jealous nature. Perhaps this was only natural after all. Here were scores of women coming every day, ready to throw themselves at him, to whom his slightest word was law. They were closeted with him alone by the hour, while I was forced to await his return from his sanctum. I often recall my first interview with him at such times, his first smile, the way in which he received me, and I wondered if many of these women were impressed in a similar manner.

I often tried to find out what developed during these secret sessions, but my curiosity was never satisfied. He would never tell me anything of his "professional secrets" as he called them, saying they were sacred and could not be divulged. I think I should say, however, in fairness to him, that I truly believe my friend did a great deal of good in the world, and helped many people by his advice. They paid money for it, it is true, often a lot, but I have never seen one of them who was dissatisfied or who wanted it back. Indeed they would often come again and again seeking further advice, more than willing to pay for it.

Let me give one or two examples of the extraordinary things that I witnessed during the period of my association with this remarkable man. One day a prosperous-looking businessman walked into the office and asked to see the "Professor" about a very private and personal matter. The businessman obtained his interview—a long one—and what do you think he wanted? He wished my friend to dispose of his wife by some psychic means. It was an astonishing request, but not an unusual one. The man hoped that my friend would exercise his powers and cause his wife's death by some occult means that would resemble an accident or illness. This criminal request should serve to show the temptations that are often put before unscrupulous persons.

The idea that all psychics are dangerous and harmful is, according to my observations, entirely wrong. I know he gave his clients sound advice and information, which they could not obtain from any other source or in any other manner. He did a great deal of good in the world, in many ways, and if people paid him for it that was their business. In many cases, the information was often worth far more than the money paid. I was often struck by my friend's wonderful insight into human nature. He could tell at a glance when a client entered his room what sort of man or woman they were, what kind of advice they needed, and what would help them the most.

I admit that my love for him increased during that eventful year. I was constantly with him, assisting him, performing in his show, impressed by his knowledge and wisdom and enjoying his society at other times, when he threw business to the winds and became intensely human. I think he was only truly happy when he was on the stage. On such occasions he and I would enjoy ourselves to the utmost. All this time I was living with him in the closest possible association. Despite the trials and hardships I often experienced, I was, in the whole, intensely contented and look back upon that year as perhaps the happiest in my life.

Then the final blow fell! I found out that he had another woman and had been carrying on with her for some time. I thought my heart would break. I could not bear the thought of leaving him or breaking off my associations with him. But events developed so that this finally became inevitable, and I was forced to leave him and return to New York a sadder but wiser woman. But even this experience added something to my life and spiritual storehouse. My romance with this man ended as it had begun, in mystery and in pain, yet with a surrounding halo of romance, love and tender memories.

"Who wrote this?" I asked Aunt May.

May declined to tell me the woman's name (today, of course, there's no doubt it was Juliana), but she looked at me with fond amusement. "That is the history of Doc's last great fling—although her version isn't *exactly* what happened. The woman who wrote this understated her 'jealous nature.' She made Doc miserable with her suspicions. She wanted to own him, and Doc wasn't the sort of man who could be owned. They had different values. Doc craved a simple, regular life and this woman was a bit of a snob who thrived in the higher social circles." Aunt May stroked her cat, which rolled over and loudly purred. "Doc was the type of person who didn't do too well by himself. Left on his own, he'd always find a way to get into trouble. He was a great mystic,

Appearing as Ramazon, Alain "Doc" DeLyle performed
extraordinary mental feats and stage hypnosis with the help of
his cast of hypnotic zombies!

but not very practical. He needed somebody to help keep him grounded. Doc was a generous soul who could never turn down anyone in need. He'd give you the shirt off his back, even if it was his last one." May sighed. "She just wasn't the right person for him. After she left Doc, she lived in New York and worked in the theater for a while. She pursued a career as a writer, with some small success, I believe. That's one of her short stories. I think it appeared in a magazine. You know, one of those *True Confessions* sort."

"And the other woman . . ." I looked at Aunt May in disbelief. She returned my gaze with a mischievous look.

"I came to Doc for a reading and fell in love with him. Don't look so shocked, dear. The other woman in that story was *me*."

CHAPTER TWENTY-ONE

Friends in High Places

IN THESE DAYS when spirit communication is a common topic on daytime talk shows, I have to admit that I never received a direct message from Doc. No ghosts, no apparitions; no spooky writing on frosty winter windowpanes. However, I've had many, many mystical experiences since Doc's passing which have convinced me that he's still around, affecting my life in subtle ways. I guess the first one was the incident involving the note I found in my pocket the day of Doc's funeral. The next one happened the summer after Doc's funeral.

It was a hot, sunshiny day. A group of us were playing a very physical game of flag football at Rebecca Simmons' house—and need I point out that these games were a thinly disguised excuse to mingle with the opposite sex? Night fell, and we wondered what to do next. Someone suggested we hold a séance, and everyone jumped on the idea. It just so happened that nobody was home but us. And I don't think it was strictly the idea of communicating with spirits that caused everyone's enthusiasm. Lights out, holding hands in the dark, who could say what might happen? The evening was full of possibilities.

We gathered around the big dining room table and held hands. Through a lightning-fast combination of instincts and elbows, I out-maneuvered Robert Davis and got the seat next to Rebecca. She smiled at me, extinguished the lights, and we began our explorations of the spirit world.

None of us really knew what to do. We sat in the dark, breathing hard, feeling self-conscious—at least, that's how I felt. I heard a feminine giggle, followed by a loud smack. "Stop it," someone said. Some of my friends were obviously taking advantage of the dark to produce manifestations of their own, though hardly of a spiritual nature.

"Don't break the circle," Rebecca scolded.

"Whoo-o-o-o, I'm the ghost of Christmas Past . . ." I recognized the voice of Robert Davis. More giggles.

I sighed. This wasn't getting us anywhere.

Rebecca said, "I think we have to ask for them by name. Who do you want to try to talk to?"

"Johnny Carson!" Robert yelled.

"He ain't even dead yet, you moron!" Chuck Peters said.

"Why don't we try George Washington?" Rebecca said.

We tried George. Nothing. I guess the Father of the Country had better things to do with his time than play party games. We tried Houdini, and got more of the same—that is to say, nothing—but Uncle Alain always said Houdini had little use for the spirit business.

That gave me an idea. "Maybe we should try to contact someone we had a personal connection with."

"Like who?" Robert asked.

"Let's try my great-uncle. His name was Alain DeLyle. He was into stuff like this."

"Everybody hold hands," Rebecca ordered. "Alain DeLyle, are you here?" she intoned. "Give us a sign. Speak, spirits!" (I had to hand it to Rebecca; she was quite a showman.)

Total silence for several long moments.

In the next room, the television suddenly came on.

Everyone jumped and gasped, and a couple of the girls screamed. We knew there was nobody in the house but us. Robert Davis cursed and got smacked on the arm again.

We jumped from our chairs, ran into the living room and stared at the television. On the screen, the Professor explained to Gilligan how his coconut and papaya rocket fuel worked. Gilligan's face mirrored our blank astonishment.

The resident expert on spooky phenomena, I stepped forward and turned off the television. "Let's try it again."

We went back into the dining room and reformed the circle. Rebecca's hand was sweaty in mine. "Go ahead, 'Becca," I urged.

She cleared her throat. "W-what was his name again?"

"Alain. Alain DeLyle."

"A-alain DeLyle, are you here?"

From the next room we heard the Skipper bellow, "Gilligan!"

After the third time, we were so freaked out we unanimously decided to give the séance business a rest. I think we played Twister for the remainder of the evening.

Had it been my uncle, answering Rebecca's call? Or was it an electronic accident, perhaps a power surge or a short in the television? A psychic occurrence generated by our concentration—what researchers call a Spontaneous Psychokinetic Event? I don't know. If it was a sign, it was a perplexing one. Doc never even liked Gilligan's Island.

Doc was always ambiguous on the question of spirits and life after death. Whenever I asked him about the subject he'd give me a lot of conflicting information and urge me to make up my own mind. I don't know if this was because he felt the subject was too intense for a thirteen-year-old boy, or if he simply tried to avoid conflicting with my parent's views on the subject. Probably a combination of the two, I decided. In his later years Doc still had very few family members who had anything to do with him. Maybe he didn't want to alienate what family he still got on with.

However, his notebooks contained volumes of information and speculation about the survival of the spirit after death. He apparently considered the subject important enough to devote an enormous amount of thought to it. "We all wonder," he wrote, "if there is an immortal component to our makeup, an inner being that contains our thoughts, perception of self and our memories, a part of us that survives the death of the physical body." Doc wondered if this immortal component—the soul—actually existed, or if it was simply an illusion generated by the fear that when we die it's like snuffing out the flame of a candle: poof, that's it—you're gone. "The thought of our own an-nihilation is a frightening one," he points out. "Shakespeare wrote about 'The dread of something after death, the undiscovered country, from whose bourn no traveler returns.' Perhaps this dread is the mother of all religions."

He clipped a piece by Woody Allen (of all people) and pasted it in his notes:

"The chief problem about death, incidentally, is the fear that there may be no afterlife—a depressing thought, particularly for those who have bothered to shave. Also, there is the fear that there is an afterlife but no one will know where it's being held."

Of course, Doc knew what his father would have said: "Yes, there is a soul, and when you die it either goes to Heaven or Hell. You'd better straighten up!" But every religion, Doc reflected, has its own vision on the afterlife. The Egyptians believed that the soul had to be prepared with knowledge and information to help them on the other side. Egyptian sarcophagi contained books, magical objects, and even food, for the soul's use. Buddhists say that the entire concept of "I" is an illu-sion, and when we die we lose all sense of self and enter a state of being that is beyond description. Some Native Americans maintain that after death, the spirit must undergo a series of tests, the results of which de-termine its status in the afterlife. Science, of course, remains agnostic on the subject. As yet, there's no way to measure or detect the existence of the spirit with scientific instruments.

Doc wondered: Were all religions true? Were none of them? Some of them? Which ones?

Doc knew he sometimes received messages or insights that seemed to come from an outside intelligence: "spirit messages." But did these messages come from The Great Beyond, or did he psychically receive the information from the grieving clients? Perhaps, he reasoned, when people die, they lived on in the memories of those who knew them. Maybe this psychic imprint could be tapped into, giving the impres-sion that the medium is communicating with the departed. Maybe when we die, we leave an imprint on the minds and hearts of those who remember us. Was this the secret of spirit messages, or did the con-sciousness survive the death of the body? Doc collected various theories from a number of sources and examined them in the light of his own experiences.

Some researchers believed that spirit communication was really telepathic images received from the lingering, bodiless minds of the deceased. Others advocate the psychometric theory, which proposes that physical objects record mental energy (bio-recordings) and that some people can psychically tune in on this energy. Proponents of this theory believe that the strength of the apparition depends on the emotional force of the original psychic imprint and the sensitivity of the observer.

Theories. Speculation. Doc wanted the *facts*.

What about ghosts? he wondered. People see them all the time, whether they admit it or not. Sometimes the ghosts seem anxious to impart information to the living. Other times they repeat a simple action or routine relentlessly, over and over as though obsessed. Some ghosts bring warnings, some act as guardians. The spiritualists of Doc's time had a very simple philosophy. They said that the spirits of the ones we love pass over to "Summerland," where everything is happy and nice. These spirits were eager to appear to those whom they left behind, in order to assure them of the existence of Heaven. Whereas most spiritualists were sincere, Doc also knew that many of them were no more psychic than a cinder block, and that a lot of these messages from "beyond" were vague, conflicting, and confused. Others, more skeptical, believed that ghosts were conjured up from a person's imagination. Psychologists speak of the hypnagogic state, sort of a waking dream wherein the person experiences visual hallucinations while suspended between sleep and awakening. "The problem I have with both of these viewpoints," he wrote, "is that neither theory completely covers all the facts."

In Doc's later years he was intrigued by the theories of Oxford University's H. H. Price. Price proposed the existence of a "psychic ether," a dimension between mind and matter where the mental images of the living are recorded. According to Price, certain sensitive people may be able to plug into this dimension and play back the stored impressions. "Makes sense," Doc wrote. "This would explain ghosts, psychic phenomena, and ESP."

Doc's newspaper ads of the '50s seem to reflect an attempt to put distance between himself and the numerous roadside charlatans whose flaming neon signs can be seen scattered across the highways even today:

Know Thyself!

Know the Truth!

Know in Time!

When in trouble, doubt or suspense, consult DELYLE:

"The Man Who Knows"

DeLyle is not a mere mindreader or fortune-teller, but a qualified Psychologist, Psycho-Analyst and Metaphysician who can and will help you solve your most perplexing problems now and without delay. What he tells you of your past and present proves his power to help your future.

Love, Courtship, Marriage

I will tell you the one who is sincere and the one who is fooling you. If affairs of the heart interest you, I give the exact and truthful revelations of all love affairs, settle lover's quarrels, and enable you to win the esteem and affection of the one you desire. I tell you if the one you love is true, the date of marriage, and restore waning affections. I can restore peace and confidence in lovers and disaccorded families. I will also give you the full secret of how to charm, fascinate and control the one you love, and how to make a distant person think of you.

$25.00—Interview—$25.00
Hours daily 1 o'clock to 8 o'clock
Look for the sign: "The Man Who Knows"
No letters answered!

No mention of crystal balls, spirits, palm reading, or tea leaves. Although Doc still used these tools on occasion, he had outgrown the need of such "psychic crutches," as he called them.

Doc always seemed to me to share the scientific agnosticism about spirits—at least, about the chain-rattling, physical kind—and yet one of his most dramatic cases appeared to be solved with the aid of the ghost of a young girl's grandmother!

In the fall of 1957 Doc was visited by two police officers. Accompanying them was a young woman, obviously beside herself with worry. He opened his door and invited them into his parlor. "How may I help you, Officers?" he asked, helping the woman to a comfortable chair. Doc's heart sank; it didn't take a psychic to tell that the two policemen—and the grieving woman—were bringing bad news.

"We're here because *she* insisted," the older of the two officers said, pointing toward the woman. "She seems to think you can help us find her daughter." The policeman's voice dripped with disgust. "I tried to talk her out of wasting her time on a witch doctor, but the Chief told us to pursue any avenue of investigation. So here we are."

Doc brought the distraught mother a cup of tea. "I take it your investigation is at a dead end, then?"

The older policeman's face turned red. "I didn't say that!"

"Yes, you did," Doc answered. "The fact that you're standing here, in the den of a 'witch doctor,' says it louder than words. My dear," Doc said, taking the woman's hands. "I don't know if I can help you or not. Finding missing persons isn't my specialty."

"I—I just thought you could give us some idea," the woman sobbed. "It's not like Rachel to just wander off. She's just five years old. Something must have happened to her. My sister is one of your clients. She says you can work miracles. Please help me!"

The policemen told Doc the details of the case. Rachel's mother had taken her to the park just across the Ohio River two days ago to play with her friends. Rachel and her pals were playing hide-and-seek when one of Rachel's friends came running to Rachel's mother. Rachel couldn't be found. A frantic search of the woods revealed no sign of the little girl.

Doc sighed. "I promise you I'll do my very best. Do you have something belonging to Rachel?"

The woman handed Doc a small handkerchief. "She was carrying this when she disappeared."

Doc took the small piece of cloth and rubbed it, then held it to his nose. He smiled slightly. The handkerchief smelled faintly of cherry lollypop. But no matter how hard he concentrated, he couldn't receive any impressions that hinted at the girl's whereabouts. He turned to the two police officers. "Can we go to where she was last seen?" The policemen, still skeptical, agreed.

At the park, Doc took one look at the Ohio River and shuddered. What if Rachel had fallen in? The current would have swept her out to the channel and pulled her under the water. However, this awful scenario didn't feel right. Nor did the thought that she'd been kidnapped. Doc knew the difference between imaginary worries and intuitive hunches. He decided to look around a bit and try not to anticipate what might or might not have happened to Rachel. He hoped that his mind would observe the scene, analyze the situation and come up with the answer.

The two police officers were talking to each other in low voices. "Do you think he'll come up with anything?" the younger officer whispered.

"Nah," the older one answered. "We went all over this place with a fine-toothed comb. All these psychics are fakes anyway. All they're after is some publicity."

Doc smiled to himself. *They must think all psychics are deaf as well as fakes.*

The younger cop cleared his throat. "She's been gone two days. If somebody doesn't find her soon . . ."

Doc was wandering around the edge of the woods when he heard a twig crack. He glanced in the direction of the sound.

He saw the shadowy figure of a woman, tall and slender, gesturing at him.

Doc peered into the dark woods. "Are you trying to tell me something?"

The shadowy woman put her hands on her hips as though to say, *"And who else would I be talking to, man?"* She gestured impatiently for Doc to follow, and he did, making sure he knew which way led back to the path outside the woods.

Hurry as he might, Doc could not catch up with the dark figure. She always kept ahead of him, barely within sight, leading him deeper into the woods. The fading light, dappled through the trees, played tricks with Doc's perspective. Sometimes it seemed as though he were peering at the woman through the wrong end of a telescope. The shadows grew longer; Doc was becoming nervous. The sun would be down soon. Suddenly, the woman held up her hand, an imperious gesture clearly meaning *"Halt!"* She pointed down a rocky embankment, then stood back. It was clear that she expected Doc to slide down the bank toward a series of rock outcroppings. Shrugging, Doc complied. After all, he never could say *no* to a lady.

At the bottom of the small ravine, Doc looked up and saw the outline of the tall woman against the fading sky, staring at him intently. It was unnerving that he couldn't make out her face. Doc explored the rocky shelves for about ten minutes when he came across a small cave. The dark opening was barely big enough for Doc to squeeze his shoulders through. But inside the cave he saw a small, huddled shape: a little girl!

"Rachel?" Doc called out. "Is that you? I'm here to take you to your mother."

"I hurt my leg," Rachel complained. "I fell down and broked it. Can you carry me, Mr. Man?"

Doc gently helped the girl out of the cave. She was burning with fever, scratched and dirty—but in remarkably good shape, considering she'd been hiding in the cave for two days. Rachel looked up at Doc. "Are you going to take me home?"

"Yes," Doc said, picking her up. "We'll be with your mother before you know it."

"I'm glad, I'm awful hungry." Rachel touched Doc's face. "Why are you crying, Mr. Man?"

Doc wiped his face. "I've just got something in my eye, Honey. Call me Doc."

There was no sign of the tall woman, but Doc really didn't expect to see her again. After all, she'd finished her job. The little girl was safe.

"I'll bet you were lonely, here all by yourself." Doc said to Rachel.

Rachel shook her head. "Nope. My Grammy was here playing with me. I was glad to see her. Mommy told me she was gone. We sang songs and drew pictures." Rachel looked around the woods. "Hey, where is Grammy?"

"I think she went back home, Sweetie. How about you singing me one of those songs?"

When Doc and Rachel emerged from the woods the two policemen looked at them, goggle-eyed with amazement, the little girl and the older man singing "Somewhere Over the Rainbow." Rachel's mother ran over and grabbed the little girl from Doc's arms and peppered her with a fusillade of kisses. Doc pulled the two policemen aside. "Rachel said she was hiding behind a tree when something chased her through the woods. Probably a fox or a wild dog. She fell down an embankment and hurt her leg. I think she has an infection; you should probably get her to a doctor."

The older cop gripped Doc's hand. "How about you, fellow? You look wrung out."

Doc removed the wrapper from a cigar and lit it, inhaling the smoke gratefully. "I'm fine. Just a little tired. I'll come by the station tomorrow and give you the details. Can you give me a ride home?"

"Sure, sure we can!" Doc smiled around his cigar. The policeman's attitude toward him had undergone a dramatic change.

Doc was too exhausted to answer any of the policeman's questions, but he went over and patted Rachel on the head. "Bye bye, Rachel, you be a good girl. Stay out of the woods from now on."

Rachel's mother poured out her thanks, but Doc waved them away. "I'm glad I could help," he said.

Rachel rubbed her eyes, almost asleep. "I wanna say goodnight to my Grammy," she said.

Rachel's mother pulled her daughter's head to her chest and looked at Doc. "Poor thing, she's so feverish she's forgotten her Grammy died two months ago."

I believe old Grammy must've forgotten, too, Doc thought. He'd never been so tired in his life.

Doc wondered about the strange incident for a long time. He wrote, "I don't know if Rachel's grandmother was actually there in spirit or if she was a construction of the imagination; a way for my mind to interpret the psychic energies sent out by the lost little girl.

The truth about the spirit world still eludes me, although I suspect I'll find out for myself soon enough. I guess the bottom line is that it doesn't matter where the message comes from, as long as it's positive and helpful."

I guess so, too, Doc.

C H A P T E R   T W E N T Y - T W O

The Rainbow Bridge

WILLIE WAS A STRAY DOG that my mother and I found in the summer of 1980, just before Charlotte and I were married. He was a mixed-breed terrier, black and gold; a street-smart dog, but not much good with tricks. He couldn't see the practical side of learning them, but he possessed an uncanny awareness of what was going on around him. Apparently he had been abused. The vet discovered he had suffered a broken rib that hadn't healed correctly. Willie was wary of men, especially men in hats, but he loved women. And he loved me. Willie was a member of our family for eighteen years. He was a "road dog," traveling everywhere with us.

Then he got sick.

It was just old age, but it crept up on us so gradually we didn't notice at first. The last year was the worst. When we moved into our new house, we began to realize just how badly Willie had declined. He kept getting lost in the new house, whining when he couldn't find us. One day Charlotte heard a commotion, followed by pitiful yelps. Willie had fallen down the steps. We realized then that Willie was practically blind. He had the other house memorized and could cruise around it without any problems, but in the new location he was totally lost.

As his circulatory system declined, we had to have part of his paw amputated. Charlotte and I realized that our poor dog was going downhill fast. He was incontinent, blind, and in pain. Finally, we decided we had to "put him to sleep." It was the hardest decision we'd ever made in our lives.

Charlotte and I handled the whole thing in a very businesslike manner. We found a wonderful female veterinarian who would come to the house and do the procedure. We made the necessary arrangements and set a date, secretly hoping that Willie would pass naturally in the meantime. But he held on a lot longer than we thought he would. He was a tough little guy.

On Willie's last night on earth I flew in from Oklahoma City where I was performing for a corporation. Charlotte picked me up at the Pittsburgh airport. "How is he?" I asked. She just shook her head. There were tears in her eyes.

From the airport, we went to Duquesne University in Pittsburgh for a show. I ran through the motions, but my heart wasn't in it. I dreaded the thought of the task that awaited us in the morning.

When we got home, Willie lay on his spot in the hall, moaning. He saw me come in and wagged his tail feebly. That night, his last, we slept with him on the foyer floor (he quit doing steps a long time ago). I held his paw—his good one—for most of the night, telling him he was a good boy. Charlotte didn't sleep much either. I think both of us hoped Willie would pass peacefully during the night.

The next morning the doctor arrived. "Are you ready?" she asked. "Yes," we said, but we were lying. Nobody could ever be ready for something like this. We went over to where Willie was lying, whimpering softly. His breath rattled in his chest. The vet was kind and gentle, and very professional. She didn't seem to think it was odd that I was wearing sunglasses at nine o'clock in the morning.

It was over quickly. Charlotte held Willie's head in her lap and I rubbed his back. The vet patted Willie's head and looked into his faded eyes. "You're going to a better place now," she told him. "You're going to a place where there's no pain, and you can run around and play all day." Willie seemed ready to go. The vet gave him the shot; he whimpered, gave a final sigh, and closed his eyes. I felt his body relax into death's embrace.

Charlotte hugged Willie to her and cried, rocking him like a baby.

I couldn't move, or feel my arms or legs. It was as though all the nerves to my body had been cut. I didn't cry. Men don't cry over the death of a dog.

It was over. The vet drove away and we just sat for a while. Charlotte looked at me. "I can't believe we did it."

I nodded. I couldn't believe it either. Charlotte clipped a lock of his hair and then we wrapped him in his favorite blanket. We buried Willie on the side of the house, marking the grave with fieldstones and a Celtic cross. We buried him next to our friend's dog, Savannah, a scrappy Scottish terrier. They never got along well in life, but I was sure they were playing with each other now.

After the ceremony we jumped into the Explorer and headed off for another show at a college in Ohio. Life goes on, and there were bills to pay. We returned from the show at about two in the morning.

"Let's go see Willie," Charlotte said. We stood over his grave for a long time as the moonlight illuminated it.

The next morning I was off to perform at Montana State University's family weekend. I thought a lot about Willie. We'd had him put to sleep and it was hard, but I couldn't very well call the college and cancel a sold-out show because my dog died. I was a grown man. On the airplane I took out my day-timer and went over my schedule: more than two hundred shows this year alone. Not bad. At this rate, we'd have the house paid off in five years.

I put the day-timer away, and at 35,000 feet, somewhere between Chicago and Bozeman, Montana, the dam broke inside me. Grief poured through me like an enormous mudslide. I covered my eyes and started to cry. I couldn't help it; it caught me by surprise.

My seatmate looked over at me. "Are you okay, buddy?" he tentatively touched my arm. "Afraid to fly?"

I looked out the window. "No . . . no." I took a deep breath. "I just lost a good friend."

■ ■ ■

For some people, the death of a pet is just as traumatic as losing any other family member. Sometimes it's harder. Pets, especially for childless couples, are surrogate children. Those who forge emotional connections with animals say it's the strongest and purest love they have ever experienced. Pets love you no matter who you are. I remember one time Doc told me there was something good to say about everybody. Trying to trap him, I asked, "What about Adolf Hitler?" Doc rubbed his chin and thought for a while. He replied, "He had a dog."

Aunt May couldn't resist adding, "True . . . however, he didn't have a cat."

Doc laughed. "No. A cat would have known the difference all right."

While looking through Doc's notebooks, I found a case in which Doc helped a woman deal with the bereavement of a lost pet in his own unique fashion.

In 1970, a woman came to Doc's office because her dog was missing; a black-and-white mixed-breed named Scruffy. "Can you help me find him? I haven't seen him in two days. He's never been away from home this long before."

Doc thought about it "Mrs. Stevens, I've never been asked to find a lost animal before. All I can promise you is that I'll try my best. I need a little information. What did the dog, ah, Scruffy, look like?"

"Here, I have a picture." The young woman rummaged through her purse and handed over a picture of the missing pet. Doc smiled at the image of the little dog; he was obviously a friendly little critter, one of those dogs that remain puppylike even in adulthood. His expression turned serious. "Mrs. Stevens, you have to take into consideration the possibility that Scruffy may be . . . well, things happen to dogs and cats, you know . . ."

Suddenly, the woman's expression turned into one of cold anger. "No." She stated flatly. "Don't tell me that."

Doc pursed his lips. A mental alarm had gone off. "Oh?"

Mrs. Stevens jumped to her feet and paced the floor. "He is not dead. He's not! My husband tried to tell me the same thing, but he doesn't know." She stopped and looked at Doc with disturbing intensity. "You have to find him. I'll pay anything."

Doc gently guided the woman to a chair. "I promise you I'll do what I can."

When Mrs. Stevens left, Doc called her husband at his office. "Hello?"

"Mr. Stevens, my name is Dr. Alain DeLyle. I'm a . . . a counselor. I'm working with your wife right now, and I have a few questions . . ."

The man inhaled sharply. "She got help? Oh my God, I'm so glad she got some help with this. She just can't let Scruffy go."

Doc made a note to the effect that there was, at least, an absent pet named Scruffy. Doc cleared his throat. "I understand that Scruffy is missing."

The man said in a quiet voice, "I guess you could say that. He's dead."

Doc rubbed the sides of his nose. "I was afraid of that. Are you sure?"

The man's voice clogged with emotion. "Yeah, I'm pretty sure . . . I found him myself. Poor little guy. Hit by a car outside our driveway. I took him to the vet but . . ." the man cleared his throat. "It was too late. He died on the table. Just licked my hand and looked at me like he was apologizing. Then, he was gone." Silence for a long, long moment.

Doc said, "I'm sorry, sir. Please accept my sympathies over your loss."

"I don't mean to bend your ear, we just were really attached to that little dog. A lot of people don't understand. They say, 'Oh, it was just a dog. You can always get another.' They . . . they just don't understand."

Doc said, "Scruffy was more than a pet, he was a family member. One of the children."

"Exactly. He was our child—we don't have any kids of our own. No two-legged ones anyway. Maybe it's harder for childless couples?"

"Perhaps," Doc said. "I wouldn't be surprised."

"I keep trying to get Sue to go to the vet with me. Scruff's there, in the freezer. I want to have a funeral for him, but Sue won't even speak about it."

Doc interrupted. "Have you thought about bringing the, ah, the body home and letting her see for herself?"

"I'm afraid of what might happen. Sue just won't accept that he's gone. She's combing the neighborhood, putting out fliers. She won't believe me that he's dead. She keeps saying Scruffy's 'missing.' Sue is very sensitive, Doctor, and I'm afraid the shock might put her over the edge. I'm glad she came to you, though. Can you help her?"

Doc knew that Mrs. Stevens's denial of Scruffy's death was unhealthy and unnatural. As long as she held out hope the dog was only missing, she would never release the grief from her heart. "I'll do what I can," he told the man. "I need to think about this." He made a few notes. "Mr. Stevens, one more question. What is your vet's name?"

It turned out that the veterinarian was one of Doc's clients. Doc drove over, the picture of Scruffy in his pocket. Dr. Spencer took Doc to the back room and let him look at Scruffy's remains. He carefully compared the sad little body to the photograph. There could be no doubt—it was Scruffy all right. He gently stroked the dog's body and shook his head. Scruffy's dog tag jingled. Doc lifted it and read: *My name is Scruffy. I live at . . .*

"What gives, Doc?" Dr. Spencer asked. "I didn't know you worked with animals."

Doc showed her the picture. "Mrs. Stevens came to me hoping I could help her find Scruffy. She's holding out hope that he will come back home. I just wanted to see for myself that the dog had passed away."

Dr. Spencer nodded. "Yes, it's not uncommon for people to go into denial over the death of a pet, but Mrs. Stevens has gone way overboard. What can we do to help?"

Doc looked at the body of Scruffy for a long time, thinking. He finally decided what to do. He touched Dr. Spencer's hand. "I need to ask a favor."

"Mrs. Stevens—Susan. I think that what we need to do is attempt to establish a psychic communication with Scruffy and try to get him to tell us where he is." He sat next to the young woman on the couch in his office. "It will require a great deal of concentration. You must be brave and determined."

She looked at Doc with flinty eyes. "Whatever it takes to get Scruffy back."

Doc nodded and held out his hands, palm up. They were obviously empty. "Give me your hands," he said. He gripped the woman's smaller hands in his. "We must not break contact, no matter what."

Doc spoke to her in his deep, hypnotic voice for a long time, urging her to relax, to concentrate on Scruffy, to remember how he felt, the sound of his bark. The smell of his fur and the way his tail wagged when he was happy. Mrs. Stevens smiled as she concentrated on these happy images.

"Now," Doc urged, gripping her hands tightly, "Send your mind out and find Scruffy. Go to him! Go!"

Doc watched the young woman's face as she went on her mental journey. Her expression went from quizzical, as she searched for her pet, to happiness as she found him. But then an expression of terrible grief overcast her features. Doc held her hands firmly. This was the moment of crisis; it had to be dealt with gently.

"No, no . . ." Mrs. Stevens moaned. "No, Scruffy . . . No . . ." Her eyes snapped open. "It isn't true! It's a lie!"

Doc gestured with his chin toward their linked hands.

Scruffy's collar was looped around the woman's wrist like a bracelet.

Doc wrote that he could *feel* the woman's grief boil up in her heart like a teakettle boiling over, and he held her tightly as she cried.

"I'm sorry, Scruffy, I'm so sorry!" she wailed.

"It's not your fault," he comforted her. "You couldn't do anything to prevent it."

"I'll never forgive myself! Never!"

Suddenly Doc had a flash of insight. *Uh oh*, he thought. *There's more to this than I realized.*

Doc handed Mrs. Stevens a handkerchief and waited until she could speak again. "What happened?" he asked.

Mrs. Stevens wiped her face with the handkerchief. "I was in a hurry," she moaned, "I was late for my club meeting." She turned the small collar around and around in her hands, the metal tags jingling. "I backed out of the driveway without looking. I felt a bump, but didn't think anything about it. When Ben . . . my husband . . . told me where he found Scruff, I couldn't . . . I didn't . . ." She grabbed Doc's arms so hard it left bruises for days afterward. *"I'll never forgive myself!"*

Doc held Mrs. Stevens for a moment, rocking her as if she were a small child. "Yes, you will, Susan. You'll have to forgive yourself, because it was just an accident, and no one is to blame. Scruffy doesn't blame you, nor does your husband. This," he touched the dog's collar that still dangled from Mrs. Stevens' wrist, "is a sign from Scruffy that he's still with you, in spirit, and that he loves you. He wants your memories of your time together to be happy ones." Doc rose from the couch and opened the door to his parlor, where Mr. Stevens was waiting. Tears coursed down the man's face. He had heard everything, and Doc stood aside so Mr. Stevens could come in to comfort his wife.

Doc wrote, "*The Stevens worked through their grief and gave Scruffy a wonderful funeral service. I felt a pang of guilt at using an old spiritualist's trick to sneak Scruffy's collar onto her wrist, but the 'manifestation' helped her release the grief that was poisoning her, and that's the important thing. Reality, no matter how painful, is preferable to madness. I gave the Stevens a copy of "The Rainbow Bridge." It seemed to help them realize that Scruffy had approached his journey's end, and that the end of that journey was just a transition, not a catastrophe.*"

"The Rainbow Bridge" is an anonymous poem based on an old Norse legend. I had a copy of it that Doc gave me the summer I spent with him. After reading about Scruffy I got it out and re-read it.

The Rainbow Bridge

Just this side of heaven is a place called The Rainbow Bridge.

When an animal who has been especially close to someone dies, that pet goes to the Rainbow Bridge. There are meadows and hills for all of our special friends so they can run and play together. There is plenty of food and water and sunshine, and our friends are warm and comfortable. Animals who were ill and old are restored to health and vigor; those who were hurt or maimed are made whole and strong again, just as we remember them from days and times gone by.

The animals are happy and content, except for one thing: they miss someone very special to them; the person they left behind. All of the animals run and play together, but the day comes when one suddenly stops and looks into the distance. His bright eyes are intent; his eager body quivers. Suddenly he begins to break away from the group, flying over the green grass, his legs carrying him faster and faster.

You have been spotted, and when you and your special friend finally meet, you cling together in joyous reunion, never to be parted again. Happy kisses rain upon your face; your hands again caress the beloved head, and you look once more into the trusting eyes of your pet, so long gone from your life but never absent from your heart.

Then you cross The Rainbow Bridge together . . .

Doc gave "The Rainbow Bridge" to me to read when I was thirteen. It didn't mean much to me at the time—but it does now. *Bon voyage*, Willie. See you later, buddy.

CHAPTER TWENTY-THREE

Into the Soft Darkness

DURING THE WEEKS AFTER WILLIE DIED I had trouble focusing on work. Intellectually, I realized the humane thing to do was to put him out of his misery. He no longer had a good life. However, my heart ached with guilt over killing my best friend. Realistically, we should have done it six to twelve months earlier, but it was so hard. I missed him.

But I pushed on. Some people think I push too hard—the term *workaholic* has more than once been used to describe me—but I remember what it was like when I first started performing. When I started performing for a living I barely made a living. The first year out I was married and living with my wife and her sister (who was still in high school) in a house in rural West Virginia that my mother-in-law owned. During those lean times we could afford to go out only once a week, and I bought my suits at second-hand stores. But I pushed and pushed, and I was doing much better now. I had my own house, wore Armani, and went out anytime I wanted.

But are you any happier? Doc's voice asked in my head.

I thought about it. Being a performer is an insecure livelihood. You don't know whether or not you'll be in demand next year, let alone next decade. You have to take the work while it's offered. That way you won't look back and say "Hey I turned down a hell of a lot of money in '01—I could sure use it now!" And, I suppose, money was a way I measured advancement and success. Nor was there anything wrong with having a good work ethic and a determination to take care of your clients, was there?

All that is true, the voice insisted. *But are you any happier?*

I had to admit that I wasn't. I was just as happy years ago making no money and going to the movies and the Shake Shoppe for a fish sandwich and a milk shake once a week with Charlotte. Maybe happier. It seemed like all I did these days was travel, attend business meetings, and do show after show. As if that wasn't enough, I had just signed a contract for my first book, *Ignite Your Intuition*, and was putting the finishing touches on the manuscript. I was so busy that I had shoe-horned the death and burial of Willie in between gigs, not even taking time out to pay proper respects. All this running around, and for what? If there was one message that came through loud and clear from Doc's teachings, it was that quality of life was the real measurement of success.

I needed to get away somewhere to decompress. I had west coast engagements in Seattle and San Francisco with a weekend off in between, so I decided to spend some time hiking on the Olympic Peninsula of Washington. I do my best thinking while walking, and I had a lot to think about. I brought several of Doc's notebooks with me, intending to study them each night before going to bed.

I stayed at Lake Quinault Lodge, a beautiful rustic resort nestled in the heart of the Olympic National Forest on the shores of a pristine mountain lake in North America's only temperate rain forest. With no phones or televisions in the rooms it was the perfect location for a weekend getaway.

As I pulled into the gravel parking area I noticed the lot was full of antique cars. Apparently a group of Model-T Ford aficionados were gathered at the lodge. I marveled at the large number of painstakingly restored antique cars lined up in the parking lot, travelers from another time. It was obvious that a lot of love and devotion went into those vehicles. One in particular stood out, black and sleek. I went over and touched it. *Doc used to drive one of those blindfolded*, I thought.

"Pretty, ain't she?" an elderly gentleman walked over and ran his hand lovingly down the glossy fender. "When I was a boy, this was the greatest car in the world."

Up close, I saw that the man was more than elderly, he was ancient. His face was as wrinkled as old leather, and his frail body reminded me of a box kite: a collection of sticks and thin fabric jumbled together. He was, without a doubt, the oldest human being I'd ever met. "Is this your car?" I asked him.

"Yup."

"She's a beauty. One of a kind."

He looked at me over his spectacles. "You here with the convention?"

"No, I'm just here to get in some hiking." I waved a hand at the dozens of cars in the parking lot. "I didn't know there were this many Model-T's in the world. Where did they all come from?"

He laughed and his eyes became just two more wrinkles in his crinkly face. "From all over, son. The convention's traveling from San Diego to Vancouver, and as we move up the coast more members join us. Me and my grandson picked up the caravan in our hometown, San Francisco. This was his idea—it's to celebrate my hundredth birthday."

"You're a hundred years old?"

"Yep," the old chap cackled. "Don't worry though, my grandson's doin' all the driving, I don't see as well as I used to." He turned his face, wrinkled but still boyish, toward me. "You travel much?"

I told him that most of my travel was work-related, but now and again—like right now—I got away for relaxation.

"What d'you do for your coffee and cakes?" he asked. "Salesman?"

"I'm a mentalist," I answered. "I read thoughts." I started to explain exactly what a mentalist was, but he nodded his head as though he already knew. I anticipated the most common response when I tell people what I do: "What am I thinking now?" But he surprised me.

"When I was a boy in San Francisco there was a feller who read minds. He was pretty good. You used to read about him in the papers a lot. He used to do horoscopes for people, read palms and such. My father knew his father. Pops said the guy's family was religious, and had disowned him."

I swear the hair on the back of my neck stood up. "What was his name?" I asked.

The old man rubbed the back of his head. "Hmm . . . the family's name was Green, I think. I don't quite remember the boy's name . . ."

"Alan!" I interrupted. "Was his name Alan Green?"

The old man looked astonished, then made his eyes disappear again as he gave a wide grin. "Now that was one hell of a good trick!" he exclaimed. "You read that right out of my mind."

"I'll be damned . . . Doc!"

The man, ignoring my outburst, continued. "The psychic fella disappeared from the Bay Area right after the big quake in '06. Some people thought he'd caused it somehow. You know how people are. Everyone missed him after he was gone . . . too late by then, though. They shoulda thought of that when they were chucking bricks through his parlor window. Green became somewhat of a legend in the neighborhood. After he left there was a lot of talk, you know. Speculation. Some folks said he went to the Four Corners area of Utah, Arizona, Colorado, and New Mexico to live with the Indians. One couple swore they saw him doin a mind-reading act in Los Angeles at the Orpheum Theater. Another guy said Green joined a Wild West show as a blindfolded trick shot artist. Then I heard he was serving time in prison for running a gambling operation. I guess nobody really knows what ever happened to him."

A man about my age called out the old man's name, and he waved. "Over here!" He turned to me, smiling again. "I'd like you to meet my grandson, uh . . ."

"Peter," the younger man said. "Pleased to meet you."

I introduced myself and the old man cackled again. "Memory sure is a funny thing. I can remember the distant past so clearly; it's yesterday I have trouble with."

"How come you remember so much about Alan Green?" I asked.

He blinked at me. "He was the fella who predicted the Great Quake. That's a hard thing to forget."

The younger man draped an affectionate arm around the old guy. "Time to go, Pappy, or they'll leave us behind." He nodded at me. "Nice to meet you, sir."

The old man, a relic from another age, held out his hand for me to shake. "Nice talking to you, young man. I hope you have a good time while you're here. That was a good trick you showed me, but I reckon a lot of people are named Alan. Take care now!"

The elderly fellow hurried off with his grandson to join the caravan, leaving me standing there with my mouth hanging open. A lot of people *are* named Alan, I thought. But how many of them were psychics living in San Francisco in the early 1900s? I shook my head, wondering if I'd imagined the whole thing.

"Have a good trip," I called after them as I started my hike. At the head of the trail is a plaque with a quote from Chief Seattle, the chief of the Suquamish Indians after whom the city of Seattle was named. The plaque read: *"This we know: the earth does not belong to man, man belongs to the earth. All things are connected like the blood that unites us all. Man did not weave the web of life, he is merely a strand in it. Whatever he does to the web, he does to himself."*

It was a bright, well-lit morning, and I remember a comment Doc made to me long ago, on Blennerhassett Island: *Like Lord Byron, I'm most religious on a sunshiny day.* As I walked, I considered Chief Seattle's quote. While the environmental message wasn't lost on me, what really got me thinking was the concept of the web of life. I thought about my dog, Willie. I guess even animals are part of the web, playing along the Rainbow Bridge while they waited for their human friends to join them. I also considered the coincidence of running into a hundred-year-old man who knew my great-uncle as a boy, as though Fate itself was conspiring to keep Doc in my mind.

Connections. Coincidences. The web. Was the universe so contrived, ticking away like clockwork?

It was incredible that I met a man who knew Doc when he was simply Alan Green, a naive young fortune-teller. It was even more incredible that the man had remembered Doc all these years. My great-uncle seemed to have left a lasting impression on everybody he met. Too bad more people didn't know about him.

I stopped dead in my tracks.

In my mind, the idea of a book took shape. It would be about the summer I spent with Doc. I even had a title for the book: *The Wizard's*

Legacy. I thought about Doc's notebooks, some of which were in my suitcase back at the lodge. I had plenty of material. I could write Doc's biography!

The idea of becoming a published author was exciting. *Ignite Your Intuition* would be out soon, and Doc's biography would make a great second book. As I thought about it, I realized that *Ignite Your Intuition* was largely an updating of some of the lessons Doc taught me. *The Wizard's Legacy* would be the perfect sequel!

By the time I finished the seven-mile trek, a rough outline had formed in my mind. I ran back to my lodge room to write it all out.

Doc would live again!

■ ■ ■

I was in Helena, Montana, appearing at Carroll College, when I received the bad news, and, like most bad news, it caught me completely unprepared. After my show I was relaxing in the lobby when my cell phone rang. "Hello?"

"Craig, it's Charlotte. I don't know how to tell you this . . ."

"What's wrong?" I braced myself. My first thought was that my mother had passed away. Mom had been in a nursing home for the past year and a half, in the final stages of Alzheimer's. We had all accepted the fact that she was going to die. In fact we prayed for it. I was prepared for the worst.

But the bad news wasn't about Mom. "Oh Craig, it's Bill. He's in the hospital."

"Bill? My *brother* Bill? Is he all right?"

"No. He's in critical condition."

I couldn't speak for a moment; I was absolutely stunned. "Was it a heart attack? A stroke?" It was my first reaction; Bill was overweight, and he smoked and drank.

"No," Charlotte said. "No one knows what happened. He was all right at work on Friday. Saturday, he came down with a fever and became delirious."

Bill, in critical condition? I couldn't believe it. He was only forty-seven years old. He'll bounce back, I thought. He'll recover.

I thought about my older brother, his kindness and love of life, his restless intellect. After spending a decade or so in the Marist Brothers teaching, Bill had left the order. By that time he had received his doctorate in psychology and became Dr. Karges. He worked a variety of jobs in the corporate sector and then went back into what he really loved—education—teaching and counseling at the prestigious Collegiate Institute in Manhattan. Bill lived in New York City most of his adult life. Three years ago he moved to the Charlotte, North Carolina, area to join the rest of the family (except for me; I stayed in Wheeling) taking a job as a teacher, head counselor, and assistant headmaster at a private school. He loved his work. His students loved him.

He'd get better. I was sure of it.

But the following day his condition hadn't improved. Charlotte stayed in touch with my father and my other brother, Brian, for updates. My "little" brother Brian was now a six-foot-one, two-hundred-ten-pound, thirty-eight-year-old man, with a wife and three beautiful children.

The next day I left from Montana to San Francisco for another corporate appearance. In Salt Lake City there was a long layover, and I took the opportunity to arrange a conference call with a client for an upcoming presentation. I was sitting at the airport, reading one of Doc's notebooks. I was bewildered by the immense amount of information the journals contained. How was I ever going to make a book out of all this? Unfortunately, writing a book isn't just a matter of sitting down and deciding to do so. Doc's journals were so full of information, and my memories of him spanned such a small portion of his life, that I didn't know where to begin.

My cell phone rang, interrupting my train of thought. I looked at my watch: ten o'clock. My client was calling right on time. I removed my day-timer and sat it in my lap on top of Doc's notebook. "Karges," I answered.

But it wasn't my client. It was Charlotte. "Bill is gone," she said. "I'm so sorry." It was August 24th, 1999, and he had apparently died the victim of bacterial meningitis.

Just then the call waiting tone on the phone went off. "Just a minute," I said automatically and switched the line over. With the horrible timing only possible during the worst moments of our lives, it was my client, ready to do business. Within a couple of seconds two of my client's associates joined the conference. An inner autopilot came on and I started to go through the motions of the conference call. I tried to speak, but my voice cracked. My client's voice seemed to come from a great distance. I took a deep breath, tried to gain control over my emotions. "I can do this," I told myself. When the client asked "What?" I realized I'd said it out loud.

"I'm sorry," I said. "I think we should do this another time. I just found out my brother died." My client, embarrassed, gave me her condolences. One by one, the others broke off the call. I switched back to Charlotte and we talked for a while. I can't really remember what we said. A single thought reverberated inside my skull, relentless and final: "Dead . . . dead . . . your Brother Bill is dead . . . dead . . ."

After we hung up I sat in the airport, running my hand through my hair. My chest felt like a metal band had encircled it, squeezing and twisting. "I can't take it, Doc," I whispered. "I just can't take it."

I glanced down at the notebook I'd been reading. One line jumped out at me, punctuated with a teardrop: "There is no complete forgetting, even in death. Death cancels everything but truth."

"What is the truth?" I whispered.

In my mind, Doc's voice—or was it Bill's?—answered, "The show must go on."

"Yeah," I said. "I suppose it must."

CHAPTER TWENTY-FOUR

Ashes to Ashes

MY FLIGHT ARRIVED ON TIME and I boarded the airplane mechanically, as I have done hundreds of times in the past. I took a troubled nap on the plane and before I knew it we were landing in San Francisco—the city where Doc was born. I'd never been so tired in my life.

In a few hours I was scheduled to appear at the Westin St. Francis, a legendary hotel with its share of ghost stories. After checking in, I left the hotel and strolled through a nearby park. The park was decorated with dramatically posed statues all along the path. I walked among the statues, trying not to think too much. I was so tired that the world around me seemed a bit fuzzy around the edges, out of synch and surreal. Suddenly I caught a blur of movement out of the corner of my eye. One of the statues was looking at me! I jumped as though I'd been tickled with an electric cattle prod. The statue rolled its eyes and muttered, "Cheer up buddy. It's not the end of the world." I rubbed my eyes and did a double take, but the statue had once again frozen into immobility.

For a moment I thought I had finally lost my mind. When the statue grinned at me I understood. These were "human statues," performance artists who wore body paint and stood absolutely motionless. The "statue" who had spoken winked at me. "Gotcha, didn't I?" I tossed a wadded twenty-dollar bill in his direction and he instantly came to life and snatched the cash from mid-air. "Thanks, buddy," he said, returning to his pose. I gave him a weak smile and moved on. It was a day completely divorced from reality, a day of living statues and a dead brother.

I walked for blocks and blocks, aimlessly. No real purpose or direction; I'd pop into a store, look around, and then hit the streets again. I remembered that Bill had loved San Francisco. He traveled to the city on numerous occasions to attend educational meetings and seminars. He had toyed with the idea of moving here a few times. In his opinion, San Francisco was the only city that could hold a candle to his beloved adopted home of New York.

Where are you now, Bill?

I'd been taught in church that when we die we go to a better place. I fervently wished my big brother Godspeed, but a part of me wondered if he could really hear me or if I was just talking to myself. The question of the afterlife has always split me into two opposing viewpoints. Part of me, the spiritual half, wants to believe that we go on. The other, more rational part, demands proof. I knew what I'd been taught in church. I'd heard what the spirit mediums on television said about life after death. I'd been reading Doc's notebooks for months, preparing to write his book, and even he was uncertain about what awaited us on the other side. What was the truth?

I stopped at the top of a hill, catching my breath. Stop it, I told myself. I was driving myself crazy worrying about questions I could never answer. Regardless of what happened to Bill's spirit, the rest of my family needed me—and I had a show to do. Now wasn't the time to lose it.

Returning to the hotel, I made my plans. I rescheduled my flight out for the next day to a red-eye that night, about an hour after my performance. My bags, packed and ready to go, were stashed in the hotel's ballroom during the show pending a quick getaway. I performed my show, thanked my client, picked up my bags, took the elevator down to the lobby, got in a cab, and headed for the airport to fly to Charlotte, North Carolina. With business out of the way I was finally free to go say good-bye to my brother.

On the plane, I caught a couple of hour's sleep and had an odd dream involving Bill. He was sitting in Doc's den smoking his pipe and playing cards with Doc and an old man whom I somehow knew was

God. As they played, Bill plied God with questions about the universe. Doc watched the debate, grinning, enjoying the conversation and a glass of Scotch. The plane landed and I awoke just as God was about to explain exactly *why* he gave us earlobes . . .

My younger brother, Brian, met me at the airport with his wife, Sandy, and their three children, Amanda, Brittany, and Christopher. We shook hands and embraced. Brian pounded me on the back. "It's good to see you, man. How are you doing?"

"I'm okay. You?"

He nodded. "It was a shock. None of us saw it coming. Dad's taking it pretty hard."

Brian drove me over to Dad's house, where I always stay when I'm in Charlotte. Punchy from shock and lack of sleep, I thought, "I wonder if I'll see Bill this trip?" Then I caught myself. Bill had been cremated; I'd never see him again.

Brian was right: Dad looked awful. We tried to comfort him. It was hard enough to lose a brother; we couldn't imagine how horrible it must have been to lose a child.

Later my wife, Charlotte, arrived via car with our dogs. After Willie's death I was reluctant to risk any more pets, but I was on the road a lot and didn't like the idea of leaving Charlotte at home by herself. Now we had two new additions to our family: Dolittle, a cairn terrier, and Dolittle's half brother, Connor P. McNasty. They swarmed over me, licking my face and generally letting me know they were glad to see me. Charlotte didn't say anything, but I could tell by the expression on her face that I must have looked exhausted.

We moved too fast to really think about our loss. There was a huge memorial service at the school where Bill was employed. Former students from New York flew in to pay their last respects. I was amazed at the number of people who loved my brother. He had quite an effect on many, many people. One phrase from the service particularly stuck in my mind: "Bill gave of his life so generously, to so many other people, that it cannot be truly said that he is gone. He lives on, in the hearts of those whom he taught and those whom he loved."

Before leaving North Carolina, I went with Charlotte and Brian's son, Christopher, to see Mom at the nursing home. When I saw her I thought my heart would break. She had deteriorated since the last time I'd visited her. Mom's condition had become so bad she was bedridden, curled in a fetal position and totally noncommunicative.

I reached over and took her thin, sticklike hand. "Hi, Mom, how are you feeling?" She just stared at the wall, unblinking.

Hospice was a blessing. Dad had tried to take care of Mom at home for almost two years, but it finally got to be too much for him. I remember visiting her in the Alzheimer's wing, where people wandered around aimlessly, speaking gibberish, or staring with dead eyes. It was horrible. My father was able to enroll her in the hospice program. They kept her pain to a minimum, and made her as comfortable as they could while we waited for her to die. We all prayed it would be soon. Alzheimer's is a vicious, terrible disease that destroys the family as much as the person with it. All we could do was watch in helpless frustration as the disease stole away our mother's life; stole her away from us.

During our visit, I held Mom's hand and talked to her, hoping that maybe some consciousness lurked beneath that staring, glassy-eyed exterior. However, there was no hint of awareness in her gaze. Mom lay motionless and unresponsive.

When it was time to leave, I bent down and stroked her silver hair, whispering in her ear, "I love you, Momma." She still didn't say anything, but as I lifted my head I thought I saw just the hint of a smile on her face. I looked at Charlotte. "Did you see that?"

Charlotte nodded and smiled through her tears. "I did. She smiled!" Christopher said he saw it, too.

The attending nurse was amazed. "What did you say to her? She's shown no recognition of anything for months."

I shook my head, unable to reply. Mom had said nothing, but at least I made her smile. This was to be the best memory I have of that time.

■ ■ ■

After "visiting" Mom, I flew to Nashville for another corporate appearance. I really didn't know what else to do. My head spun with questions. What dates do I cancel, how many do I cancel, how long should I be in mourning for my brother? I decided to push ahead.

I was booked literally every day, plus my work on Doc's project was causing me a lot of trouble. *Ignite Your Intuition* was structured as a series of lessons, sort of a workshop in book form, but I didn't want to take this approach with Doc's book. I wanted to bring him alive; make the reader feel like they knew Doc. I decided that under the circumstances I should suspend work on the book until I was able to devote more energy to it. Nor did I feel like performing, but people were counting on me and the show must go on, right?

To make matters worse, word had leaked out on the college circuit that my brother had died. People called and e-mailed Charlotte, asking about it. "It must be some kind of mistake," they said. "We knew his mother was sick, but his brother? What's that all about?" I told Charlotte to ask everyone not to talk to me about it. I was afraid I might crack. Terms from my college psychology classes flitted through my mind, words like *denial* and *avoidance*, but I didn't have time to deal with such issues. There was work to do; a living to make.

The next three weeks were a blur as I lost myself in the routine of traveling, performing, and traveling again. On September 15, I was in Nashville again. I had flown in from Toronto to do another corporate appearance. Ironically, I was returning from the show connected with the conference call I was on when I heard that Bill died. I was also scheduled to appear at a trade show in conjunction with my publisher to show off and hype *Ignite Your Intuition*. I arrived late that night in Nashville, picked up my rental car and drove to the hotel. I was painfully tired and looked forward to collapsing on the bed.

At the hotel, the clerk took my name, rummaged around the reservations, then looked back at me. I could tell by the look on his face that something had gone wrong. "What is it?" I asked.

"I'm sorry sir, it looks like someone accidentally gave your room away . . ."

"Can I get another one?"

"No, we're completely full."

I leaned against the counter, sighing. "Great. Just great."

The clerk was busily typing away on his terminal. "Don't worry, Mr. Karges, we'll find you another hotel. I'm terribly sorry for the mix-up. We'll pay for it." The clerk finally located another room for me, all the way across town, of course.

Naturally, I got lost while trying to find the hotel. After driving around for an hour asking directions, I finally stumbled across it by accident. I checked in, completely exhausted, went to my room and called Charlotte.

"How are you?" she asked.

"It's good to hear your voice," I told her. "I've had a hell of a day."

We talked for a while about small things, and I thought she sounded a little distant and tired. I attributed it to the recent strain we'd been under. Suddenly, her voice cracked. "Oh, Craig," she choked out.

"What is it?" I asked, gripping the receiver.

I heard her take a deep breath. "Craigy, your Mom died today. Her heart finally gave out."

I felt a totally indescribable sensation, of both relief and tremendous sorrow, like ice water and hot lava running together inside my heart. The waves of conflicting emotions literally paralyzed me.

Charlotte's voice broke through the wall of pain. "Are you okay, Honey? Are you going to be all right?"

I took a deep breath and said all the things you were supposed to say at such a time. "Yeah, I'll be fine. We were expecting it. It's a blessing. I'm glad she's out of her pain."

We talked for a while, then I hung up the phone and tried to get some sleep. My mind raced with thoughts. Mom died almost three weeks to the day of Bill's passing. I knew that Mom's passing was a blessing. She'd been in terrible pain and her mind was gone. What kind of life was it, I told myself, to lie in a bed, day in and out, with no mind left? I knew I should have been grateful that she was gone, just as I was when my beloved grandmother passed away in the mid-'80s, after a series of strokes left her helpless and ready to die. However, losing Bill and then Mom so quickly was just too much. Our little Karges clan of five people—Mom, Dad, Bill, Brian, and me—had taken a big hit in a three-week period.

As I stared at the ceiling tears rolled down my face, the hot kind, the ones that burn like molten wax. Before her illness Mom had been an active, social woman who loved to play bridge, loved to travel, and was a soft touch for stray animals. She always fed birds and couldn't walk past a dog without petting it and trying to feed it. Being Irish, she had a bit of a temper and was always up for a bit of verbal debate with Dad, Bill, or Brian. She and I hardly ever tangled. She loved life. Being bedridden and inactive for so long must have been really hard for her.

At least I know the last time I saw Mom I made her smile.

About 3:00 A.M. I finally rolled over and cried myself to sleep. I had a show to do the next afternoon and needed to rest up for it.

Some things in life seem beyond explanation. Losing Mom, Bill, and Willie so suddenly didn't allow me enough time to put my feelings into perspective. So, typically, I threw myself into my work, picking up *The Wizard's Legacy* once again.

One of Doc's notebooks begins, "Part of my job as a counselor is to help assure people that their departed loved ones are happy and healthy on the other side of life. The most tragic feeling is that of having left something important unsaid, and now it is too late to say it. Sometimes I act as the messenger or the mediator between the two worlds, ensuring a closure to whatever issues remain unresolved."

But who counsels the counselor? In early 1960 Doc received a tragic blow. One morning a letter from a distant cousin appeared in his mailbox. He was surprised, to say the least, since most of his family had severed all ties with him decades ago. Sensing that the letter must contain news of some importance, Doc retired to his den and fortified himself with a glass of his favorite tonic.

The letter was brief and brutally to the point:

> "Alan, I hope this letter finds you in good health and prosperous circumstances. I regret to inform you of the sad news that your mother has passed away following a lingering illness. Please accept our condolences. Enclosed you will find a picture that your mother wanted you to have. Out of respect for her, my brothers and I went to a great deal of trouble to locate you and see that you received it per her last request. Please make no efforts to contact me or any other member of the family. This is a bad time for us and we do not wish further aggravation. Once again, please accept our sympathy over your recent bereavement."

The signature was a name Doc barely remembered. In the envelope was a picture of Doc—Alan—as a child of twelve, holding his mother's hand as they posed for the photographer. In the picture, his mother gazed at him lovingly. His fingers lingered across the photograph. Doc's mother must have kept this picture with her for almost sixty years. On the back was a single sentence in his mother's hand: "Alan, remember that I'll always love you."

Sharp agony seared though Doc's heart; grief for the lost decades apart from his mother; grief for the destiny that gave him gifts and talents that, while enabling him to help people find peace in their lives, had forever isolated him from his own family; grief that he couldn't even return to his home to pay last respects to the mother who had given birth to him. And what must it have been like for her, he thought, estranged from a son whom she never stopped loving? "Why do we work so hard to make each other and ourselves so unhappy?" he lamented in his journal. "Is it so hard to simply accept each other for what we are?"

Doc had helped hundreds of people come to terms with his or her own bereavement, and now he faced the same agony himself. "Physician, heal thyself," a hollow voice echoed in his head.

But how?

Doc smiled. A distant memory floated to the surface of his mind, summoned by the faded, yellowing photograph. His mother knew how to heal the old wound—that's why she sent him that particular photo. It was a final act of love for her absent son; a reminder of a lesson he had learned from her a long, long time ago.

I remember seeing the framed picture she'd sent him on the mantelpiece in his den the summer I studied with him. "That picture serves to remind me of a lesson I had forgotten, Craig," he told me when I asked about it. "My mother once told me that each moment of a person's life exists forever, an endless series of frozen moments exactly like that photograph. In one sense my mother and I are still holding hands and smiling at each other, just as we are in that photo, and we always will be. No one can ever take that moment away from us. Nothing ever ends, Craig, never forget that. Nothing ever ends."

We had a joint ceremony for Bill and Mom in Wheeling a month later, in October. Just as Bill had been, Mom was cremated. I flew every-

Craig Karges returns to the grave of his great-uncle, Alain "Doc" DeLyle, for inspiration. Doc's headstone can be found at Mount Calvary Cemetery, Wheeling, West Virginia. —Photo by Mark Campbell, Prestige Photography, Wheeling, West Virginia.

one up for the ceremony—Dad, Brian, Brian's wife and children. It was a beautiful sunny day when we buried the cremains in Mount Calvary Cemetery, a stark contrast to the cold sleety day of Doc's burial almost twenty-eight years ago. A cool breeze blew varicolored leaves around the tombstones.

After the ceremony Charlotte drove the family back to our house. I stayed behind, intending to visit Doc's grave, which was just a stone's throw from Mom's and Bill's. I remembered what Doc said when I asked him if he could really talk to spirits. "It's easy to talk to spirits," he had said. "The trick is getting them to answer back."

I'd saved a flower from Mom's grave to place on Doc's. The headstone was just as I remembered, although it was weathered a bit and speckled with moss, *Alain DeLyle 1887–1971.*

"Are you there, Doc?" I said quietly. "Is there something you want to tell me?"

No answer. I wondered if he was lonely without Aunt May. She had been buried in California with her brother after passing away in 1986 at the age of eighty-nine. Her spirit and sense of humor had always been a source of inspiration to me. She had been my last link to Doc and I missed her. It seemed sad that two people, so much in love, were now separated in death. But then again, maybe time and distance didn't mean anything in the spirit realm. I felt certain that if there was an afterlife Doc and May were walking through it hand in hand.

I was alone in the graveyard, my only companion the wind. It was calm and peaceful. The autumn leaves whispered and chuckled like spirits trying to be politely unobtrusive as they spoke among themselves. I bent down to pull away some weeds that obscured the tombstone, thinking about all the work that needed to get done on Doc's book. Suddenly, I shivered; I had the creepy, persistent feeling that someone was watching me.

Still kneeling, I turned my head and saw a small dog sitting in the long shadows near the bushes looking at me. Its gaze wasn't unfriendly, just curious. I stared at the dog and it stared back. Then the creepy feeling came over me again and I felt the hair rise on the back of my arms. Something about the dog's black-and-gold color, the tilt of his head, reminded me of Willie. In fact, the little dog looked a *lot* like Willie . . .

"Here boy." I extended my hand. "Come here, boy."

The black-and-gold dog gave a single bark and disappeared into the bushes.

CHAPTER TWENTY-FIVE

Madame Bernice
Deals the Cards

BETWEEN MY DEMANDING PERFORMING SCHEDULE and my recent losses, I'd almost forgotten about Doc's book. But Doc wasn't through with me. He appeared again, if a bit indirectly.

It began when our friends Bill and Bonnie Poole invited us to a party New Year's Eve—the day before the Great Millennium. I'd received some lucrative offers to appear professionally that evening, but I declined. I rarely work on New Year's Eve. I have a firm belief that mentalism and alcohol don't mix! Inebriated audiences have trouble maintaining the concentration necessary for a successful performance; plus, they can be unbearably obnoxious.

The Poole residence was in the fashionable Shadyside district of Pittsburgh, an 1865 Gothic Revival home that they have completely renovated and that has been designated as an historic home by the Pittsburgh History and Landmark Foundation. It was quite a party. All the guests in formal wear, tables groaning under the burden of foods of all variety, a live swing band. One of the activities was a fortune-teller. A long line of partygoers in various stages of sobriety waited to have their palms or cards read. The fortune-teller seemed to be doing a brisk business; most returned from her table quite impressed.

Charlotte and Bonnie nudged me. "Go over there and see what she says," Charlotte said.

"She's really very good," Bonnie added.

I know when I'm outnumbered. The line was long, but I waited patiently for my reading. Finally, it was my turn and I sat down at the table. The fortune-teller, a middle-aged woman with dark hair and eyes, really looked the part. She even wore a gypsy robe and a turban! A placard read MADAME BERNICE: PAST PRESENT AND FUTURE REVEALED.

"Sit down, dear," she said. "What's your name?"

"Craig," I told her.

She rubbed her hands together, smiling. "Hmm . . . Craig, from the Gaelic word for 'rock' or 'crag.' A stony name. Are you a stony man?"

I shrugged. "I don't know. You tell me."

She shuffled her tarot cards and dealt them in a row. "I see you have a lot of ambition. You'll go far. You have some creative ability that you haven't completely developed yet. Sometimes you overextend yourself. I see you come from a conservative family, and that your family is scattered around the country. You'll probably make a great amount of money doing what you enjoy. I see travel, several short journeys, and at least one over water. You probably enjoy flying a lot."

So far it was a pretty ho-hum reading. Fortune-cookie stuff. Doc wouldn't have been impressed.

Suddenly she looked up from the cards. "You're not really buying this, are you, Man-Who's-Named-After-a-Stone?"

I was taken aback by the abruptness of the question. "Oh, no," I said, trying to be nice. "It's really good. Keep going."

But something in the tone of my voice, or something in my eyes, told her the truth. She smiled; her dark eyes glittered with amusement. "You see, when I do these parties I have to keep things sweet and nice," she explained. "My livelihood depends on me being lighthearted and nonthreatening. If I told most of these people what I really see, I'd scare them to death."

"Really?" I said.

"Oh, yes."

"So what do you really see for me?" I asked, not expecting much.

She looked at me for a moment with those disquieting eyes. "Are you sure?"

"I can handle it."

Madame Bernice redealt the cards and looked them over. "1999, for you, has been a year of significant personal loss. You've had to deal with letting go again and again. I see a great struggle within you as you try to understand the interplay of love and death. I see an older male who has passed to the other side. His spirit is trying to contact you. Do not turn away from him. He's like a father-figure, or perhaps an uncle. The presence of The Hierophant tells me he's definitely a mentor." She pointed to a card. "This card refers to a job left undone, work unfinished. Something probably connected to this male spirit."

Now I was interested. Could she be talking about Doc's book?

Madame Bernice turned over another card. "The Wheel of Fortune says that the time to complete this work is approaching. Putting it simply, he wants you to quit dilly-dallying and get started on it. Don't worry; someone will appear to help you." A serious expression crossed her face. "He's also saying that you must not let your fear of death keep you from your work. Have faith in the Magic, he says. That's all I see," she said. Madame Bernice began packing her cards and candles away. "I have to run now, Rocky. Got another gig on the other side of town. This is the busiest night of the year for me. Everyone wants to know what the New Millennium will bring! Ta-ta." With a swirl of gaily-colored skirts, she was gone. I sat there for a long time, with a lot to think about.

A hand landed on my shoulder and I jumped. "How was it?" Bill Poole asked. "Was she any good?"

I stood up. "Yeah, she was great."

Bonnie came over. "I told you so!"

"Where did you find her?" I asked. I thought I might like to see her again in the future.

Bill chuckled. "Bonnie found her. I think in the phone book."

Bonnie looked puzzled. "No dear. You found her, remember? You were in charge of the entertainment."

"It wasn't me. It had to be you."

"No . . . I'd remember it if I'd hired her . . ."

Bill and Bonnie had an amusing argument before it became clear that neither one of them had booked the fortune-teller. We all looked at each other, shrugging. Strange!

Unbeknownst to me, the final pieces were clicking into place. A couple of months after the Pooles' party I was driving late at night through the Southeast. I had a show at the University of Tennessee in Knoxville the following afternoon and I wanted to get there in time to grab a full night's sleep. I encountered a patch of heavy fog on the highway. The fog was so dense in places I literally couldn't see three feet in front of my hood. It was as though the entire world had vanished, leaving me alone in a cloud of white mist. I slowed down to avoid rear-ending any car that might be in front of me. I wasn't too worried, though. I was less than an hour away from Knoxville and making good time.

Suddenly the fog lifted just enough for me to see a lone figure standing on the side of the road, an old man dressed in black. His face was very pale. My breath caught in my throat. *God*, I thought, *that old guy better get off the road. Someone's going to hit him!* I saw him for just an instant, a photo-flash of recognition, and then I drove past him.

Doc? I thought.

I looked in the rear-view mirror, but the fog had closed back again like a thick curtain. I was uncomfortably reminded of the dream I had the night Doc died, where I saw him disappear into a similar fog. Don't be silly, I reminded myself. The old man wasn't Doc. He couldn't have been Doc. I'd just imagined that he looked like him.

Nevertheless, a feeling of apprehension came over me. The thought entered my mind that I should pull off the highway and stop for the night. Something just didn't feel right. I pulled off the next exit and checked into a hotel in Dayton, Tennessee. I was extremely tired and fell asleep almost immediately.

The next morning I awoke refreshed and went down into the hotel restaurant, feeling a little foolish for overreacting the night before. The fog had lifted and a beautiful day greeted me. Over a cup of coffee I picked up the newspaper and saw the headline: *Forty Car Pileup on I-75 Kills 25.*

Stunned, I read the details. Apparently, a tractor-trailer had collided with a slow-moving car just a couple of miles from the exit where I had decided to pull off for the night. Because of the extremely poor visibility, the initial wreck caused a chain reaction involving forty vehicles. Thirty-four people were injured and twenty-five died in the tragic accident. If I hadn't pulled off when I did, I might have been one of them.

I didn't know what to think. Was that solitary figure standing on the shoulder of that foggy Tennessee highway Doc, trying to catch my attention and warn me? Or was it just some poor old man wandering around on the side of the road?

It's easy to explain away such incidents as coincidence or imagination, but by now even my skeptical nature began to crumble. It seemed that a powerful synchronicity was at work; a sequence of events that began the day I found Doc's notebook in my briefcase on the plane and continuing to the present, one event leading to the next like dominos tumbling toward some inevitable final goal. I decided to quit trying to explain the series of coincidences and just accept them. After all, we don't always have to know *why* something works in order to accept that it does. At least, that's what Doc always said. The older I get, the more I'm beginning to think he was probably right.

My show at the University of Tennessee was well attended and went smoothly, considering I was still a little shaken up over the previous night's near-miss. The material played strongly; people applauded and cheered in all the right places. There was only one bad moment. A feature of my show is a version of the table-tilting phenomenon Doc had taught me. An audience member and I lightly rest our fingertips on a table and concentrate. Soon, the table begins to vibrate and move around the stage, finally floating several feet above the floor while the spectator and I are still touching it. I've performed the stunt for years with nary a mishap. That afternoon, while the table was in mid-air, it gave such a violent jump that I almost lost control of it. Had that happened, it could have conceivably flown out into the audience and landed in somebody's lap! I chalked it up to residual jitters from last night's almost-accident.

Or perhaps it was another sign, an attempt to get my attention. After the show, I was autographing copies of *Ignite Your Intuition* when

I noticed a large, burly bear of a man standing off to the side. Something about his eyes reminded me of Doc—but by now, Doc's presence was so pervasive that practically everything reminded me of him! The man was obviously waiting for the crowd to subside to talk to me. Probably another performer, I decided. After I had autographed the last book he walked over.

"Good show," the man said, shaking my hand. He proceeded to give me a detailed analysis of my performance, exhibiting a deep knowledge of the techniques and history of mentalism. One remark he made especially caught my attention. "It looked for a moment like your table was about to take off on its own. But then again, this theater is loaded with spirits—like most old theaters."

I was fascinated by his comments. I wondered if perhaps another piece of the puzzle had fallen into place. "What's your name?" I asked.

"Jon Saint-Germain," he said. "Pleased to meet you."

I discovered in Jon a passion for magic and mentalism rivaling my own. Coming from a family of psychics, Jon was a walking encyclopedia of mystical and supernatural phenomena. He'd retired from the engineering field to investigate hauntings, perform on the stage, and work as a psychic reader. He'd also authored a number of books on magic, mentalism, and psychic phenomena. In fact, I'd read some of Jon's books without ever having met him. Now I had a face to go with the name.

We continued our conversation over dinner, and Jon told me about a screenplay he was working on about psychic phenomena. One of the characters reminded me of Doc! As we talked about the screenplay an idea started to form in my mind. I mentioned the problems I was having getting started on the book. I told Jon about the summer I'd spent as Doc's apprentice, and the series of events that convinced me that Doc *wanted* the book written. "I want to concentrate on the lessons Doc taught me and the people who came to see him," I said, "but I don't want it to be a series of lectures. I'm beginning to think it should be presented as a fictionalized work, like a historical novel."

Jon thought about it. "The problem is trying to weave together three different story lines." He ticked off the points on his fingers. "First, your summer with Doc; second, Doc's distant past as revealed in his notebooks; and third, how all this is meaningful to you today. You have so much material that trying to organize it is overwhelming. I suggest you concentrate on your summer with Doc—sort of a coming-of-age story, and then synopsize his notebooks in a separate section. Deliver the facts, but use the techniques of narrative fiction to tell a good story."

But I had another idea. "Why don't you help me write it?"

"Ehh . . . how much money are we talking about?" Jon is a mystic, a spiritual man—but he's also practical. We struck a bargain on the spot. The final piece was in place. Doc's book was on its way to becoming a reality.

With that out of the way, there still remained one piece of unfinished business I had to attend to. I only hoped it wasn't too late.

CHAPTER TWENTY-SIX

The Victoria Revisited

A LONG TIME AGO I had promised Doc that I would one day perform my show at the Victoria Theater. It seemed unlikely that it would ever happen. At the time of Doc's death the Old Vic was in an advanced state of decrepitude, slated for condemnation and, everyone assumed, demolition. But the old girl wasn't ready for retirement. Apparently she had a guardian spirit watching over her.

A local real estate developer bought the Old Vic, along with approximately half of Wheeling. The developer was an admirer of Donald Trump. He was a visionary of sorts, and rumor had it that he had a particular vision calculated to bring fame to the city, hopefully attracting droves of tourists. According to the rumor, he planned to put a light display in the shape of a large cowboy boot on top of one of his downtown buildings. Beneath the boot would be a pile of manure, carefully crafted in lights. On New Year's Eve at the stroke of midnight, the boot would come down and land in the manure, a wacky parody of the Times Square ball drop. Thankfully, the project was never completed.

Eventually the developer leased the Victoria to a church, and thus commenced the period of the Old Vic's comeback. The church group was heavily into the performing arts, incorporating dance, music, and drama into their services. Craftsmen from the church's congregation donated their time to completely restore the old building. They scraped the paint down to the original colors, then repainted everything to match perfectly. It was truly a labor of love. The workmen tapped into the spirit of the antique building. They refurbished the balcony and re-upholstered all the seats—all in return for not paying rent. The workmen obviously took a shine to the old theater and did an incredible job, and when they were finished I could only wish that Doc had been alive to see it.

At this point the history of the Vic gets a little strange, but I swear it's true. Towards the end of the church's lease a chiropractor who moonlighted as an Elvis impersonator wanted a permanent theater for his show. He approached the owner, bought the church out of its lease and set up shop, performing his tribute to the King every Friday night. "Elvis" also added state-of-the-art sound and lights, and the transformation of the Old Vic was complete. She had risen, Phoenix-like, from the ashes of neglect.

Now the stage was set, so to speak, for me to enter the picture. In January 2000 a television executive approached me with the idea of taping a special. Location, it seemed, was an important consideration. The network wanted a classy, elegant place with character that would look good on television. Remembering the promise I'd made to Doc when I was thirteen years old, I immediately thought of the Victoria. The executive and I scouted the location, escorted by the chiropractic "Elvis."

I was amazed at the beauty of the old theater. It looked even better than I had imagined in the dream Doc inspired, graceful and gleaming, spacious and, well—proud of itself. Buildings are like people and pets in one respect, I thought. All respond joyously to a loving touch.

We walked onto the stage and looked out over the rows and rows of seats.

"Check out those lights," Elvis pointed to a vast array of suspended lights with a hand that twinkled with gold rings. "Really perks up the show, adds that Vegas glitter, if you know what I mean."

"This is a great theater," the executive observed.

"Yeah it is." Elvis pulled out a comb and ran it through his ebony hair. "You sure you don't want Elvis on your show? I think an appearance by the King would really class things up." Elvis went into his pitch: "You gotta catch the show sometime. The best in country-western music, slapstick comedy, and me. A different show every Friday night."

"No, uh, I'm afraid it really wouldn't fit the theme of the program," the executive said.

"Too bad," Elvis said. "I'm waiting for my big break. You know, take it to the next level."

As we left the Victoria, Elvis hit the main switch and all the lights went out. All, that is, except one lone light, nothing more than a bulb attached to an upright stand, that sat at center stage. The television executive pointed to the solitary light. "What about that one? Are you leaving it on?"

Elvis laughed. "That's the Ghostlight," he said. "It stays on."

I turned around, interested. "What's a Ghostlight?"

Elvis smoothed a hand through his hair, straightening a stray lock. "You never, ever let a theater go dark, son. You always leave a light on in an empty theater to keep the ghosts away. Otherwise, bad things can happen during the show, accidents and mishaps. Know what I mean? And if there's already a resident ghost and it's a friendly one, the light keeps him company." He looked at us through his aviator glasses. "Of course, the Victoria was dark for a long time. Who knows what spooks may have taken up residence? Maybe the King himself! See y'all later. Call me if you want to do business." Elvis locked up the theater and went over to a big white Cadillac, tossing his keys in the air and singing "We-hell, that's uh ONE for uh the money . . . TWO for the show . . ."

"What do you think?" I asked the executive.

"About Elvis? He's great."

"No, the theater."

"Oh that. I think it's perfect." So we rented the Victoria for the shoot and scheduled it for sometime in April. With *The Wizard's Legacy* taking shape I decided to present the show as a tribute to Doc DeLyle, and even work a few spooky effects into the presentation. I smiled at the thought; Doc would have loved it.

259

■ ■ ■

April 6th, 2000.

Every arrangement had been taken care of, the film crew was in place, and the house was filled to capacity. All that remained was to do the show.

I sat in the dressing room collecting my thoughts, possibly, I imagined, the same way Doc used to prepare himself before showtime in the old days when he packed the Victoria time and again. I reminisced about the summer I'd spent with Doc and how much I'd learned from him in that short time. It occurred to me that I was still learning from him, as I applied his lessons to my own life. And perhaps, I was ready to admit, he still made his presence known to me in subtle ways.

Wherever you are, Doc, I hope you can see me performing in your favorite theater tonight.

There was a brisk rap at my door. "Showtime, Mr. Karges."

I was ready. I walked onto the stage to keep the promise I had made to Doc so many years ago.

It was a night I'll never forget; the culmination of every lesson Doc had taught me. The combination of the beautiful Victoria and the excitement of a television shoot resulted in a very enthusiastic crowd. The show opened in the lobby of the Old Vic, where I related some of the history of the theater to an audience volunteer named Becky. I talked for a little while about Alain DeLyle, mentioning that he had performed in the Victoria Theater many times during the '20s and '30s. "Tonight," I told the viewing audience, "I'm going to try to coax him out of retirement. The truly extraordinary thing about this is that he's been dead for almost twenty-nine years!"

I performed the usual staples of my act: sightless vision, where my eyes are sealed shut with tape, my head wrapped in cloth and then I "read" the serial number from a borrowed piece of currency with my fingertips (I thought that I'd come a long way from the time when I'd stumbled around Doc's kitchen, trying to make tea with a bandana wrapped around my face); the dancing table—this time it remained under perfect control—and the Question and Answer Act, where I told complete strangers their birth dates and other personal information. I wasn't as dramatic as Yandee had been, but the audience seemed to love it.

In memory of Doc, I incorporated several of his original effects and props into my performance. Jill, a volunteer from the audience, randomly selected a page from one of Doc's favorite books—a treatise on fortune-telling with cards printed in 1933—and then held the book firmly between her hands. Next, I introduced an empty picture frame and placed it in full view. "Everyone concentrate on the book, please," I requested. When the volunteer opened the book, she discovered the selected page was missing! I gestured toward the picture frame; there was a flash of fire, and the missing page appeared in the frame. A little magicky, Doc might have said, but the audience ate it up.

To end the show, I used the Dunninger challenge box that Doc had given to me in 1971. Before the show, audience volunteer Becky had selected a word from my book *Ignite Your Intuition*, and in absolute secrecy wrote the word on a piece of paper and sealed it in an envelope. Next she placed the envelope in the book and wrapped the whole package with several rubber bands. She held on to the book and envelope throughout the show, never allowing anybody near the package nor revealing her secret word to anyone.

Next, two more volunteers—Chuck and Jennifer—came on stage to act as a committee. I teased the audience by explaining there was one other committee member, my late uncle! I gave a brief discussion of the challenge box, explaining that it was invented by the skeptical mentalist Dunninger, who didn't believe anyone could make the pencil write. "My uncle, however, believed otherwise, although he could never do it himself."

Chuck, Jennifer, and Becky initialed a single white index card and then placed it inside the box. From the top of the box dangled a pencil, just touching the card's surface. I placed a chair next to the table to make Doc comfortable in case he decided to arrive. After all, if he were alive today, he'd be well over a hundred years old.

We all stood away from the table and I turned to address the audience. "My uncle never got a chance to see me perform. He passed away before I began actively performing. Hopefully, he will see me tonight." I raised my hands and a hush descended upon the theater.

"Uncle Alain . . . hopefully you are with me here tonight . . . Uncle Alain, I'd like you to come back to the Victoria one last time . . . Come back, be with us one last time . . . Uncle Alain, if you can, please come back. Please show us a sign . . ." Long moments stretched out. Nothing happened. Chuck and Jennifer shuffled their feet nervously. Then the table began vibrating. Before long, the pencil in the box was scribbling furiously. Chuck slowly backed away from the vibrating box, and the audience laughed.

The pencil's frenetic movement ceased. I asked Chuck to remove the index card. "Is there anything written on it?" I asked.

Chuck cleared his throat. "The word 'opposite' and the numbers 90 and 91." Becky unwrapped the rubber bands from the book, tore open the envelope and verified that her word was indeed "opposite." Furthermore, the envelope had been placed between pages 90 and 91! The audience erupted into enthusiastic applause.

I thanked the volunteers and sent them back to their seats. When the applause subsided I turned toward the chair. "Uncle Alain, thank you for coming back to the Victoria. You're free to go now." The chair folded and collapsed to the stage. Needless to say, the audience gave a collective gasp of astonishment before exploding into applause.

It was a great night, not just for me, but for the memory of Doc DeLyle. None of the spooky effects I presented that night were really caused by spirits, of course, but I knew somehow that Doc was there watching, and that he approved.

After the show everyone prepared to go to Bugsy's, my favorite restaurant at the time, for the wrap-up party. I retired to my dressing room. "I'll be along in a few minutes," I told Charlotte. "I want to change my clothes." This wasn't entirely true; I needed a little time to decompress from the show and to spend some time alone to think about Doc. I truly wished he had been alive to see the show. And how I longed for Mom and Bill to have been there this special night.

I sighed. It was the one sad aspect of an otherwise thrilling experience. Maybe they did see it, from wherever they were now. I wished I knew.

■ ■ ■

As soon as I changed into my "civvies" there was a knock at my door. I looked at my watch, puzzled; by now everyone should have left the theater for the wrap-up party. "Come in," I called out.

A thin, elderly man wearing a clerical collar entered, peering into the room over his glasses. "Mr. Karges?"

I stood up to greet my visitor. "Yes, I'm Craig Karges."

The elderly gentleman held out his hand. "I don't know if you remember me. It's been a long time. My name is Brother Carl Simon . . ."

I searched my memory, then the light came on. I took a good look at the elderly gentleman's face, a face I hadn't seen in a long time. "Yes! I remember you. You presided over my great-uncle's funeral. Come in, have a seat. What can I do for you?"

Brother Carl made his way into the small room and sat on the small sofa in the corner. "Mr. Karges, I'm here on an errand; one that's long overdue. You see, before your great-uncle Dr. DeLyle passed into spirit, he left certain instructions with me. In particular, he left me a letter I was to deliver to you on the evening of your performance at the Victoria Theater . . ."

"A letter? For me? From Doc?"

"Yes, and about damned time." Brother Carl's eyebrows came together in a frown. "My instructions were to hold the letter until the night of your first show at the Old Vic and to deliver it to you at the successful completion of your first show here. I was beginning to give up on you. What took you so damned long?"

I gestured with my hands, temporarily at a loss for words. "I . . . I don't know." I shook my head and shrugged.

Brother Carl's face broke into an engaging grin. "Doc was right about you—sometimes you take things too seriously." He reached into the breast pocket of his jacket and pulled out a faded envelope. "All that matters is that you made it. Who cares how long it took? All the experts tell us time is just an illusion, so what does it matter? Here you go, son." Brother Carl handed me the envelope. I took it gingerly; almost afraid the old document would crumble to pieces at my touch.

Brother Carl rose to his feet and shook my hand. "I watched your show, Mr. Karges—Craig. You did well. I'm sure Doc was proud of you. See you." And just like that he was gone.

"See you," I said absently, turning the envelope over in my hands. My name was scrawled on the front of the envelope in Doc's handwriting. A sensation of unreality swept over me, and for a moment all I could do was sit and stare at the envelope. I imagined Doc, knowing that his time was short, writing this letter and trusting that it would find its way to me at the appropriate time. Nothing happens by accident, I thought; everything has its place in the universe. Life, death, life-after-death, a cycle of birth and rebirth, all part of the rhythm of the dance and the web of life. I thought about the incredible chain of coincidences that first reintroduced me to Doc's notebooks, led me to write a book about him, and finally brought me to the Old Vic to honor Doc with a televised performance.

Let's see what the old Wizard had to say.

I began to open the letter but a sudden impulse stopped me. No, not here in the dressing room, an inner voice prompted. There was a more appropriate place for Doc's final message. I grinned. The old Wizard still craved the spotlight, even in death!

I walked out onto the stage of the Old Vic, footsteps echoing through the empty theater. The only illumination came from the Ghostlight, shining center stage. I looked out upon the rows and rows of empty seats. It was kind of sad; the old theater looked abandoned. I broke the seal of the envelope and removed the letter. Of course it was on Doc's trademark magenta stationary.

> Dear Craig,
>
> I hope this letter finds you well and happy, assuming it finds you at all! You've accomplished much in your life so far, and although your happiness has been tempered with loss and disappointment, I'm proud to see that you continue to push on. At times you may feel you're not progressing as fast as you want; that you're running out of time. Don't worry. All good things take time and you have plenty of it left.

I felt a chill run down my spine as I continued:

I'm glad you took care of your education before embarking into show business. After all, if you hadn't gone to college you never would have met the love of your life, eh? By now you've learned the meaning of loss; you've learned that nothing is forever, that life is a temporary, ephemeral thing; nothing more than sandcastles on the beach. All we have are brief moments on the shore before the tide comes in and washes us away. The name of that tide is Time; and the ocean is called Eternity. But do not think for a moment that Death is the end of life—far from it. Death transforms us into the pure energy of Life Itself, the energy that is Light and Vitality: the Light that allows your physical eyes to see; the Light that allows your mind to think; the Light that allows your spirit to soar above the clouds!

Think of death as stepping into a better-lit room.

Sorry for the sermon, but I knew you'd be disappointed if I didn't lay a few heavy insights on you right off the bat. So much for the metaphysics; now let's get down to business.

Your life is rich and full. You've met and married your soulmate, made a great success in your chosen field. Probably no children of your own, but like May and I, you have your pets. Your brother Brian became a man of great heart, a wonderful father. Brian always did things in threes; the number three rules his life, so I think he'll probably have three children. Your older brother Bill, sadly, is destined to have a short but intense life. A flame that burns as intently as his cannot burn long. However, he'll positively touch a great many people before he goes.

You've traveled the world, seen wondrous sights. You should be happy. Are you?

Perhaps the nagging you have felt in your heart is unfinished business. There is a promise you made long ago, in the shell of a once great theater. Have you kept this promise? Or has this unfulfilled promise stood in the way of you and the rest of your life? If you're reading this letter, you've kept that promise. The Victoria is a magical place, Craig. I knew that as soon as my foot crossed its threshold. Expect magic here and it will happen.

I never told you, but I think you knew. I love you, son. If May and I had been blessed with children we could have asked for none better. You kept me company in my old age, you listened as I rambled on, and you were my friend. For that I thank you. I knew the day we first met that the spark of Magic burned within you. Some people approach conjuring as a hobby, and a damn good one it is. But for some of us, either cursed or blessed (I still do not know which) who are bitten by the bug, Magic becomes an obsession; a thirst that is never sated. Magic is more addictive than any drug crafted by the hand of man; smokier than the finest Scotch. You share that magnificent fever, and I hope it has been as much fun for you as it has been for me. No regrets son. If I had it to do over again I wouldn't change a thing. What an adventure it's been!

But as I stand here on the edge of an even greater adventure I have a few predictions for you, if you'll bear with me. You'll continue to be successful. You inherited your father's work ethic and will be good at whatever you turn your hand to. Your restless mind will make you seek a myriad of new experiences. I see that you have several books in you, some of which you'll write yourself, others with partners. There's no shortage of material; the mind is an inexhaustible subject. If nothing else, I left you my notebooks, and if you find anything of interest worth sharing with the world by all means do so. Write about our adventures on Blennerhassett Island if you like. Imagine: A book about Alain "Doc" DeLyle, the West Virginia Shaman! It's too funny!

Emily Dickinson once wrote that thought is the property of he who originated it, and since all thought comes from God, everything I learned came from studying God's finest creation: the human mind. Avoid the sin of intellectual arrogance. There is truly nothing new under the sun. Everything that ever will be discovered is already there, waiting to be noticed. Everyone, no matter how humble, has something to teach you if you'll just listen with your heart.

In my naïve youth I wrote a series of lessons called The Wonderful Power which I sold to my clients for a small fee. I don't have any of the booklets left, but I can pretty much sum it up in a few words: The Wonderful Power is nothing more nor less than the permission to love freely and totally, to not only love others unselfishly, but to also love yourself and to recognize the infinite potential of your heart and mind, to embrace the myriad possibilities that lie within your grasp. To realize that you have the power to change your life and to become the Alchemist of your own destiny. It all boils down to what I told you years ago: Never, ever, let the light go out!

That's it. Not very much—but everything.

Craig, performing is not just a job; it is a calling. The performer is summoned to serve just as the preacher is called to the pulpit. When you stand on the stage you're not merely entertaining the audience. You're sending out messages about life and love and magic. Make sure all your messages are positive ones. Do this, when you look back on your life at the end of your journey and ask if it was well spent, the answer will be yes. Life on the road can be a grind, however. If things start tasting a little stale take this little piece of advice: just look at their faces. This always worked for me. See that look of amazed delight. You did it! You reached them! It never gets any better than this! Do the show, Craig. Do it with all of your heart. The audience deserves nothing less. You deserve nothing less.

I love you, Craig, and love doesn't end with death, it only moves to a higher level. By now you will have lost many loved ones, but keep this in mind at all times: We're not gone, none of us. Those who loved you in life are still with you, watching your show from the balcony and cheering you on. Listen for us in the rustle of the leaves in autumn; watch for us in the dance of dust motes in a sunbeam in your den. Keep us in your heart and in your mind. I'm not far away, son—and the lessons are only beginning. Get it?

Your respectful friend,
Alain "Doc" DeLyle

PS: If you haven't gotten it by now, you never will!

"I got it Doc," I whispered. "I finally got it." And I did get it. I finally understood that Mom, Bill, Willie—and Doc, the old Wizard of Wheeling himself—weren't gone; they hadn't vanished forever from my life; they had merely moved to another level. They still lived on, alongside of Charlotte and Dad and Brian and everyone else whose imprints were forever engraved in my heart and mind and spirit. "I love you guys," I said aloud. "I love you, Mom, Bill, Doc, Willie. I love you."

We love you too. We always have, and always will.

I looked out into the darkened theater and sitting in the front row, silhouetted by a shimmering cloud of silvery light were my family: Mom, smiling quietly at me just as she did when I was a child practicing card tricks; Bill, nodding as he smoked his pipe and contemplated the nature of the universe; my grandmother and grandfather, holding hands like two kids in love; Aunt May, eyes bright and shining. And wriggling around in my Mom's lap was Willie, barking with the pure joy of being young and healthy and with his family. As one they stood up, clapping their hands and cheering. But where was Doc? I wondered.

Don't worry; he'll be along soon.

I took a deep bow, my heart swelling with such happiness that I thought it would burst. I could feel them, all of them, surrounding me with their love and approval, and I knew that I would never be alone again. I laughed and cried at the same time, the barriers of grief and denial finally collapsing and allowing me to see my departed family with a clear, inner eye, and they were beautiful beyond description. "I got it, Doc!" I yelled, laughing, not caring who heard me. "I got it!"

"Bravo!" I heard behind me, a resonant baritone I hadn't heard in almost three decades.

"Doc?" I spun around. There was nobody. Of course there was nobody. Nothing was there. Nothing except the mingled aromas of cigar smoke and single-malt Scotch.

■ ■ ■

I took a last look around the stage of the Victoria Theater, the stage so well loved by Doc, dimly illuminated by the Ghostlight. I smiled at

Craig Karges returns to Alain "Doc" DeLyle's theatrical
home, The Victoria Theater in Wheeling, West Virginia,
to inherit the wizard's legacy and tape a television
special in the process. —Photo by Art Limann
and courtesy of *The Wheeling News-Register*,
Wheeling, West Virginia.

the old superstition. It was too late for the light to do any good, I
thought. The Victoria already had a ghost. Not the King of Rock and
Roll, as my chiropractor friend hoped, but the celebrated King of the
Clairvoyants!

"Goodnight Doc," I said. I turned the Ghostlight off and made my
way to the stage door by the dim glow of the exit sign. My family and
friends—my living family and friends, that is—were waiting for me at
the wrap-up party.

Then I felt a tingle between my shoulder blades, an unmistakable
sensation that I was not alone. I turned to look at the darkened theater
and dimly made out a shadowy figure walking toward the Ghostlight.

It must be Elvis, I thought. I grinned. Apparently, he still was in the building. "Did you forget something?" I called out.

Suddenly, the Ghostlight came back on. The stage was absolutely empty. Never let the light go out, Craig.

I nodded. "Don't worry, Doc—it'll never go out again."

I went to the party to join my friends and family.

Epilogue

WE'VE REACHED THE END of Doc's notebooks and the end of as much of Doc's story as I know how to tell. I've tried to provide a mix of stories from Doc's journals—from the mundane to the extraordinary—to provide a glimpse into this remarkable man's life and a sense of exactly who Alain "Doc" DeLyle was and how he affected the lives of others. There are hundreds of other stories in the notebooks, and there are still many, many unanswered questions. What happened during Doc's missing years after he left San Francisco? Was he really a trick shot artist with a Wild West show? Had he actually performed on the celebrated Orpheum vaudeville circuit as a crystal gazer? Did he live for a while among the Native Americans of the southwest and learn his shamanistic skills from them? Did he spend time in prison because of his love of a good card game? How did Doc get the interesting scar under his left eye? How do we explain the actions of a man who apparently feared nothing, yet always slept with a candle burning in his bedroom? And why did Doc always make sure he never sat with his back to the door?

We may never know. However, the answers may be out there somewhere, in long-forgotten leather-bound notebooks gathering dust in attics or basements or on library shelves, waiting to tell their secrets.

My little brother, Brian, grew up to be a great guy and a wonderful father. He's apparently completely recovered from the trauma of Doc's ghost stories. My father is still alive and doing well in Charlotte, North Carolina. Even after reading this book, he still thinks Doc was "full of it."

Our two dogs, Dolittle and Connor P. McNasty, have made themselves quite at home and often accompany Charlotte and me on the road. Willie rides along with us in spirit sometimes, but these days he spends most of his time on the Rainbow Bridge, chasing cats.

I still love performing and I'm doing it with a renewed passion. There is something extraordinary about imparting some of Doc's lessons to a cynical businessman during a workshop; to see the light come on as he watches a "mystical" pendulum respond to his mental commands. Or the face of a jaded college student light up in amazement as I tell him his birthday from the stage during my show. Entertaining through the creation of mystery and wonder while opening minds to unlimited possibilities.

Despite the rewards of my work, I am slowing down a bit. Doc taught me that life's too short for nothing but work. Sometimes you have to slow down and dig in the garden a little. It's not enough to smell the roses; Doc would have said you have to grow them first. Charlotte agrees. Whenever we can, we take the dogs on long hikes through the woods of nearby Oglebay Park. I took up skiing again, an activity I love, after being away from it for fifteen years. I plan on doing a little traveling (pleasure, not business) and I also plan on spending more time at home. I may even write another book. Not too soon, though. Doc taught me that although life is short, it's also paradoxically long, and there's plenty of time to fill it with love and experiences. As he told me many years ago:

"Love is action, not words. Love happens when you hold your beloved's hand and watch the sunset, or when you pet your dog, or sometimes when you just look at each other and let your hearts speak what the lips cannot. Keeping a loved one's memory alive in your heart after they've passed away is perhaps the greatest love of all."

In the last notebook I found the complete story of the summer I'd spent with Doc in 1971. Toward the end of the journal—and his life—Doc wrote, "My young apprentice helps me remember that life is just like show business. We each have our turn on the stage and then it's time for us to take a bow and make room for the next act. Preparing Craig for his turn has been the most satisfying period of my life."

Thank you, Doc. It was great for me, too. Goodnight, you magnificent old Wizard, see you soon.

INDEX

Index